A History of Enterprise Policy

Governments in developed and developing economies have increasingly turned to entrepreneurship and small businesses for economic growth, dynamism and economic and social inclusion. Policies seeking to encourage, support or otherwise influence these forms of economic activity are varied but virtually omnipresent, recommended by organisations such as the OECD and World Bank and implemented by governments of many political ideologies. With a range of activities across government labelled as enterprise policy, it is vital to unpick the different policies, initiatives and interventions and to understand their development in order to subject them to scrutiny and evaluate the actions taken in the name of enterprise.

This book provides the first in-depth, historical analysis of enterprise policy in the UK. Successive UK governments have been particularly active, with the number of initiatives estimated recently at 3000 and expenditure reaching as high as £12bn, yet facing continuous criticisms for its use, value or relevance. This historical study of UK enterprise policy represents a case study of different forms of enterprise policy and how they have developed, or failed to develop, over time, contributing to understanding of government, small business and entrepreneurship. It will be of value to researchers, academics, policymakers, and students interested in the history of small business and entrepreneurship as well as standing as a history of a specific policy area and the ways in which policies involving many different areas of government develop over time.

Oliver Mallett in an associate professor in Work and Employment at the University of Stirling, Scotland. Oliver's research interests relate to employment relationships in small businesses and to government and private sector support for small businesses.

Robert Wapshott is a senior lecturer in Entrepreneurship at the University of Sheffield, UK, where he is a member of the Centre for Regional Economic and Enterprise Development. Robert's research studies small businesses and entrepreneurship with a particular focus on small business management and on regulation.

Routledge Studies in Entrepreneurship
Edited by Susan Marlow and Janine Swail
(University of Nottingham, UK)

This series extends the meaning and scope of entrepreneurship by capturing new research and enquiry on economic, social, cultural and personal value creation. Entrepreneurship as value creation represents the endeavours of innovative people and organisations in creative environments that open up opportunities for developing new products, new services, new firms and new forms of policy making in different environments seeking sustainable economic growth and social development. In setting this objective the series includes books which cover a diverse range of conceptual, empirical and scholarly topics that both inform the field and push the boundaries of entrepreneurship.

For more information about this series please visit: www.routledge.com/Routledge-Studies-in-Entrepreneurship/book-series/RSE

A History of Enterprise Policy

Government, Small Business and
Entrepreneurship

Oliver Mallett and Robert Wapshott

Routledge
Taylor & Francis Group

LONDON AND NEW YORK

First published 2020 by Routledge

2 Park Square, Milton Park, Abingdon, Oxon OX14 4RN
605 Third Avenue, New York, NY 10017

Routledge is an imprint of the Taylor & Francis Group, an informa business

First issued in paperback 2021

Library of Congress Cataloging-in-Publication Data
A catalog record for this book has been requested

ISBN: 978-1-138-33730-5 (hbk)
ISBN: 978-1-03-217546-1 (pbk)
DOI: 10.4324/9780429442483

Typeset in Sabon
by Apex CoVantage, LLC

Contents

Acknowledgements

While as authors we bear ultimate responsibility for our work, undertaking research on such a wide topic necessarily reflects the support (and goodwill) of various people. The research underpinning this book took several years to complete and was supported by our respective colleagues and institutions.

In particular we acknowledge:

The Institute for Small Business & Entrepreneurship's Research and Knowledge Exchange fund provided a small grant to study the 'enterprise industry' of business support, which informed some of our thinking. Participants at ISBE annual conferences also provided comment and feedback on early versions of some of the ideas included in the book.

The Department for Business Innovation & Skills (now BEIS) funded a project on the effects of regulation on small businesses.

The University of Sheffield supported a small project on identifying contemporary enterprise policies, which informed the final section of Chapter 11; thanks to Nazila Wilson for support on this task.

Thanks also go to staff at The National Archives and The British Library (London and Boston Spa) for their assistance in making the most of the fantastic resources they look after.

Oliver would especially like to thank Rebecca, Lacey and Lola for all their love and support.

1 What Is Enterprise Policy and Why Is it Important?

The classic BBC sitcom *Only Fools and Horses* features a self-employed market trader ('Del Boy') and his work (often within the informal economy) and home life with a younger brother (Rodney) and their elderly grandfather (in later series a great uncle). Del Boy is a stereotypical wheeling and dealing entrepreneur who takes risks, has great ambition and looks for opportunities, seemingly convinced through each scrape and caper that 'this time next year we'll be millionaires.'

The first episode of the series, broadcast in 1981, includes a scene where Del Boy explains his attitude towards Value Added Tax, and by extension government in general, to Rodney. Del explains that their business gives nothing to government, no income tax or national insurance, and in return they expect government to give nothing back. The story reflects something of a stereotypical portrayal of small businesses' and the self-employed's attitudes towards government: they want to be left alone to get on with their business without the impediments of taxes or other burdens such as 'red tape.'

Nearly 40 years later, another high-profile (but this time not fictional) UK entrepreneur, Rohan Silva, wrote an article for the *Evening Standard* newspaper entitled 'Why is the government making life so tough for small businesses?' Silva is a very different type of entrepreneur from the fictional Del Boy stereotype, focused on high technology and innovation. He had previously worked as a senior advisor on business support initiatives for the UK government before becoming an entrepreneur and co-founding a social enterprise that provides services to small businesses and entrepreneurs. He also shapes the public perception of small businesses, with newspaper articles and a BBC podcast. In this particular article, Silva argues that the Conservative government is actively hostile to small businesses, giving examples of personal comments from key ministers and also of high taxes and business rates as well as a lack of advice and support.

These apparent tensions between government and small business, self-employment, entrepreneurship or, more broadly, 'enterprise', is perhaps surprising. There is a political consensus in the UK and internationally that these businesses are of central importance to a modern economy. If, for example, we look at UK political manifestoes across the mainstream political spectrum we can see this understanding of the importance of small business consistently hailed as key to economic plans:

> The Conservative Party is the party of enterprise and of the entrepreneur.
>
> (Conservative Party, 2017)

> . . . we will put small businesses at the centre of our economic strategy.
>
> (Labour Party, 2017)

> . . . the role of entrepreneurs and small businesses in delivering a thriving economy is fundamental.
>
> (Liberal Democrat Party, 2017)

Suggestions that government does not seek to support small business appear even stranger when we consider that, in the UK, the number of schemes and initiatives targeted at these businesses has reached as many as 3000 (!). Precise figures on expenditure levels and the impacts of such expenditure are fiendishly difficult to pin down, with spending figures typically withheld by governments (Fotopoulos and Storey, 2019), but estimates for UK expenditure have been as high as £8bn or, sometimes, even higher (e.g. Richard, 2008, estimated over £12bn). In this commitment and consensus, the UK is an exemplar of an international trend towards the 'entrepreneurial economy' (Gilbert et al., 2004: 313). For example, between 2006 and 2012 the World Bank averaged support of $3bn per year targeted to Small and Medium-sized Enterprises (SMEs) (World Bank, 2014). We believe that this policy agenda, which we will refer to as 'enterprise policy,' is a fascinating area to explore in order to try to make sense of these apparent tensions and contradictions.

The huge number of enterprise policy schemes and initiatives partly reflects the heterogeneity of categories such as 'small business,' for example in terms of targeted sectoral support, as well as the regional nature of some policies. However, it also reflects the complexity of enterprise policy agendas with 'virtually all organs of government [having] programs which qualify as either EP [entrepreneurship policy] or SMEP [small and medium-sized enterprise policy]' (Lundström et al., 2014: 946). Governments intervene in a range of ways, acting as '. . . a regulator, incentiviser and facilitator, or as a supplier' as well as a supporter of other, non-governmental forms of influence and support (Bennett, 2014: 25). However, the vast number of schemes and initiatives also raises important questions about the effectiveness of such policies. For example, why does deregulation to remove barriers and free up small firms remain a prominent political concern when successive governments have actively pursued deregulation (and later 'better regulation') since the 1980s? The UK has an Ease of Doing Business Rank of 9 out of 190 countries (following the US at number 8), reflecting the extent to which the country's 'business regulation affords micro and small firms the opportunity to grow, innovate and, when applicable, move from the informal to the formal sector of an economy' (World Bank, 2019: 1). Given this apparent success, and the extent to which a belief in the importance of small business and entrepreneurship is shared across the political spectrum, it can be surprising the extent to which the present situation is often described as problematic and the position of small businesses as endangered, requiring urgent government action (which will be taken if you vote for whichever party is making this pitch at the next General Election).

We have written this book during the prolonged period of political and economic uncertainty following the UK's referendum vote to leave the European Union ('Brexit') in June 2016. We believe that, at times of such significant political turmoil, there is value in deepening our understanding of important areas of policymaking. Where does a policy agenda come from? How has it developed over time? What unquestioned assumptions are underlying the policy agenda? Can things be done differently? It is in an attempt to answer questions of this sort that we have written a history of enterprise policy in the UK. In this opening chapter, we will set out the aims of this book and the structure we have adopted to address those aims. We define important terms and ideas that we rely on in the book and we highlight the value of an historical perspective that places the development of enterprise policy in a broader political, economic and social context. We conclude the chapter with an overview of the book, which will serve as a quick reference guide to readers seeking a particular focus for their reading.

Aims and Purpose

Before launching into the detail, it is useful to locate ourselves in relation to our research and how we came to write this book. Our starting point for the original research project was a shared interest in how governments provide support for an enterprise and entrepreneurship agenda. We previously wrote a book about management in small businesses (Wapshott and Mallett, 2015) and, in analysing the factors shaping small businesses' management practices and employment relationships, it became clear how important government policies and initiatives are. Moreover, we have had some involvement with the UK government's Better Regulation Executive and also delivering content under the growth vouchers scheme. Such activities led us to want greater understanding of the development of enterprise policies.

Developing our understanding of this topic it became apparent that, while associated commonly with the Conservative governments of Margaret Thatcher, and perhaps the Bolton Committee before that, governments had been intervening to assist small businesses for decades earlier. Further, during nearly 100 years of such policies, we became interested in how they were influenced by and were designed to respond to changing economic, political and social contexts. To fully explore these contextual factors, we focus exclusively on the development of enterprise policies in the UK. More specifically, we tend to focus on England—there is sufficient complexity without considering the variations in Scotland, Wales or Northern Ireland (for example in the administration of the European Regional Development Fund, where institutional variations led to more effective working in Scotland), especially after devolution. However, these variations are of interest in their own right and certainly worthy of further future study.

When one begins to study the history of enterprise policy something that jumps out very quickly is the recurring themes. As we will discuss throughout the book, the core areas of enterprise policymaking (financial assistance, regional focus, management guidance and support) were established in the 1930s and have been somewhat persistent areas of focus ever since. Taking a long view of government actions targeting small businesses and entrepreneurship captures the repeated framing of small businesses as struggling, for instance in accessing finance or with government 'red tape' and regulations, and the ongoing efforts of governments to support these ventures. Building an account of enterprise policy in the UK over 100 years offers an opportunity to understand the development of approaches to support small businesses and entrepreneurs and, in light of persistent concerns about the lack of effectiveness of many of these approaches, potentially identify lessons from past experiences.

To this end, we are not political history scholars but rather researchers of small business and enterprise who have developed an interest in the past in order to understand more fully a central aspect of our field. As authors, this project has been about advancing our understanding of how enterprise policy has developed in order to provide insights that can help us to navigate the contemporary landscape. The Methodological Appendix sets out the different kinds of sources we have consulted and the specific assistance from which we have benefited. For our readers, we hope that we have achieved our objective and communicated our work effectively in order to stimulate further discussion and inquiry.

The Story of UK Enterprise Policy

The traditional disinclination of UK governments to become involved in matters of industry (Millward, 1995) began to change after the First World War and then underwent a significant shift during the 1930s and

1940s when, dealing with war and economic crises, there were wide-ranging changes in the relationship between government and industry. In broad terms, post–Second World War and through to the late 1960s, 'big was still seen as beautiful and growth was seen as the key to the treasures of increased economies of scale' (Curran and Stanworth, 1982: 3; Gray, 1998). In this environment, while early examples of enterprise policies existed, small businesses were not a major concern of national governments, even as their numbers declined.

By the mid-1960s, attitudes towards small businesses among politicians appeared to be changing with increased prominence in Parliamentary debates (Beesley and Wilson, 1981). Business owners were concerned about the decline of their relative status (Middlemas, 1986) and the development of 'a small business sector consciousness' (Middlemas, 1990: 182) established a more vocal constituency seeking to protect its interests. Following a short period of pressure building for some action addressing the complaints of small business owners, the government launched its Committee of Inquiry on Small Firms (1969–1971) chaired by John Bolton. The Report of the Bolton Committee was published in autumn 1971 and has been credited with playing a significant role in the emergence and development of government policy towards small businesses in the UK (Curran and Stanworth, 1982a; Gray, 1998; Dannreuther and Perren, 2013). Described as forming 'the bedrock of virtually all research, analysis and policy making' relating to small businesses in the subsequent decade (Curran and Stanworth, 1982: 3), the Bolton Report (1971) both reflected and contributed to an increasing interest in small firms.

Economic restructuring and other political, social and economic changes in the 1970s and 1980s led to an increase in the number and prominence of small and medium-sized enterprises, with implications for the working lives of many people who were now more likely to work as self-employed, freelancers or members of smaller organisations. The Conservative governments of the 1980s under Margret Thatcher embraced and encouraged these changes, promoting a new 'enterprise culture.' This prominence of small business and forms of self-employment has continued, in many ways, to the present day: according to the most recently available Business Population Estimates from the Department of Business, Energy & Industrial Strategy (BEIS, 2018), SMEs represent 99.9% of all private sector businesses, contributing 60% of total private sector employment and 52% of total private sector turnover (where SMEs are defined as having 0–249 employees).

The complexity characterising enterprise policy throughout this period is reflected in the sheer numbers of different interventions, although marked by changes in the emphases placed on small businesses and entrepreneurs as forming a politically significant constituency and the ends to which policies affecting these enterprises have been deployed (Beesley and Wilson, 1981; Greene et al., 2008; Dannreuther and Perren, 2013). Keeping track of these interventions has been complicated by a tendency for interventions to be 'piled on top of each other with little policy termination' (Bennett, 2014: 85), leading to a '"patchwork quilt" of policies' (Storey, 1994: 304). This is a point not lost on government, for example then-Chancellor of the Exchequer Gordon Brown announced in the Labour government's March 2006 budget (HM Treasury, 2006):

> There is concern at all levels that the proliferation of business support schemes has created a complex picture making it difficult and time consuming for businesses to access relevant support. The Government will work with RDAs [Regional Development Agencies, see Chapter 11] and other local and national bodies to reduce the number of business support services from around 3,000 now, to no more than 100 by 2010.

Clearly, in the face of such size and complexity, any endeavour to tell a history of each and every enterprise policy intervention would fall far short of completeness. Instead, our focus is to develop a cohesive overview of the different approaches to enterprise policy across the past 100 years, focusing on particularly significant examples and placing the developing enterprise policy agenda in its economic, political and social contexts.

Is Enterprise Policy Effective?

Enterprise policy has been deployed to address a wide range of economic and social problems, from the consequences of industrial restructuring and regional unemployment (Hudson, 2000) to objectives such as 'social and community cohesion' (Bridge, 2010: 6), poverty alleviation (Hart, 2003) and 'cutting off the corners of regional disadvantage' (Greene et al., 2008: 79). However, despite significant efforts and expenditure, enterprise policies have been challenged as to their effectiveness in achieving the aims of policymakers (Bridge, 2010; Fotopoulos and Storey, 2019) and as to whether these policies represent value-for-money (Curran, 2000). Critical considerations of specific policies have identified fundamental problems with displacement and deadweight effects (Curran and Storey, 2002) as well as a lack of understanding of the challenges identified (Nightingale and Coad, 2016) or of the available research evidence (Arshed et al., 2014). For example, if government intervenes to address a specific problem (say, incentivising businesses to hire new employees in an area of high unemployment), it is often unclear whether any jobs created are truly additive (i.e. a result of the intervention and would not have been created anyway), whether the intervention really tackles the underlying problems and whether such a policy is evidence-based and fully evaluated. Consequently, government ministers and policymakers have faced questions regarding whether they are well-placed to intervene effectively (Bennett, 2008).

Blackburn and Schaper (2012) present three persistent obstacles to the development of effective enterprise policy: a lack of progress due to poor learning from previous experience; poor use of the evidence base or rigorous evaluation of policies; and poor collaboration and information sharing between relevant actors. Greene et al. (2008: 4) identify 'a distinct tendency to recycle particular interventions even when they were not successful when they were tried previously.' As Curran and Storey (2002: 168) describe it: 'The blinding hegemonic dazzle surrounding "entrepreneurship", "enterprise", and "the enterprise culture" has placed them almost beyond question and resulted in policies not being scrutinized as closely as might normally happen.' The result is what Nightingale and Coad (2016) discuss in terms of a fixation on a core set of assumptions that drive enterprise policy and an inability to look critically at the past. It is this critically informed understanding of the past and of the development of enterprise policy that we seek to achieve with this book.

Historical Institutionalism

To guide our research and analysis we have adopted an historical institutionalist perspective. Institutions can be understood as 'sets of regularized practices with a rule-like quality [that] structure the behavior of political and economic actors' (Hall, 2009: 204). Analytically, institutions provide a useful way of segmenting the normative order. Combinations of formal institutions, such as rules and regulations, and informal institutions, such as norms, values or codes of behaviour, are therefore understood as '. . . activities, beliefs, and attitudes [which] have come to acquire taken-for-granted or rule-like status . . . thus in turn enabling and constraining entrepreneurship' (Bruton et al., 2010: 423). For example, a heavily regulated economy might deter a business from taking on employees or encourage business operations to exist in the informal economy, not registering with government or paying appropriate taxes. It might support consumer confidence and boost sales for those businesses that are regulated. Informal institutions, such as societal norms and values associated with, for example, being self-employed or an 'entrepreneur' might also shape someone's choice of career path or social attitudes towards informal economic activity and taxation may influence a decision to formally register one's business.

In this way, institutions create the 'incentive structure' of a society that shapes economic outcomes (North, 1990: 7). Tolbert et al. (2011:

1336) highlight that prior research provides 'compelling evidence that prevailing institutions—consisting of normative expectations and understanding of acceptable organisational structures and practice—exert considerable influence on decisions about appropriate structures, practices, and behaviors of entrepreneurial ventures.' Institutions can influence not only the number of businesses that are created (e.g. through encouraging or discouraging people into starting businesses) but also the nature of those businesses and how they operate (e.g. through tax incentives for certain organisational forms or cultural norms shaping management practices). However, the effects of institutions are not universal, they can impact members of society and particular social groups in different ways, helping some while hindering others, for example in perceived fit with entrepreneurial norms.

An institutional perspective therefore has clear advantages for studying enterprise policy in that it is, ultimately, 'the incentive structure of a society' and associated supports that many enterprise policies seek to shape. Enterprise policies have often had as their targets changing the nature of the economy (e.g. the quantity of small businesses) or how it operates (e.g. the behaviour of particular actors such as investors or the 'quality' of small businesses, how they are managed or what their objectives are). Calls for deregulation are often framed as reducing barriers to entrepreneurship and small business, changing the 'rules of the game' (North, 1990: 3), just as forms of business support and advice aim to help businesses to navigate their institutional environments, helping them to play the game more effectively.

In such descriptions, institutions can appear as static and determining of actions undertaken within the framework of appropriate, established activities, beliefs and attitudes and studies of entrepreneurship and institutions have tended not to engage with detailing the processes of how institutions develop (Aldrich, 2010). For example, emphasising the relatively enduring, stable nature of institutions has highlighted the difficulties for those seeking to bring about institutional development to reorient rules, norms and social values towards greater predisposition to entrepreneurship (Williams and Vorley, 2015). Evidently, efforts to explore the history of UK enterprise policy over 100 years must engage with questions of change. Drawing on the work of political science scholars who have been engaged for some time on the challenges associated with the stability inherent in institutions and the fact of observable institutional change over time has provided a valuable framework for how we have approached this task.

A common explanation for institutional change has been to highlight the exogenous shocks that do away with an existing state of affairs and replace them with a new regime. Such a punctuated equilibrium model holds that institutions endure until the point they give way to a new order, that is, '. . . institutions create stability and have causal efficacy, until they don't' (Schneiberg, 2007: 51). Such approaches suggest a dualism between periods of stability or change, whereby exogenous shocks, such as a financial crisis or a radical new political leader, create critical junctures that set events off on new paths. Within these accounts is a recognition of path dependency, that is how institutions created at critical junctures continue to exert influence, sometimes long after the events have passed; to this extent, institutions are forces for stability. State structures and policy legacies can act as filters for policy-relevant ideas that exclude alternatives and narrow the spectrum of what is considered or seen as legitimate (Blyth, 2002). More broadly, the particular economy or labour force that has been shaped by prior policies (for example in the development of a socialist economy) may preclude the adoption of policies at odds with this environment which would not provide the contexts or support necessary for the policy to be a success (see, for example, Williams and Vorley's, 2015, study of the introduction of liberal market economy enterprise policies in a former socialist state). However, path dependence is not path determination. Often in order to survive, institutions must flex and adapt. As Thelen (2004: 8) argues, 'it is not sufficient to view institutions as frozen residue of critical junctures, or even as "locked in" in the straightforward sense that path dependence arguments adapted from the economics literature often suggest.'

Studies informed by a particularly historical approach (broadly labelled 'historical institutionalism') have sought nuanced accounts of institutional *development* where 'elements of stability and change are in fact often inextricably intertwined' (Thelen, 2004: 31) and are not simply reflections of changes in the balance of power or the interests of the powerful. Such an approach might be broadly termed a process-centric approach to institutional development (Aldrich, 2010; Khavul et al., 2013) as the focus is placed on processes of development, on how institutions are formed and re-formed over time. Clemens and Cook (1999: 443), for example, detail a project of reframing institutions, working to 'disaggregate institutions into schemas and resources; decompose institutional durability into processes of reproduction, disruption, and response to disruption; and above all, appreciate the multiplicity and heterogeneity of the institutions that make up the social world . . .'

Work by political scientists in the historical institutionalism tradition has therefore been framed as '*historical* because it recognizes that political development must be understood as a process that unfolds over time [and] *institutionalist* because it stresses that many of the contemporary implications of these temporal processes are embedded in institutions—whether these be formal rules, policy structures or norms' (Pierson, 1996: 126). Pierson (1996) recognises the role of intentional actors seeking to shape institutions but crucially distinguishes intentions from outcomes. The distinction is vital to informing the study of questions such as the development of enterprise policy because it demonstrates the importance of visiting contemporary sources as opposed to just looking back with the certainty of how events played out and inferring intentions from outcomes.

Pierson (1996: 127) demonstrates how intentions of actors cannot be inferred from outcomes, and how '. . . the current functioning of institutions cannot be derived from the aspirations of the original designers. Processes evolving over time led to quite unexpected outcomes.' Firstly, institutions (e.g. a set of enterprise policies) have multiple effects making it hard to trace back from specific outcomes to particular interests and motivations. Secondly, institutional designers (e.g. enterprise policymakers) might work along isomorphic lines to achieve what seems 'appropriate' rather than work to secure the particular interests of those interests driving the establishment of the institution. Thirdly, institutions might outlast the period of interest for those seeking to establish the institution, creating longer-term by-products as distinct from the shorter-term objectives desired by an institution's designers. Fourthly, the complex environments in which institutional designers are operating mean that realised outcomes might be unanticipated as opposed to stemming directly from designers' intentions and wishes. Finally, the passage of time means that the interests that served to establish a particular institution might change, and those agents who established the institution will be replaced by others, who might have different interests.

Drawing on Pierson's work, among others such as Orren and Skowronek, Thelen observes that given the complexity of how institutions come about and develop, and the way that various institutions will be involved in a given area of political action, 'there is no reason to think that the various "pieces" will necessarily fit together in a coherent, self-reinforcing, let alone functional whole' (Thelen, 2004: 285). Reflecting on the relevance of this perspective for the study of enterprise policy returns us to the tendency noted previously for interventions to be 'piled on top of each other with little policy termination' (Bennett, 2014: 85), leading to a '"patchwork quilt" of policies' (Storey, 1994: 304).

For our purposes, being influenced by an historical institutionalist perspective means that in seeking degrees of cohesion around important themes in our account of enterprise policy, we must balance this by acknowledging the inherently messy and uneven processes of institutional development and change. In developing our analysis of enterprise policy and presenting it in this book, we follow Wilks (1999) in so far as, while historical institutionalism has informed our perspective and underlies our broad approach, for clarity of communication the chapters have been organised along thematic and chronological lines.

Structure of the Book

Our analysis of the development of enterprise policy is explored through the following 11 chapters, grouped in terms of the following themes: pre and early enterprise policy (Chapters 2–4); formalising an enterprise policy agenda (Chapters 5–7); Thatcher and the enterprise culture (Chapters 8–10); post-Thatcher, new ideas? (Chapter 11); and a conclusion (Chapter 12).

Pre and Early Enterprise Policy Agendas

In Chapters 2–4, we explore pre and early enterprise policy agendas. In Chapter 2, we provide a brief overview of the position of small businesses and their relation to government in the UK prior to our study's period of focus. What emerges is a regional orientation with the role of government focused predominantly on supporting relevant institutions and discouraging rent-seeking behaviours.

In Chapter 3, we focus our analysis on the identification of a funding gap for smaller businesses in the 1931 Macmillan Committee report. We set out the context for industrial policies following the First World War up to the 1929 stock market crash and subsequent economic depression. In one of the key patterns that would come to shape the history of enterprise policy and the development of key institutions, the tough economic conditions of the 1930s saw an upsurge in the number of people entering self-employment, prompting greater attention to these businesses and their concerns. The so-called Macmillan gap implied a market failure in terms of the provision of business finance that is perceived as harming not only the daily operation of small businesses but also to act as a brake on business growth. We trace the development of this line of policy, from the 1934 Special Areas Act (which included a loan fund targeted at supporting small enterprises) to the establishment of the Industrial and Commercial Finance Corporation in the 1940s, involving not just government but a range of organisations including the Bank of England and the clearing banks.

Chapter 4 takes up the 1934 Special Areas Act in more detail. The Act was broader in scope than addressing a perceived finance gap, it sought to address economic deprivation, for example by encouraging businesses to relocate to deprived areas. This established an important link between enterprise policy and regional policy, in part due to the localised nature of many start-ups and small businesses. However, such fledgling enterprise policies remained limited in scope and ambition, and we trace how the link has developed, including several regionally focused initiatives in the 1960s.

Formalising an Enterprise Policy Agenda

The next thematic grouping of chapters, Chapters 5–7, explores the refining and formalising of enterprise policy, both within government and in relation to lobbying for small business interests. Chapter 5 takes up the political context of the 1960s when there were growing tensions between governments' national strategies focused on large-scale organisation and the interests of smaller businesses. Voices calling for greater acknowledgement and representation of the interests of small businesses led to the 1969 appointment of the Bolton Committee of Inquiry on Small Firms. We discuss the establishment and work of the Bolton Committee and the subsequent influence of the Committee's report.

Chapter 6 traces events in the early 1970s, when the Conservative government attempted to reduce regional spending and subsidies but this proved impossible after a series of shocks and challenges: the first half of the 1970s was a time of high unemployment, economic crises and recession, and smaller businesses became more prominent as a result of significant economic restructuring. As large firms decreased the size of their operations, they created more opportunities for small businesses. We discuss how organisations such as the National Federation of the Self Employed (NFSE, now the Federation of Small Businesses, FSB) were formed, principally in response to government national insurance changes that were perceived as unfair to the self-employed. As now, a key focus of the NFSE's activities was to lobby government and lead public campaigns, and it is in this way that the development of such organisations and the interests they represent are relevant for understanding the development of enterprise policy.

As a focused enterprise agenda developed in UK politics in the 1970s, the UK was also debating and then joining the European Economic Community (EEC) in 1973. The Treaty of Rome viewed state aid as distorting the market and therefore being incompatible with the Common Market. In Chapter 7, we discuss the emergent compromise which allowed (partial) exemptions for SMEs, especially in particular (deprived) regions and to support particular areas of development, such as training, consultancy and technology. These exemptions were crucial for shaping subsequent UK enterprise policy.

Thatcher and the Enterprise Culture

Chapters 8–10 discuss the Thatcher governments of the 1980s and early 1990s that saw a substantial increase in the prominence and extent of enterprise policymaking. In Chapter 8, we focus on the emergence of a new political discourse around entrepreneurship that promoted an 'enterprise culture,' with government rhetoric encouraging particular social values based on self-reliance and self-help (and in opposition to a so-called dependency culture). These values were portrayed as being embodied in the independent entrepreneur and government set out to influence public attitudes towards small business and entrepreneurship.

As small businesses have received increasing attention in relation to economic and social goals, so too have the effects of regulations on these firms as part of a broader shift towards market liberalisation. Business start-up and small business growth in particular have been highlighted as key rationales for deregulation, and in Chapter 9, we discuss these policy initiatives in relation to enterprise policy. We analyse high-profile commitments to remove 'red-tape' and improve the institutional environment in which to start up and grow a small business.

In Chapter 10, we discuss the increasing emphasis on improving management skills, in particular by encouraging engagement with consultants. We focus in particular on Business Link as representative of this agenda and a substantial development in the support of business support services and promotion of consultancy that, for some, represented a nationalisation of business support. We draw out an important and ongoing tension between government and private sector support for small businesses and entrepreneurship, complicating the institutional environment in which small businesses and entrepreneurs had to operate as well as provoking significant questions about the place of enterprise policy.

Post-Thatcher, New Ideas?

In Chapter 11, we examine the late 1990s and 2000s, which saw the New Labour government introduce new approaches to governance and broaden the objectives for enterprise policy by encouraging a push towards equality of opportunity for enterprise. While enterprise policy has a long history of involvement in relation to economically deprived areas (as discussed in Chapter 4), under New Labour it was extended in scope to targeting a perceived 'enterprise gap' among particular, underrepresented social groups. In effect, this broadened the range of questions to which 'entrepreneurship' was the answer and therefore shifted the emphasis of enterprise policy. In this chapter we will also briefly consider the more recent enterprise policy agendas developed in response to the financial crisis, austerity and Brexit.

Conclusion

The final chapter of the book provides an extended conclusion, drawing out the key themes and insights from the preceding analysis in relation to a broader international context. It draws out and discusses in detail the lessons for understanding the development and interplay of institutions, interests and ideas relating to enterprise policy. Examining the interplay of institutions, interests and ideas allows us to explore why particular policies emerge at particular times but not at others and to develop a rich set of insights enabled by the analysis throughout the book. Chapter 12 concludes with an assessment of enterprise policy and suggests ways forwards that underpin the practical contributions of the book, including beyond the specific UK context.

2 Government, Small Firms and Entrepreneurship in the Nineteenth Century

Before we begin our analysis of the development of enterprise policy in the twentieth century, it is valuable to understand something of the history leading up to this period. What emerges is the invaluable role of government in supporting entrepreneurship, for example in the stability of the rule of law and relevant institutions, and in discouraging rent-seeking behaviours. However, while the role of the State in the development of private commerce was well-established (for example, supporting chartered companies such as the East India Company), enterprise policy was not a significant focus for UK governments before the twentieth century. This is not to suggest that small businesses were outside the scope of government intervention, but that the focus tended to be more sectoral or at a local level, and small businesses were not viewed as a discrete grouping.

For much of nineteenth century, Britain's economy was dominated by small businesses and independent traders and we begin this chapter by sketching the types of small business in the UK economy at this time. We focus in particular on the second half of the nineteenth century as things began to change, highlighting some of the early indications of larger scale developments that were to follow. The chapter then draws out discussions relating to individualism, which has often been highlighted in historical accounts and modern political discourse to characterise the entrepreneurs of this time, and the laissez-faire approach ascribed to nineteenth century governments, especially in their approach to industry. The chapter concludes by outlining the increasingly difficult position small businesses found themselves in at the turn of the twentieth century.

The Nineteenth-Century Small Firm

The nineteenth-century UK economy was dominated by owner-managed small-scale enterprises, locally based and hyper competitive (Elbaum and Lazonick, 1986). In many areas these businesses operated in response to high levels of demand, supporting a large number of individual operations so that even in industries (such as metal or chemicals) dominated by large businesses, smaller concerns still proliferated. While today mass production and economies of scale, especially through the use of technology, are taken for granted, this orthodoxy was not an immediate result of the industrial revolution. As Piore and Sabel (1984: 48) identify: 'like so much apparently commonsensical truth, the mass-production paradigm had unforeseen consequences: it took almost a century (from about 1870 to 1960) to discover how to organize an economy to reap the benefits of the new technology.' Commenting on the processes of mechanisation, More (2000) observes that, by 1850, there were some 600 000 workers in textiles factories, or about 6% of the total workforce. By contrast, at the same point 1.8m men worked on the land and more industrial workers were using tools than minding machines.

In the research reported in *The Age of Entrepreneurship*, Robert Bennett and colleagues (2020) conducted 'the first large-scale, long-term and whole-population assessment of the history of entrepreneurship in Britain in detail from the nineteenth century to 1911' (p. 3), utilising a significant new database drawn from census data and covering in excess of 9 million entrepreneurs. Their analysis of this database identifies that, in the period 1851–1881, the majority of firms (60%) were microbusinesses (less than 5 employees), with much of the remainder (26–33%) composed of small businesses (5–19 employees). In 1851, only 157 firms had 500 or more employees (433 firms by 1881; p. 113). These micro and small businesses included enterprises across a wide range of sectors.

Henry Mayhew, in *London Labour and the London Poor* (published in the 1850s and 1860s), provides a more qualitative record of the huge variety of street sellers selling food, drink, literature, manufactured items, second-hand goods, coal, scrap metal, as well as more illicit and illegal sales. Mayhew (2017) presents the following scene which is worth quoting in full to get a sense of the variety of what we might now consider forms of entrepreneurial activity:

> The street sellers are to be seen in the greatest numbers at the London street markets on a Saturday night. Here, and in the shops immediately adjoining, the working-classes generally purchase their Sunday's dinner; and after pay-time on Saturday night, or early on Sunday morning, the crowd in the New-cut, and the Brill in particular, is almost impassable. Indeed, the scene in these parts has more of the character of a fair than a market. There are hundreds of stalls, and every stall has its one or two lights; either it is illuminated by the intense white light of the new self-generating gas-lamp, or else it is brightened up by the red smoky flame of the old-fashioned grease lamp. One man shows off his yellow haddock with a candle stuck in a bundle of firewood; his neighbour makes a candlestick of a huge turnip, and the tallow gutters over its sides; whilst the boy shouting

"Eight a penny, stunning pears!" has rolled his dip in a thick coat of brown paper, that flares away with the candle. Some stalls are crimson with the fire shining through the holes beneath the baked chestnut stove; others have handsome octohedral lamps, while a few have a candle shining through a sieve: these, with the sparkling ground-glass globes of the tea-dealers' shops, and the butchers' gaslights streaming and fluttering in the wind, like flags of flame, pour forth such a flood of light, that at a distance the atmosphere immediately above the spot is as lurid as if the street were on fire.

As this extract suggests, in addition to market sellers and itinerant traders, the nineteenth century saw an increased number of small-scale shops, often with a local focus responding to the demand from urban concentrations of the working class. In turn, such shops relied upon extensive supply chains to fill their shelves, often including a variety of other small businesses.

In manufacturing, the dominance of small businesses began to change with mechanical innovations to the manufacturing process and the introduction of steam power led to new possibilities in economies of scale and the growth of larger factories and modes of organisation. However, these processes of change in scale were gradual and did not lead overnight to huge, factory-based organisations (Cain and Hopkins, 1980). For example, even in the cotton industry, 'where the scale economies were internal to the firm, they appear to have been exhausted at a scale well below the full extent of the market, so that no firm had a dominant share of output' (Hannah, 1983: 10). That is, the types of economies of scale familiar to us today were not at first available and, with significant market demand, the industry overall maintained large numbers of small firms rather than a small number of large firms. In other industries, there was not yet the technology or the division of labour to support large economies of scale, preserving small businesses. Further, the growth of factories as a form of organisation and employment 'was accompanied by an upsurge in the number and variety of smaller-scale units, and a notable continuation of self-employment' (Hudson, 2004: 37). This included forms of subcontracting to small-scale workshops and of homeworking, with domestic labour remaining a significant part of the manufacturing industry.

Agriculture was, broadly, a system of landlords, tenant farmers and farm workers. The second half of the nineteenth century saw a decline in agriculture, for example due to large-scale importing. There were also significant impacts from the international economic effects of the 'Great Depression' during this time (see the following discussion). These challenges accompanied forms of 'industrialisation' in some aspects of agricultural work and ongoing areas of demand supported by, for example, the distribution possibilities of the railway network. Despite the declining numbers of those engaged in agriculture, throughout this tumultuous period agricultural enterprises often showed resilience and, from the 1860s, reduced their reliance on labour and were more likely to operate as sole proprietors, often relying on family members (Montebruno et al., 2019).

Individualism

Nineteenth-century small-scale economic activity has been recalled by some enterprise policymakers as a halcyon period of self-sufficiency and personal responsibility. Bechhofer and Elliott (1981: 193), writing in the early years of Thatcher's government (see Chapter 8), identify in the moral economy being promoted the values of 'an eighteenth- or early nineteenth century market economy—or rather some highly abstracted and idealised version of this.' Invoking an idealised image of the past was used by the Thatcher government to promote a mode of economic activity led by market forces shaping the economy, complemented by a small state.

In the second half of the nineteenth century, some of this idealised image was already being deployed. The rise of industrialisation in Britain is often told as a story of individuals, an image promoted not-least by Samuel Smiles, an author and campaigner whose accounts told of men who had risen to transform their chosen fields of occupation (for detail on the entrepreneurial activities of women in the period that are excluded from such accounts, see Bennett et al., 2020). Smiles presents short biographies of apparently ordinary men who applied themselves tirelessly, and won through, which Bendix (1956: 115) describes as establishing a 'new entrepreneurial ideology.' In *Self-Help: With Illustrations of Conduct and Perseverance*, Smiles (2014, originally 1859) emphasises the ability of anyone, regardless of rank, to improve themselves through dedication and hard work:

> . . . strenuous individual application was the price paid for distinction; excellence of any sort being invariably placed beyond the reach of indolence. It is the diligent hand and head alone that maketh rich—in self-culture, growth in wisdom, and in business. Even when men are born to wealth and high social position, any solid reputation which they may individually achieve can only be attained by energetic application; for though an inheritance of acres may be bequeathed, an inheritance of knowledge and wisdom cannot.

In his chapter on *Leaders of Industry—Inventors and Producers*, Smiles accounts for the rise of Arkwright (textiles manufacture), Peel (calico printing), and Wedgwood (pottery) among others, their industrious spirit and drive seeing them through against numerous circumstances that would otherwise thwart their achievements.

> Men such as these are fairly entitled to take rank as the Industrial Heroes of the civilized world. Their patient self-reliance amidst trials and difficulties, their courage and perseverance in the pursuit of worthy objects, are not less heroic of their kind than the bravery and devotion of the soldier and the sailor, whose duty and pride it is heroically to defend what these valiant leaders of industry have so heroically achieved.

Reflecting the individualism highlighted by Smiles, Coleman and Macleod (1986: 600) argue that, owing to the initiative and endeavour of small business owners, absent of coordinating efforts, 'the British industrial revolution gave rise to powerful currents of individualism in business behaviour.' Tracing such attitudes across industries and across the country, Coleman and Macleod argue that many small businesses were resistant to standardisation of products and instead continued by serving niche markets. The apparent preference for individualism might also be explained, in part, by a preference for ownership and control to be held privately or within the family, as opposed to the corporate arrangements of separating ownership and control associated with the very large enterprises created at the turn of the century (Payne, 1972; Hannah, 1983).

Moreover, Winstanley's (1983) analysis of shopkeepers identifies how individualism and open competition were sometimes used as a rhetorical attack on larger organisations rather than existing as a deeply held ideology. It was argued that cartels and corporations were responsible for a decline in national industry, restricting the industrial improvements that could only develop out of the individual enterprise of smaller concerns. Further, it was argued in some quarters that being an employee could limit ambitions, removing the possibility of their becoming independent businesspeople themselves one day. For Winstanley (p. IX): 'Historians . . . should not be so gullible as to believe that such men were motivated by the individualist, entrepreneurial ideals that they professed.' Ultimately, small business owners were pragmatic businesspeople trying to make a living.

Reluctant to Change?

The high-profile entrepreneurs of the late eighteenth century were noted for their engagement with technological innovation. Bendix (1956: 27) cites how, in each of the three decades following 1760, there was a significant increase in the numbers of patents issued and details how the 'veritable outburst of inventive activity was accompanied by much popular excitement.' However, a central plank of the critique of entrepreneurs in the latter part of the nineteenth century was their apparent resistance to the adoption of new technology (Crafts, 2012; Ciliberto, 2010). Although the critique is associated with the work of Aldcroft (1964) writing in the mid-twentieth century, concern over the apparent reluctance of British manufacturers to invest in new equipment and technologies was also noted at the time. Presenting comments from the Committee on the Machinery of the United States of America, Coleman and Macleod (1986: 592) relate concerns that American progress in machinery would soon see American producers exporting 'not only to foreign countries, but even to England, and should this occur, the blame must fall on the manufacturers of England . . . for want of energy in improving their machinery.'

However, even if a case can be made for failures to adopt the latest technologies, there remains a question of business-owner motivation. More (2000) notes that innovations came to depend less on the learning-by-doing practical knowledge that contributed to early industrial progress, and increasingly on scientific and technical skills. Against this backdrop there was a shortage of the advanced skills required to both invent new processes and machinery as well as to realise how innovations could drive improvements. Arguably associated with this outlook, and amidst highly competitive domestic markets dominated by small firms, independent business owners might have seen little incentive or opportunity to take on the costs of increased investment. So long as they were able to run a viable business, retain family ownership and control, it is understandable that business owners may choose to develop other pursuits beyond the business. What interest did they have in taking on the challenges of exporting even if this could have benefited the international standing of Britain at the time?

An Era of Laissez-Faire?

Today, the adoption of new technologies or the decision to export would be seen, even for some free market politicians, as an area for government to create incentives or forms of support. State intervention did play a vital role in the development of the UK economy and industry and can be seen, for example in the extensive regulations introduced during the eighteenth century relating to the regulation of production, labour, the movement of people, trade and interest rates. However, a great deal of this regulation was abolished in the first half of the nineteenth century (Harris, 2004), reflecting questions about the role of the state and a significant shift towards laissez-faire and belief in free trade, competition and their connection to individual liberty. As the processes of industrialisation continued to unfold, questions around the role of government persisted and the nineteenth century continued to balance a tension between laissez-faire and state intervention (Brebner, 1948).

Harling and Mandler (1993) trace the emergence of laissez-faire government in Britain to the end of the French wars in the early nineteenth century. Public disapproval of the state as serving the interests of those close to it restricted its legitimacy and created pressure to reduce the burden of taxation that could be justified in times of war. In what Harling and Mandler present as a move to maintain the general social order, and in an era where expectations on governments for social and economic intervention were relatively few, laissez-faire was a way of reducing expenditure popularly perceived as being unnecessary and responding to calls for 'cheap government': a government that did less, and therefore spent less required, less contribution in the form of taxes (recall Del Boy in *Only Fools and Horses* and his view that he would contribute nothing to government and expect nothing in return).

The second half of the nineteenth century was a time of wide-reaching political change. Between 1852 and 1886, with changes including an expanding electorate, the UK moved from a Parliamentary government, where the cabinet governed subject to the support of the House of Commons, to governments selected by political parties that held electoral mandates and attempted to achieve internal ideological consensus (Hawkins, 1998). This changed political debate, moving it, to some degree at least, further outside Parliament and to the development of party machinery across the country. At this time, the two main political parties were the Conservatives (also known as the Tory Party, which had moved away from some elements of laissez-faire capitalism, including the recognition of trade unions) and the Liberal Party (which had emerged out of a coalition of Whigs and free trade advocates and who had dominated politics for many years previously). As the century moved on, and by the 1880s, both parties broadly adopted 'the prevailing Victorian preference for curtailing government in favour of local autonomy and economy' (Pugh, 2002: 60), albeit with protectionist tendencies lingering within the Conservatives.

Nonetheless, the extent to which laissez-faire can be used to characterise much of nineteenth-century Britain requires further consideration (in this discussion we omit consideration of government behaviour in overseas parts of the Empire, see Hobsbawm, 1968). As Polanyi (2001) established, the economy is embedded in society, and therefore in political, cultural and social institutions, and 'free markets' can never be entirely free. UK political and legal institutions were necessary for the effective functioning of the 'free' market and had been an important aspect of the industrial revolution. Bennett (2014) argues that one of the primary advantages for the UK in its industrial development was a result of how its institutions encouraged entrepreneurship through the rule of law and property rights together with a broadly legitimate, stable ruling elite. This produced a 'positive "business enabling environment"' (p. 77).

Invariably, as social and industrial changes arose, the state responded with regulations. Examples of legislation affecting matters of industry and business development include interventions in factories, railways, communications, mines and so on (see Brebner, 1948). There were also different forms of intervention beginning to be introduced later in the nineteenth century, such as the increasing emphasis on technical education, which served as a means to improve the efficiency of labour (Tomlinson, 1994). However, in general, government did not involve itself with how businesses were run (e.g. not pursuing significant anti-trust legislation). Further, passing legislation does not mean that it is effectively enforced. For example, limited resources devoted to a system of inspection and practical problems of identifying breaches limited the impact of legislation entered into the statute books (Bartrip, 1983). Bendix (1956: 37) cites an 1833 Commission of Inquiry into evasion of the previous factory legislation that commented on how parents with a tradition of, and a financial interest in, their children working were inclined towards misrepresenting these children's ages to avoid child labour legislation. Problems of effective enforcement of the factory acts was a particular problem in small workshops employing under 50 people, which were not covered by the acts until 1867. While acknowledging the increased intervention found on the statute books, Bartrip (1983: 83) concludes that there were clear distinctions between that and the 'the degree of intervention actually felt on the factory floor and at the coal-face.'

However, this was beginning to change, for example in the development of civil government and its budgets and in the enforcement of regulations in terms of its effectiveness and the number of inspectors (Harris, 2004). In this way, central government intervention began to increase in terms of calls for it to intervene in industry and of its impact when it did so. This included in relation to business-related regulations, especially those providing consumer protection such as the Weights and Measures, Merchandise Marks or Sale of Goods Acts. There was less emphasis on protecting labour, at least until public outcry over working conditions prompted government action (e.g. in the largely ineffectual Shops Acts of the early twentieth century, see the following discussion).

In trying to make sense of the tensions between laissez-faire and state intervention, it is helpful to follow Brebner's conclusion (1948: 69) that 'in the historical view, neither laissez faire nor state intervention was the engine of change in nineteenth-century Britain. Instead, both were constant accompaniments of the basic force—industrialization.' Politics remained a vital means by which society responded to and sought to shape significant changes and, ultimately, the state came to have greater influence in wider sections of society and the economy. In understanding how this mixed political picture related to small businesses, it is also useful to consider small business voice and political influence at a more local level.

Local Politics

To fully understand small business politics it is important to engage with the local context in which these businesses tended to operate and with the local politics in which they could exert significant influence. Shopkeepers, for example, were enfranchised by the 1832 Reform Act, giving them political influence including, in some constituencies, acting as the largest group of voters (Winstanley, 1983). They often voted for laissez-faire liberalism but also involved themselves in local decision making and interventions. Taylor (1972) identifies that even Samuel Smiles, who celebrated the economic individualism of industrial entrepreneurs, opposed laissez-faire being invoked against reforms targeting improvement in public health, which often required action at a local level. Jones' (1983) study of Birmingham during the period 1860–1900, does not identify evidence of corruption or shady deals but finds 'entrepreneurs did use their control of the council to advance sectional interests, in that they projected on to the community their own philosophy of politics' (p. 254). This would have included in areas where business owners could exert local power, for example through membership or control of local institutions providing for poor relief, health or policing.

While the involvement of local businessmen in municipal politics was therefore well-established alongside that of merchants, Jones' analysis of Birmingham tracks a transition in who represented business interests. During the 1860s, Jones notes a shift from small-scale entrepreneurs and traders to the general and commercial managers of the larger industrial firms growing up in the city. With this shift, Jones identifies a change in the rhetoric and dealings of the council towards a focus on policies representing value for money and being cost-effective. The adoption of business principles, as opposed to those that were strictly political or ideological, is seen in the justifications for an extension of municipal trading in domains such as water, electricity and gas. Elsewhere business principles also seemed to incorporate a combination of business and political interests. Speaking in favour of a building programme for technical schools, William Kendrick is quoted by Jones as arguing on the basis that without skilled artisans to support the city's industries and manufacturers, the city and wider district would suffer.

Challenging Times for Small Businesses

While the number of businesses continued to grow, this expansion started to slow (Bennett et al., 2020) and, as the nineteenth century neared its end, conditions became increasingly difficult for many small businesses. The economic situation was challenging, especially in agriculture, with some referring to the last quarter of the century as the 'long depression' or the 'great depression' and with consequences internationally, including famine in Ireland in 1879. The degree to which this can be described as a continuous period of depression is limited (Saul, 1985), for example, falling prices encouraged consumer spending and there were also techno-logical advances that supported forms of growth, producing a very mixed picture. Nonetheless, the international nature of the economic recession and the downward trend in prices did have important effects and sig-nalled the types of crisis that would shape key periods of the twentieth century, which will be discussed later in this book.

The biggest issue for many small firms was the increasing competition from larger businesses, although these processes were uneven. Taking the example of the mid-nineteenth-century textiles industry, Mathias (1969) details how changing commercial and technical pressures led to a rise and then fall in the role of large, integrated plants (also see Ciliberto, 2010). Nonetheless, the overall direction of change was to increasing competi-tive pressure from larger businesses, especially after the 1860s, as they began to more effectively leverage economies of scale. In the analysis of Bennett et al. (2020: 107), this represents 'the turning point for the end of the Victorian "age of entrepreneurship", with a profound re-balancing after 1901 between own-account proprietors in favour of those employ-ing others.' For shopkeepers, for example, competition from department stores and cooperatives (Winstanley, 1983) led to greater self-exploita-tion and intensification of work for those family members drawn upon to extend opening hours. In staying open as late as there remained potential customers, shopkeepers and their families extended their own working hours or those of any assistants they employed.

The threat from large businesses created through mergers and acquisi-tions, potentially creating monopolies and increasing competitive pres-sures was generally not viewed politically as an area for government intervention, despite calls for the protection of the individualism and free competition that some argued small firms represented. Bennett (2014: 80) notes that 'Alfred Marshall, a founding figure of economics, in writings over 1890–1920 saw no need for small firm or entrepreneurship policy in Britain' (p. 80). Marshall regarded there as being effective competition between large and small firms, although he identified changes relating to the advantages gained by the rise of the limited liability company, inter-nal economies of scale from mergers and changing institutions that could unsettle this situation. In order to compete, many small businesses relied on the intensification of labour and this, in turn, did lead to some politi-cal action in response to public concern. In the case of the shopkeepers, this resulted in the poorly designed 1904 Early Closing of Shops Act. This required that two-thirds of the members of a given trade in a local area should be supportive before a local authority could enforce restric-tions on opening hours. Given their large numbers, this framing of the regulation created the opportunity for small businesses to resist attempts to restrict their opening hours and the possibility of competing in this way. The issue was not fully resolved until after the First World War.

Where once small businesses had been politically active and at times influential, the second half of the nineteenth century saw a retreat to focusing on more immediate financial concerns such as those around business rates. Disputes over rates continued into the twentieth century with the Liberals, who largely ignored the issue, losing significant ground to the Conservatives, who now presented themselves as the party of low taxation. Winning back these voters would become a force shaping Liberal politics as they began to lose ground to both the Conservatives and the new Labour Party (see the following discussion).

The shaping of important institutions also came to be more prominently influenced by the concerns of large firms and the shifting nature of industrial relations, often limiting the influence of skilled self-employed workers or artisans. For example, the development of training through apprenticeships in the UK became entwined with trade unions, in contrast to other countries such as Germany. For their part, the trade unions focused on a strategy of localised labour control contested by employers who sought to limit the influence of skilled workers (Thelen, 2004). This led, by the late nineteenth century, to a lack of a developed framework or institutional support around apprenticeships or, in turn, artisans. As apprenticeships became situated in large firms, prolonged as a form of cheap labour, they also developed expertise only in relation to the specific operations of that business; they were not learning a trade that might one day support self-employment. Further, as small firms increasingly sought to compete through work intensification, regulations developed through collaboration of large employers and unions (for example in the printing industry with the 1912 Apprentice Training Scheme) attempted to limit the scope for small firms to make use of cheap labour provided by apprentices and to compete on price.

The lack of political influence found some echoes in social attitudes too. Bennett (2014) discusses the loss in status of small business owners and family businesses by the end of the nineteenth century, not only in comparison to those with inherited wealth but also those highly educated people working in government or as managers in large businesses. In this way, various factors compounded to contribute to the beginnings of what some would later come to refer to as the decline or even the demise of the small firm in the UK.

Politics at the Turn of the Century

The increasing influence of organised labour within the changing economy also gave rise to a powerful new political force amid concerns that the working class was not represented in Parliament. As it became apparent that this representation could not be fulfilled by the Liberals, the Independent Labour Party (ILP) was formed in 1893, resisting formally labelling itself as socialist, though it was heavily shaped by socialist intellectuals. This was followed by the Labour Representation Committee (LRC) in 1900, an organisation established to sponsor and support left wing, trade union and other working class political candidates. It was the LRC that then became the Labour Party in 1906, with the ILP affiliated to it and formed of those Members of Parliament within the earlier groups. As we will see in the next chapter, the Labour Party would quickly grow in support and influence, especially with universal male suffrage in 1918.

The beginning of the twentieth century also saw several political debates of relevance to small businesses, though often focused on particular sectors or in relation to specific issues rather than a wider concern with 'small business' or 'enterprise' as a political constituency or agenda. Debate continued between the free trade Liberals and the increasingly protectionist Conservatives, for example in relation to how to respond to international market forces in what was a highly globalised world of the early twentieth century. For example, debates around tariff reform that would potentially protect struggling small businesses. From 1905–1908 there were several minor acts to encourage smallholdings and, perhaps more significantly in terms of the creation of a political constituency, the exclusion of the self-employed from the 1911 National Insurance Act. However, the focus of central government, and its attitude towards state intervention, would become dominated by the experiences of the First World War.

The Great War

In 1914 the First World War (1914–1918), known as the Great War (reflecting the extent to which the magnitude and horror of the conflict was assumed to be something that could not be repeated), brought social, political and economic change. In the first half of the war, with restricted supply, there were significant profits for some businesses, including the self-employed, though these were limited to an extent by taxation and price controls (Tomlinson, 1994). As the war continued, its demands also necessitated a greater degree of coordination, state ownership and modernisation of mass production and technology. The coalition government imposed controls on factories and mines, including regulating prices and profits. Government negotiated with organised labour to facilitate women entering areas of the workforce affected by labour shortages with these negotiations also producing welfare reforms. This suggests the changing nature of how the state related to industry and specifically to labour.

The war ended with victory for the UK and its allies but at a cost of millions of casualties, military and civilian, including the deaths of 723 000 British and 200 000 Empire soldiers (Rubinstein, 2003). It also left the country with substantial debt and a significant set of changes for industry and politics that will be explored in the next chapter. The war saw the weakening of the UK position in international markets. This deepened calls for protectionist measures, especially in relation to those less developed industries that had filled the gap left by German imports. For industries that had benefited from government support and contracts during the war, there was a tendency to pursue similar support through tariffs and subsidies after the country returned to peace.

Conclusion

In the nineteenth century, the UK economy had been dominated by small (and often micro) enterprises, often without government support or subsidy but nonetheless as an object of government action. Interventions often sought to protect consumers or, in response to public outcry, to provide some measure of protection for workers. While small business owners could exert significant influence at a local level, this began to lessen in the last third of the century, and increasingly the political focus of these individuals became concentrated on demanding lower business rates.

As we will see later in this book, a particular sense of the individualist entrepreneur operating in a laissez-faire, free market system would be an important mythology for future enterprise policymakers. However, it is debateable whether this mythology was ever a reality and, in the later nineteenth century, it was already being utilised as a mythical past and as a form of political discourse to frame the position of small businesses struggling to compete against their emerging larger competitors. This approach to lobbying government and calling for public support was largely unsuccessful, however, and there was little that could be considered in terms of modern enterprise policy to support or to relieve the burdens on small businesses. The growing dominance of large businesses would reshape the economy and government approaches to industrial policy. For some commentators, this meant that the period at the start of our analysis marked the beginning of the decline of the age of entrepreneurship (Bennett et al., 2020).

3   Filling the Finance Gap

We stated in our Introduction that UK enterprise policy is widely seen as having begun with the Bolton Committee (1969–1971) and the report it released in 1971. This report, as we will discuss in Chapter 5, certainly entrenched a lot of the terms of subsequent enterprise policy debate. However, it also drew on what had happened previously, with the identification of the 'Macmillan gap' as a particularly significant foundation. It is therefore important that we understand how forms of what we may now consider to be enterprise policy looked prior to the Bolton Committee. This involves two core, interrelated themes of finance and regions that we discuss respectively in this chapter and the next.

The changing political landscape produced in the early twentieth century a very different approach to national government, largely ignoring regionally focused, limited-scale small businesses, concentrating instead on continuing to support mergers and large businesses throughout the majority of the first half of the twentieth century. This new approach to centralisation and state intervention also extended much further, into welfare and the economy, with the financial crises that followed the Great Slump in the 1930s. However, while the first half of the twentieth century was an era of concentration and very large businesses, we must not ignore important changes outside of these trends that would carry significance as foundations for the events of the late 1960s and beyond. Beyond the dominant focus on large firms, small businesses did continue to feature in political considerations and actions, albeit often in ad hoc or incidental ways (Beesley and Wilson, 1981).

In this chapter we will argue that the 1930s saw the emergence of enterprise policymaking and consideration of small businesses as a distinct grouping. In particular, the crises of the 1920s and early 1930s led to the development of one of the central recurring themes in enterprise policymaking: access to finance. After setting out the political context of the time, we therefore focus in detail on an analysis of the identification of the Macmillan gap in finance for small businesses and the policies that resulted. We discuss Credit for Industry as an example of the type of response that would set some of the patterns for future interventions, including what was arguably the most prominent result of enterprise policymaking in the first half of the twentieth century. We then discuss in detail the Industrial and Commercial Finance Corporation, a long run organisation seeking to address the finance problems of small firms.

Beginning the Interwar Years

As discussed in Chapter 2, the nineteenth century saw various forms of state intervention, but a laissez-faire approach to government predominated, especially in relation to industry. This began to change with a series of significant political changes that arose out of the Great War (1914–1918) and developed during the interwar years (that is, until the Second World War in 1939). The war had necessitated the development of large-scale bureaucracy and regular consultation between central government and key non-governmental interests with government policy encouraging mergers, for example in the engineering industry, that saw small firms merge into large combines. Large businesses therefore often came to replace the small, family businesses that had traditionally existed, often through the 'absorption and competitive elimination' of small firms (Hannah, 1983: 1).

This applied not just to areas such as manufacturing but also to services. The 1918 Treasury Committee on Banking Amalgamations (also known as the Colwyn Committee, after its chair) was established to examine changes in the financial industry. Specifically, it considered the development, through mergers and a competitive marketplace (i.e. failure of competitors) of the Big Five banks, which had systems of branches in place of local, independent banks. While it was not apparent at the time, more recent analyses of the interwar years have demonstrated a resultant cartelisation and a tendency for the large banks to confine their activities to the formal provision of short-term loans to largely captive markets, reaping monopoly profits (Scott and Newton, 2007).

The implications of these changes in the financial sector for small businesses would come to form an important factor in the emergence of enterprise policy (see the following discussion), but they were largely ignored at the time. Carnevali (2005) argues that the Colwyn Committee too was influenced by banking interests instead of, for example, considering the impacts of a reduction in competition for customers such as small businesses. Bank representatives argued that their practices had increased the flow of financial support to the 'small man' (see, for example, analysis of the evidence presented in Billings et al., 2019). The one manufacturer to speak to the Committee gave contrary evidence but, as a lone voice, his representations of local businesses unable to access finance were unlikely to have had much impact (Carnevali, 2005). The Committee ignored the concerns of small business, believing that the future of British industry should be led by large, centralised banks best suited to supporting the needs of large businesses. However, the Committee did lead to future mergers being regulated in the financial sector, effectively ending the merger boom.

The end of the Great War had also contributed to the creation of a mass electorate designed to enfranchise men over 21 who had fought for their country but also extended to women aged over 30. In turn, this led to wider political developments in the interwar years, including the fracturing of the governing Liberals and the development of a Labour Party which, with a new constitution, separated from the Liberals whose governments it had predominantly supported since it was established in 1906. While Labour lost the 1918 General Election to a Liberal–Conservative coalition led by David Lloyd George, its socialist constitution and trade union support would come to have important implications.

The Doldrum Twenties and the Intractable Million

The 1920s saw the growth of a relatively affluent middle class (see, for example, discussion of regional disparities in Chapter 4). For the 'bright young things' these were the 'roaring 20s.' However, the interwar period was, after initial economic gains following the Great War, predominantly one of uncertainty and recession, exacerbated concerns about maintenance of the British Empire and its international power and influence. Pigou (2016: 42) referred to the 1920s' economic struggles as 'the doldrums' and the persistent unemployment that accompanied them as the 'intractable million.' The second half of the 1920s also witnessed significant labour unrest, including a General Strike in May 1926 in support of coal miners who were in a dispute over their pay and conditions.

The scale of the changes affecting the nation at this time is reflected in artwork and commentary, such as in Robert Flaherty's film *Industrial Britain* (1931). Contrasting idyllic scenes of traditional work, from windmills and small-scale manufacturing, with 'the world that coal has created' [4.30], smoke-filled urban centres and 'bewildering acres of streets' [4.48], the film highlights the radical changes to the economy and to wider society that were still not fully realised when faced with the long-term presence of 1 million unemployed workers and the associated social impacts.

In addition to unemployment insurance, significant government subsidies, industrial intervention and infrastructure projects attempted to stave off the persistent unemployment, although, in contrast to more recent times, without recourse to the promotion of self-employment or small firms. While business formation rates increased, especially during the slump that followed (1929–1931), Foreman-Peck's (1985) analysis of regional business formation rates during the interwar years concludes that 'the great majority of new firms and the small business sector should not be regarded as seedcorn, but as chaff in the wind of economic recession' (p. 403). While much of UK industry was still organised as small-scale units, these struggled to compete with larger, more efficient plants abroad. Radical changes in the industrial makeup of the country were underway in terms of what Foreman-Peck (1985) describes as 'the formative years of the corporate economy increasingly dominated by giant, multi-divisional firms' (p. 42). This saw increases in productivity and output compared to the pre-war period but without the needed reductions in unemployment.

In 1925, Chancellor of the Exchequer Winston Churchill took Britain back onto the gold standard (which had been largely abandoned after 1914), with the potential to improve perceptions of the stability of the economy. However, it also meant significantly increasing the price of UK exports, deflation and further damage to industry, contributing to the persistence and severity of unemployment. Limited available finance and high interest rates are likely to have further restricted the activities of new businesses and small firms and contributed to the challenges of restructuring industry, including the new industries that might have responded to the high levels of unemployment.

Throughout this period, there was an unfolding shift in emphasis from traditional laissez-faire to forms of government intervention. While engaging local authorities in efforts to encourage local infrastructure projects, there was also a centralisation of the relationship between government and industry. Such developments moved emphasis away from small businesses and contributed to the problem of these businesses lacking a central voice to speak for their interests at a national level. This will become a significant issue throughout the book.

Political Responses

In the 1929 election the three main political parties understandably focused on unemployment as they tried to win over the country's largest ever electorate (women could now vote from age 21, a further increase in the size of the electorate). With no wage flexibility or international free trade and increasing welfare state commitments, a return to the laissez-faire approach of the past was not possible. This left political debate focused on the form and limits of state intervention.

The Liberals, while fractured and in decline, would continue to be relatively radical in their responses to crises. Led by former Prime Minister Lloyd George, they built on the Liberal Industrial Enquiry of 1925 (whose membership included influential economist John Maynard Keynes) and produced a raft of policy proposals. The development of these proto-Keynesian ideas made the case for state intervention, including significant funds for infrastructure projects (with a focus on roads, housing and the telephone network). However, the underlying economic arguments for this approach had yet to fully develop or to garner sufficient support.

The Conservatives, in contrast, ran under the slogan 'Safety First.' They made concerted efforts to discredit the general approach proposed by the Liberals, trumpeting their successes in government and proposing to limit intervention in industry. However, as Rubinstein (2003: 164) notes, 'The Tories appeared to have no issues to run on, and no really successful record of legislation or achievements in office.' For their part, Labour, who had themselves previously proposed state investment to tackle unemployment, now sought to account both for why Lloyd George's ideas stole from them and also for why these ideas would not work. They produced a 'slovenly' pamphlet (Skidelsky, 1967: 60) that attacked investment in roads and argued for the value of central planning.

Nonetheless, Labour won the 1929 election, forming a minority government with Ramsay MacDonald as Prime Minister and Philip Snowden as Chancellor of the Exchequer. MacDonald's administration did not fundamentally challenge the idea that industry should not be supported by government but that there was scope for public works to try and create employment. They also attempted to achieve a balance between international and domestic agendas, for example in seeking to secure tariff reductions. This agenda, and the government's efforts more generally, demonstrated a 'failure of imagination' (Skidelsky, 1967: 89). There was a lack of new ideas that were needed to tackle the scale of the challenge confronting the government as they moved into the 1930s:

> Lack of education, lack of talent, bad administrative arrangements all tended to make Labour ministers timid when they should have been bold. But irrelevant doctrine exposed their intellectual vacuity to the civil servants who, in effect, took over the running of the country.
>
> (Skidelsky, 1967: XXIII)

In terms of our focus, Labour's work on 'home development' and attempts to address unemployment did not lead to small business–focused enterprise policy.

The Great Slump

While the exact causes of the stock market crash of 1929 are complex and disputed (Galbraith, 1992: 187, ties it to the 'great speculative orgy [that] occurred in 1928 and 1929'), what resulted was a financial crisis and subsequent depression that was international in scope, reflecting the complexities of the global finance system and the vast international loans that had been made during the Great War. The global nature of the crisis and 'the complicated interaction between political, economic, social and psychological factors [meant that it] profoundly affected and changed the lives of ordinary men and women throughout the world, condemning millions of them to destitution, misery and despair' (Rees, 1970: 282). As America began to drastically reduce international lending, the new vulnerability of the UK currency became increasingly apparent. The Great Depression that followed the crash saw UK unemployment rise from 1.2 million in March 1929 to 1.7 million a year later. We discuss the wider impacts and the extreme poverty that resulted in some areas of the UK in Chapter 4.

The crisis and Labour's inability to address it, especially from the position of a minority government, led to the formation of a coalition government of all parties. Then, with the General Election on 27 October 1931, coalition-supporting politicians were returned, with Ramsay McDonald continuing as Prime Minister. This National government had intended to establish business and international confidence but failed to do so and this period saw the 'flight from the pound' (Skidelsky, 1967: 384). The country left the gold standard (again) and introduced a form of imperial trade protection. With subsequent crises (in particular the Second World War in 1939), national and coalition government would continue to be the norm, generally dominated by a substantial parliamentary majority for the Conservative Party, albeit with shifts in emphasis and control, until the Labour government that was elected after the war in 1945.

This period saw an intensification of key debates that had existed since the end of the Great War, for example significant lobbying for a reduction in the 'burden of taxation' by politicians, banks and business groups including the National Confederation of Employers' Organisations and Federation of British Industries (Skidelsky, 1967: 297). Government engaged with economists in debates around the degree and form of investment in public works, how to increase exports and free trade versus tariffs and protectionism (with political opinion largely now opting for the latter).

Despite the dominance of the Conservative Party in the coalition governments, the 1930s saw significant state intervention in the economy and industry, including government loans for shipbuilding, the continuation of agricultural marketing board schemes and, in 1933, the nationalisation of the passenger rail and bus system in London. Hannah (2004: 92) attributes this process to an acceptance among 'a wide range of middle opinion' that public corporations could offer a solution to problems encountered in parts of the national economy, just as earlier interventions at municipal level were generally accepted in response to sets of pressures (also see Millward, 1995).

In one of the central patterns that will come to shape the history of enterprise policy and the development of key institutions, in the 1930s tough economic conditions saw an upsurge in the number of people entering self-employment, prompting greater attention to these businesses and their concerns. However, the specific issues of small business and how they might relate to exporting or reducing unemployment struggled to gain traction in political debates.

A Near Miss in Proto Enterprise Policymaking

In 1930 Lloyd George, together with Kerr and Seebohm Rowntree, produced *How to Tackle Unemployment. The Liberal Plans as Laid Before the Government and the Nation*. They argued that 'the healthy life of the State depends upon free and abundant enterprise' and that enterprise was restricted by excessive taxation, especially where it prevented reinvestment into a business. While largely focused on industry and the 'industrialist,' their conception of enterprise also extended to 'the inventors, the born organisers' (p. 27). In this vein, they criticised the big banks for not doing enough to support industry (especially in comparison to other countries such as Germany) in a way that prefigures a core theme of enterprise policymaking to come: 'Nor have they catered for the smaller businesses which are so important in the aggregate, and which represent the kernel of the big businesses of the future' (p. 27). They proposed an Industrial Bank to be staffed by private sector expertise but publicly supported:

> The Bank would not remain a permanent investor in the businesses helped, though it would feel responsibility for seeing that its advice to investors was justified in the event. It would act as intermediary between smaller manufacturing concerns and the investor [and provide some protection/confidence for small investors].
>
> (p. 28)

This idea of small businesses being disadvantaged by the practices of the finance sector would come to be one of the central themes of UK enterprise policy (see the following discussion) but did not become established from these proposals. An area that received greater immediate attention related to smallholdings as an area of industry where small business should be actively supported by the state.

In contrast to a factory farming approach, the Liberals proposed actively supporting family farms. The rationale was that such an approach would support a large number of people on the land more productively and that 'if proper marketing and co-operative facilities are available, the family farmer can live successfully in face of the fiercest competition' (p. 43). Lloyd George and his collaborators recommended that the state acquire land for family farms, investment (in technology, new family farms would have to agree to use modern methods) and lower tax (especially death duties), with the state acting in the traditional landlord role. Detail was provided on how to develop family farms, applicant selection processes and additional support (e.g. a continuation of Unemployment Benefit for the first year). As we will see later in the book, in many respects the different aspects and general approach of this plan (support for disseminating industry best practice, subsidies through tax exemptions) would have pre-empted a lot of what was to become standard enterprise policy design.

The idea of creating a class of smallholders had been around for a while, for example in the Irish Land Purchase Act of 1903, which sought to provide funds to buy out the estates of large landowners. A version of the Liberal farming plan was taken up in the Land Utilisation Bill that was hinted at in the king's speech at the end of October 1930 and made it to a second hearing in Parliament. The Bill had two key elements, one large- and one small-scale. The first involved a £6m fund for an Agricultural Land Corporation to invest in large-scale innovations and experimentation that involved a form of compulsory purchase that was attacked in some quarters as representing a form of nationalisation. The second part centralised the provision of smallholdings, taking this power from county councils in order to enable the minister to provide land for the unemployed and other applicants. Skidelsky (1967: 257) records that 'no financial limit was set to this section, but it was calculated that it would cost about £1m for each 1000 holdings, agreeing with the Liberal estimate of £100m for acquiring and equipping 100,000 small-holdings.'

However, while the plan was brought forward, it gradually fell apart through debates around costs and Conservative attacks on the element of perceived nationalisation that was contrasted with their own calls for protectionism. Speaking in the House of Commons, Minister of Agriculture Dr Addison explained what he saw as the reason for the impending failure of the policy:

> The second line of advance was the development of schemes for the utilisation of land. The Land Utilisation Bill, which was read a Second time before last Christmas, is still not on the Statute Book. That is not the fault of the Government. Is it my fault that I am still unable to take a demonstration farm? Is it my fault that we cannot take land that needs draining, and put men on to it? The responsibility rests with hon. and right hon. Members opposite and their friends. Is it my fault that we cannot take land and put men on to smallholdings? Hon. and right hon. Members opposite and their friends at the other end of the passage are to blame. Their main complaint is that the Land Bill is too courageous; that it attempts to do too much.
>
> (Hansard, HC Deb. 20 July 1931 vol.255 col.1199)

In this way, the plan to promote and support smallholdings in the agriculture sector failed. However, this period would produce a lasting influence on enterprise policy, not directly through the proposals of Lloyd George and his Liberal colleagues but in a small but (eventually) influential detail of an investigation into finance and industry.

The Macmillan Committee

The Committee on Finance and Industry was established 5 November 1929, chaired by Hugh Pattison Macmillan, a Law Lord. It proceeded to hold 49 meetings, examine 57 witnesses and receive written submissions from a range of representative organisations and individuals (Macmillan Report, p. 1 and pp. 187–189). Chancellor of the Exchequer Philip Snowden set up the Macmillan Committee and the Treasury Minute (dated 5 November 1929) directed that it should:

> . . . inquire into banking, finance and credit, paying regard to the factors both internal and international which govern their operation, and to make recommendations calculated to enable these agencies to promote the development of trade and commerce and the employment of labour.
>
> (Macmillan, 1931: VI)

However, its initial plans were quickly overtaken by events and the Committee was required to make sense of the slump of the 1930s rather than the doldrums of the 1920s. This meant even higher rates of unemployment to consider but also introduced an international element to reflect the nature of the crisis emanating from the US's stock market crash. This included the rapid rise of securities marketed by industry, reflecting wider changes with important implications for the economy and industrial makeup of the UK.

The membership of the Committee faced with this task included a range of political, academic and industry interests, including Reginald McKenna, a Liberal politician who had previously been Chancellor of Exchequer and Home Secretary; Ernest Bevin, General Secretary of the Transport and General Workers' Union and future Labour Party government minister; and influential (and soon to be even more influential) economist John Maynard Keynes (who had lost a fortune in the stock market crash himself). Keynes authored the Committee's report and dominated many of the debates and questioning of witnesses. However, the report produced did not represent a unity of opinion: Bradbury registered a dissenting memorandum, feeling that there was already too much management of economic and monetary issues and there were also other noted reservations and forms of disagreements that emerged as the Committee worked (Kindleberger, 1987), perhaps reflecting the newness and uncertainty of many of the challenges they faced.

Emerging ideas in economics around prices, wages, business cycles and the national and international monetary system were discussed. A great deal of attention was paid to monetary policy and the role of the Bank of England, such that Gordon (1972: 970) described the Committee's report as 'midwife to the birth of modern central banking.' Even different 'language' was spoken by different participants, for example those 'talking in pre-War language' or those unsure of the 'new terminology and the new ideas which [Keynes had] introduced into the science' (The National Archives [TNA]: T200/6/1). Expert witnesses interviewed included representatives of banks and industry. A range of economists (e.g. including

Pigou) also spoke to the Committee, with debates often quite complex and with little clear evidence with which the Committee could reach a conclusion. Macmillan summed this up:

> The thing that appals [sic] me, after listening for many days to this discussion, is this: That while the fate of everyone apparently to a large extent is determined by decisions which are taken upon knowledge and upon principles which seems to me extraordinarily recondite, extraordinarily difficult to understand, and upon which you do not find agreement among the professors of the science.
>
> (TNA: T200/6/5 p. 204)

Macmillan was concerned with the Committee's work being beyond the scope of a layperson, but this equally applied to politicians and political decision making. Nonetheless, the Committee was keenly aware of the importance and implications of their considerations. As Gordon (1972: 961) notes, they realised the significance of their work, the dangers involved and 'sooner than most English-men, they accepted the development of mass unemployment in 1930 and 1931 as a problem that was not transitory, and bent their energies to this new test.'

Before 1931, monetary policy only rarely entered cabinet discussions. Williamson (2003: 14) records a famous statement from Labour cabinet member Sidney Webb, Lord Passfield, who was president of the Board of Trade in 1924, regarding the suspension of the gold standard that 'nobody even told us we could do that.' In contrast, Skidelsky (2003: 426) argues that things were very different afterwards and that 'Keynes's appearance before the Macmillan Committee marks the start of the Keynesian Revolution in policymaking.' It is worth quoting a portion of the Committee's deliberations to get a sense of this context:

MR. KEYNES: . . . if we assume that the Bank of England balance sheet tells the truth, they are as near as possible 'bust', and we ought to do something about it.

LORD BRADBURY: I think it is a safe assumption that that is not correct.

MR. KEYNES: If one has to consider what sort of amount of reserve they ought to hold, one is very much in the dark.

CHAIRMAN: The important point is whether the reserves as disclosed justify the assumption that they are so inadequate as to embarrass the Bank of England in the pursuance of monetary policy.

MR. KEYNES: Whatever the figures of the concealed reserve may be, their earnings must have been declining very greatly in recent times, so that while they may have had a sufficient margin at one time it does not seem to me certain that they might not reach a point which the Federal Reserve Bank reached some years ago, in which their policy in the management of money was really influenced by the desire to earn a given revenue. It seems to me frightfully important that in all readily conceivable circumstances the Bank of England should feel quite free not to be influenced in the slightest degree by the necessity of earning a given income.

MR. FRATER TAYLOR: We are considering a very serious situation. Why should we be so much in the dark?

MR. KEYNES: I do not know.

(TNA: T200/6/5 p. 178)

Not everyone who spoke to the Committee saw the country's problems in monetary terms. Others saw problems with management and productivity in industry and called for intervention, albeit with few concrete suggestions (and a return to ongoing political debates around tariffs).

The Macmillan Committee finished its report in May 1931 and it was published in mid-July. The primary policy recommendation was to work with the US and France to expand credit and that this required the intervention of governments, not the private institutions of central banks, and the stimulation of international trade and international loans, a 'grand design for world reflation' (Skidelsky, 1967: 296). However, assessments of the immediate impact of the Committee's work present it as underwhelming. The report was largely ignored in the press and by a public engrossed by developments elsewhere, not least in Germany as the Nazis gained prominence (Skidelsky, 1967). Reviewing the report for the *Economic Journal*, Stamp (1931: 431) observed that:

> The worst that can be said about the Macmillan Report is that, in the face of our present tremendous and urgent problems, its recommendations for immediate relief seem feeble and nerveless; but no one ought to make this criticism unless he is prepared to assert that there actually exists a field of active possibility which has been unexplored.

Later assessments of the Committee report's impact echoed Stamp's contemporary evaluation. Kindleberger (1987) was critical of its 'confused' contribution to policy, citing differences among Committee members. Moreover, Kindleberger (1987) and Gordon (1972) each highlighted the limited impact of the Committee's report on the scale of problems faced by the UK (and world) economy at that time. In contrast, Alford (1972) describes how the May Report on National Expenditure published soon after Macmillan 'carried a much clearer message and a more easily assimilated programme for action than the Macmillan Report' and that it was taken up despite being 'intellectually bankrupt as an analysis of the country's economic ills' (p. 38). Nevertheless, Gordon (1972: 972) observes that 'in the history of social thought, and in particular of thought on economic policy, the Macmillan Committee occupies a significant place.' For our purposes, the point of interest in this report rests in the brief consideration given to the position of small businesses.

Representing Small Firms to the Committee

The traditional small family businesses had raised money privately, without recourse to the market, and this may partly explain the lack of interest in these businesses in discussion of the financial sector. However, Keynes' belief in the causes of the financial failure as related to a savings glut could potentially be tied to a lack of finance available for small firms and entrepreneurs. Nonetheless, for Keynes and many others, small businesses' individualism and unpredictability placed them beyond government policy, and this had traditionally led to limited government intervention in these forms of economic activity. Small businesses were almost entirely excluded from discussion in the Committee and the submissions it received.

The one exception was William Perring, who represented the National Chamber of Trade (NCT), which was the central organisation of 360 chambers and associations of traders. Perring was a former member of Parliament but was also a businessman speaking in terms of his practical experience and conversations with fellow traders. The NCT submission stated that, while many businesses were able to obtain the financial resources required to expand their business, there remained:

> . . . considerable doubt as to whether traders in a small way of business, and those who are in their early stages, and who may be unable to deposit full security, do get that consideration from the banks which, we submit, should be forthcoming in those cases where character, personality, enterprise, and general business acumen exist. Where the position of a business is fully disclosed, and all the necessary documentary evidence produced, we feel that the foregoing considerations ought to be taken into account more fully than they are at present.
>
> Some risk is inseparable from progressive business, and the banks should be prepared to take it in such instances as those cited, and after all it would be slight compared with that which the banks have accepted in connection with larger financial operations.
>
> (TNA: T200/8/6 p. 226)

Small businesses were identified in relation to the lack of finance for industrial growth, in the range of £5000 to £200 000. In highlighting their concerns, the NCT presented a view contrary to the submissions of the large banks that had shaped the Colwyn Committee a decade earlier. Developing this contrast further, the submission presented potential reasons for this problem, citing the loss of discretion by bank managers at a local level, the refocusing on speculative activities instead of supporting 'legitimate industrial and commercial enterprise' (p. 226) and banks supporting the merger and consolidation of larger businesses. The

NCT suggested that: 'traders should enjoy the benefits of cheap money in regard to their borrowings from the bank in higher degree than is extended to them at present' (p. 226).

In discussion, Perring emphasised the severity of the challenges faced outside of London, in particular in the North and Midlands, and extensively challenged the suggestion that the answer to the country's difficulties was the continuing consolidation and growth of large-scale businesses. In outlining an argument that large businesses had often grown from small beginnings through financial support, Perring explained his view:

> I think it is much more difficult for a small man, a man with brains, to start as a master man to-day, to build up an industry, than it used to be. He finds it more difficult to use his brains and organizing capacities in developing industry for himself, on the somewhat more competitive lines that are in vogue to-day. I mean the banks do not extend to that type of man the same type of support that they would have done 30 or 40 years ago.
>
> (p. 228)

Perring was challenged repeatedly by the Committee on this line of argument and his inability to support arguments and anecdotes with data, although this had been a common theme across many areas of debate. Perhaps unsurprisingly, the position of small businesses was also not an issue that was highlighted by the representatives of the large banks and big businesses that spoke to the Committee, and the topic was not among the primary issues that focused the attention of the economists. Nonetheless, what was to become known as the 'Macmillan gap' in available long-term finance for small businesses did make its way into the final report.

The Macmillan Gap: The Birth of UK Enterprise Policy

The report outlines financing of industry, including the appropriate function of 'financial organisations' (which includes financing new enterprises as well as 'acting as intermediaries and financial advisers in the case of mergers,' Macmillan, 1931: 172). The report emphasises that 'these functions . . . are often difficult, which entail considerable risks and which may involve the temporary locking-up of large sums' (ibid). Almost as an afterthought, the report then notes:

> It has been represented to us that great difficulty is experienced by the smaller and medium-sized businesses in raising the capital which they may from time to time require, even when the security offered is perfectly sound. [. . .] The expense of a public issue is too great in proportion to the capital raised and therefore it is difficult to interest

the ordinary investor by the usual method; The Investment Trust Companies do not look with any great favour on small issues which would have no free market and would require close watching; nor can any issuing house tie up its funds in long-dated capital issues of which it cannot dispose. In general, therefore, these smaller capital issues are made through brokers or through some private channel among investors in the locality where the business is situated. This may often be the most satisfactory method. As we do not think that they could be handled as a general rule by a large concern of the character we have outlined above, the only other alternative would be to form a company to devote itself particularly to these smaller industrial and commercial issues. In addition to its ordinary capital, such a company might issue preference share capital or debentures secured on the underlying debentures or shares of the companies which it financed. The risks would in this manner be spread, and the debentures of the financing company should, moreover, have a free market. We see no reason why with proper management, and provided British industry in general is profitable, such a concern should not succeed. We believe that it would be worthwhile for detailed inquiries to be made into methods by which other countries attempt to solve this particular problem.

(pp. 173–174)

This single paragraph devoted to the difficulties experienced by small- and medium-sized businesses is presented by the Committee towards the very end of its report. Nonetheless, while hedging its conclusions ('It has been represented to us'), the report implied a market failure in terms of the provision of business finance that is perceived as not only harming the daily operation of small businesses but also acting as a brake on their business growth: firms are not able to invest and thereby expand, for example, by developing new products, entering new markets or through hiring new employees. It also recommended, albeit provisionally, that government should take action in considering this problem.

This one paragraph, while brief and unobtrusive, was published in a context where the issue of small business finance and the position of smaller enterprise in the economy more widely was beginning to be discussed (see, for example, the Liberals' *How to Tackle Unemployment* discussed previously). The report focused these debates in relation to consideration of a severe national crisis. It highlighted small businesses as experiencing a challenge specific to this otherwise apparently heterogeneous grouping. It also began to establish them as an interest group distinct from larger businesses. This produced an object of enterprise policy and a key path for enterprise policymaking, attempting to fix supply-side problems in small firm access to finance. The identification of what came to be known as the Macmillan gap can therefore be considered the birth of enterprise policy in the UK.

This section of the report was therefore to have greater immediate impact than much of the complex economic debate that had informed the preceding 170 pages of the report. Frost (1954: 181) records that only the Committee's 'authorship of the Gap keeps its name alive—and quite vigorously alive—in the City today.' For Piercy (1955: 1), an economist, chairman of the Industrial and Commercial Finance Corporation (discussed further later in this chapter) and director of the Bank of England, 'Nothing in the report attracted such lasting attention as the signalling of this "gap."' This significance is reflected in the ways in which the Macmillan gap spurred several policy initiatives that we can retrospectively label 'enterprise policies.' In the next chapter we draw out and focus on the regional policy aspects of these early enterprise policies. There we will explore these issues in relation to the 1934 Special Areas Act, which included a £1m loan fund targeted at supporting small enterprises. In the present chapter, we focus on the provision of finance more generally. However, before considering the policies that sought to address the Macmillan gap, it is useful to briefly consider whether the gap existed.

Was There a Macmillan Gap?

Archival studies have struggled to definitively demonstrate the presence or absence of the gap in finance for small businesses (Alford, 1972), a key problem being a lack of demand side evidence. However, there were significant changes in terms of investment behaviours and wider banking practices. As Frost observes (1954: 189), 'the development during the 1920s of a large-scale market for quoted industrials was the result of a change in the taste of the investing public away from unquoted and in favour of quoted issues, and that this created the Macmillan Gap.' With potential investors able to invest in a range of relatively attractive opportunities, such as large businesses, overseas opportunities or government bonds, there were few incentives to invest in the potentially problematic small businesses (Cox, 1986).

Moreover, the increased costs to lenders owing to information asymmetries, associated with lending to small businesses, have been identified as a barrier. Developing this line of argument, Carnevali (2005) suggests that the existence of such information asymmetries stems from the concentration of the banking sector in Britain, rooted in the 1920s, resulting in there being few regional banks possessing sufficient local knowledge of small businesses within their locality to reduce information gaps. The large, national banks had changed the nature of banking, moving away from the traditional forms of 'relationship banking,' which Scott and Newton (2007: 892) describe as underpinned by close personal monitoring of clients by bank directors embedded in their local business milieu. Instead, this was replaced with a more bureaucratic 'transaction banking' approach involving highly liquid asset portfolios, careful screening of applicants for loans, collateral securities, short-term lending and regular monitoring of a business client's account but in a more superficial way than may have been the case in the past (Baker and Collins, 2010). So, while definitive evidence for a Macmillan gap is lacking, changes in investment patterns and banking practices heightened problems of information asymmetries and perceptions of risk that would be expected to contribute to small businesses finding it more difficult to secure finance. With or without definitive evidence, identification of the Macmillan gap led to several initiatives that can be considered early forms of enterprise policy.

Unemployment Continues to Grow

To establish new policies and dedicate sufficient resources, an agenda would need support from the Treasury. This department of government had been forged in the age of laissez-faire, and this shaped its approach to controlling government expenditure and balancing the budget. Skidelsky (1967: 390) records that 'its conceptions did not embrace the new government departments created before and during the war, which it starved of money,' that it was 'no instrument for initiating policy, though through its control of money it was admirably placed to block it.' This can be seen, for example, in the Treasury undermining the scope of public works for creating employment.

In the first half of the 1930s, unemployment never dropped below 2 million and almost reached 3 million. These distressingly high figures 'were based upon insured workers, they excluded categories such as the self-employed, agricultural workers, and married women who did not sign on for the dole [unemployment support]' (Stevenson and Cook, 1994: 65). In the 1930s, the disaffection and protest in response to high levels of unemployment, from hunger marches to the activities of the National Unemployed Workers' Movement (as well as other, potentially more dangerous, organisations such as the British Union of Fascists) created significant alarm in government. This produced legislation to assert control over extra-parliamentary movements but fewer initiatives relating to economic policy (Stevenson and Cook, 1994).

However, there were several attempts (public and private) to address the Macmillan gap. Carnevali (2005: 27) lists the following initiatives:

> Charterhouse Industrial Development Co. Ltd (connected to the insurers Prudential Assurance Co, Lloyds Bank, and the Midland), Credit for Industry (a subsidiary of the finance company United Dominion Trust, 50 per cent owned by the Bank of England), and

Leadenhall Securities (created by the merchant bankers, Schroeder and Co.) were the main institutions that tried to provide small amounts of capital to the smaller firms.

We will focus on the example provided by Scott and Newton's (2007) detailed analysis of the Credit for Industry scheme. This scheme is representative of the key theme of access to finance that has persisted in enterprise policy ever since.

Credit for Industry

Scott and Newton (2007) studied the initiatives established to address the Macmillan gap through archival evidence (internal business records, reports and memoranda to the Bank of England and the clearing banks) and found that, excluding Credit for Industry (CFI), the schemes predominantly targeted depressed areas and firms that would be ready to issue shares within the near future, that is, they did not get to grips with the heart of the finance gap. CFI did more directly seek to address this gap when it was set up in 1934 as a subsidiary of United Dominions Trust. It was established as a small-firm finance company 50% owned by the Bank of England. The CFI's press release of March 1934 claimed that 'this new company will meet a specific criticism of our banking system made by the Macmillan Committee' (cited in Scott and Newton, 2007: 909) and it was specifically available to make long-term loans of capital up to £50 000 for up to 20 years. It originally planned to establish advisory networks, but this was superseded by the Special Areas Reconstruction Association (see Chapter 4).

It is worth noting that, in directly addressing the Macmillan gap, CFI posed a threat to the banks in terms of taking away business but also, if successful, it would demonstrate their own shortcomings, perhaps creating renewed public pressure for change. The CFI was reliant on the support of the banks, as shareholders in its parent company and providers of a lot of the finance it was offering, and it was not difficult for them to limit its expansion. Scott and Newton (2007) demonstrate how the CFI's 'operations were severely constrained by the clearing banks, which undermined its viability by "poaching" clients it had vetted and approved. . . . [arguing that the banks] acted as "jealous monopolists"—frustrating officially sponsored attempts to foster the development of specialist medium-long-term industrial lending institutions' (p. 885). This form of poaching after CFI had invested time and resources in vetting a business meant that CFI administrative costs were significantly increased while reducing potential investments by as much as 75%. Moreover, the firms the CFI assisted were still dependent upon banking facilities and therefore 'the banks held an effective veto over CFI's clients—by threatening to withdraw facilities' (Scott and Newton, 2007: 912). Finally, and in addition to the difficulties discussed, CFI proved reluctant to take risks on new ideas or new companies and it was ultimately unsuccessful in addressing the Macmillan gap: by 1943 it had made loans to just 173 firms.

The Second World War

Despite the hopes of 1918, by 1939 the country again faced a catastrophic war with wide-reaching implications for the UK and the wider global order. Many more millions died around the world, both as a direct result of the war and also due to the disease and famine that it fostered.

Domestically, the advent of the Second World War is associated with a marked increase in levels of state influence in the economy. The war centralised control and administration of society and the economy, including higher rates of taxation. Discussing the case of aircraft industry business Short Brothers, which was nationalized in 1943, Howlett (1995) argues that there was no great plan to nationalise private industries. Rather, nationalisation was a last resort and applied in cases of strategic importance. In the case of Short Brothers, it came about in response to 'strategic and political pressures associated with the high profile heavy bomber programme, pressures to which the management of the company seemed impervious' (Howlett, 1995: 253).

In other instances, the government had been able to use its position as the dominant consumer in the economy and through legislation to shape the economy and influence the actions of those operating within it. However, while the Second World War impacted the structure and levels of concentration of British industry, Millward and Singleton (1995: 313) suggest that the war '. . . seems at most to have accentuated or reinforced trends that can be observed before 1939 and after 1945.' Nonetheless, as Rubinstein (2003: 226) argues, the 'forced equalitarianism and quasi-socialism of the war years plainly benefited the ideals of the Labour Party, as did the fact that the Second World War was a "people's war" against fascism.'

The Post-War Labour Government

Labour won the post-war election and established a government that would last until 1951 (following a narrow election victory in 1950). Despite the challenges of rationing and austerity, Labour established radical change and a new political consensus that would stand for decades to come. Amidst a sense of a 'national' agenda and national policymaking that was a legacy of the war effort, changes included the creation of a welfare state and National Health Service. The Bank of England was nationalised (although the financial industry was left alone), as were many key industries including transport, utilities and iron and steel industries. The nationalisation of road haulage, which was not a natural monopoly, was opposed and left smaller businesses outside the nationalisation programme. However, while clearly significant, the nationalisation programme was not as radical as it could have been: the nationalised industries were generally centrally controlled and managed by boards in ways that often did not significantly differ from when they were in private hands. The control of these industries (and the means of production) were not placed under the control of the workers.

This political momentum established a consensus that formed around social democracy, broadly Keynesian(ism) interventionist policies, a mixed economy, the welfare state and full employment. Many of these policies were popular, the government was relatively successful in keeping unemployment low (and supporting those who were unemployed), and changes such as the health system were to become a core part of UK national identity and pride for generations to come. In the late 1940s, the Conservatives accepted Keynesianism and the priority of full employment, though with much greater emphasis on the private sector. As we will see, this consensus would hold until it began to wobble in the 1970s before a new consensus of free market neoliberalism emerged under Thatcher after 1979. For our purposes, what is of particular interest are the enterprise policies that were developed as part of the reconstruction efforts after the war within this interventionist political consensus. Politicians re-engaged with the Macmillan gap (and therefore an enterprise policy agenda), establishing the Development Areas Treasury Advisory Committee (discussed in Chapter 4) and the Industrial and Commercial Finance Corporation.

The Industrial and Commercial Finance Corporation

The Industrial and Commercial Finance Corporation (ICFC) was perhaps the most prominent manifestation of a UK enterprise policy agenda in the first half of the twentieth century, with its longevity and its explicit focus on targeting exclusively smaller businesses. At the time of ICFC's establishment in 1945 it represented an institutional formation combining (with some significant tensions) government, the Bank of England and clearing bank interests. It was explicitly to address the Macmillan gap which, while remaining disputed, was now a phrase in common usage to refer to the failure of the UK finance industry to provide long-term finance for investment in small businesses. It was exclusively focused on smaller firms (in terms of the amounts of finance sought), with a different organisation (Finance Corporation for Industry) established to support large businesses. In enacting these activities, ICFC came to be what Coopey (1994: 263) characterises as 'the first venture capitalist' and it eventually became Investors in Industry, a multinational private equity and venture capital company.

A new organisation to address finance for small businesses was first discussed by the Committee on Post-War Employment (CPWE) in 1943. While the Board of Trade wanted greater scope and a focus on specific sectors, the Treasury and the (not yet nationalised) Bank of England resisted this. Instead, an alternative approach was developed, establishing ICFC as a Public Limited Company receiving no public subsidies but funded by the Bank of England and the major clearing banks to provide loans to those firms seeking between £5000 and £200 000 (in line with the figures quoted by Macmillan). This still involved discussion with the clearing banks throughout 1944, with some resistance to the initiative. Given that the banks viewed these firms as not appropriate for long-term investment and that there had so far been little to prove them wrong, it is perhaps unsurprising that they would view the scheme as doomed to failure.

While the Bank of England was also sceptical, it 'felt the creation of the ICFC was a necessary evil to prevent Labour's original hopes for a national investment bank' (Merlin-Jones, 2010: 5). The Bank of England opposed any plans to link the ICFC to government policy or to approach funding regionally (the more political focus of enterprise policy at the time, see Chapter 4), but it did play an important role in convincing the clearing banks to participate. According to Coopey's research (1994: 264), the Bank of England convinced the clearing banks that it would not look good for them to be seen as resisting rather than leading this type of initiative, especially 'given the adverse publicity they had experienced, the threat of nationalisation which was still being mooted in some quarters, and the fact that the war had left them with a high level of liquidity.' Eventually, the banks and the Bank of England subscribed up to £15m of share capital, with facilities for ICFC to borrow a further £30m (Frost, 1954).

The first ICFC chairman was William Piercy, a Labour supporter (he was made a baron by the Labour government in November of 1945) with experience in the Inland Revenue and the London Stock exchange, he would go onto to become Director of the Bank of England in 1946 (whilst retaining his ICFC role until 1964). Piercy had a background in economics, the City and the civil service and sought to drive forward ICFC with a hands-on approach to the details of the applicant businesses and in handpicking many of the staff (Kinross and Plant, 1967). Nonetheless, there was a distrust of Piercy amongst the clearing banks, in part because of his perceived socialism (as a Labour supporter). Coopey and Clarke (1995) also suggest that he may have been viewed as 'devious' because of his ability to work within the political system and to engage with an area of investment where the banks were alleged to have underperformed.

ICFC adopted stringent criteria, generally avoiding any proposals where involvement would be below around £25 000, avoiding those firms, including sub-contractors and many small businesses, viewed as too risky and unstable for long-term investment (Frost, 1954, records that, by 1953, ICFC had increased the average size of its investments to about £50 000). Crucially, ICFC avoided firms that would not relinquish equity, potentially excluding many small business owners whose degree of engagement with the business may preclude them being willing to share ownership. For those firms that did proceed, ICFC continued to be rigorous in its exploration of potential risk through technical and market assessments. Coopey (1994: 265) describes ICFC as creating an internal 'industrial department' rather than relying on consultants as banks commonly did at the time, focusing in particular on the quality of management within the firms it assessed. A later study by Mitchell and Clay (1979) concluded that the application of ICFC's exclusion criteria 'leads to quite widespread feeling (even among its customers) that ICFC drives a hard bargain' (p. 67).

This led to some concerns that ICFC was not focused on addressing its central objectives, for example in 1947 when ICFC supported the National Gas and Oil Engine Company. Questions were raised in Parliament about why this company could not have accessed finance through normal channels and whether government would take steps to ensure ICFC would focus its 'future activities to providing accommodation for small businesses which have difficulty in raising finance in the market and so not superseding existing sources for the supply of capital' (Hansard, HC Deb. 1 April 1947 vol.435 cols.1837–1838). The response largely failed to engage with this question, confirming Treasury consent for the actions and that the primary concern was 'that money goes into useful and productive enterprises' (ibid). Subsequent to this debate, further questions were raised seeking assurance that the government would not intervene in the operation of ICFC and that it would not compete with existing financial provision (e.g. Hansard, HC Deb. 15 April 1947 vol.436 col.27).

While ICFC limited its criteria, Coopey and Clarke (1995) describe how the banks widened the scope of their operations such that there were fewer businesses to refer to ICFC, and those that were referred had significant weaknesses. One might wonder if this extension of bank lending is an indication that ICFC was fulfilling its core role in addressing the Macmillan gap. However, having such organisations at a distance from government and being largely apolitical can exclude such considerations. More problematically, and similar to the experience of Credit for Industry (discussed previously), Coopey and Clarke describe banks actively seeking to take business from ICFC once it had spent time evaluating potential investments. A tension therefore continued between the banks and the ICFC, Coopey and Clarke (p. 73) providing the example of ICFC's celebratory dinner at the time of its tenth anniversary when 'all the shareholders declined to send a representative.'

Tensions between ICFC and the banks continued through the 1950s as the ICFC diversified its activities, for example through the formation of the Estate Duties Investment Trust in 1952. ICFC opened a branch in Birmingham in 1950, then in Manchester, Edinburgh, Leicester and Leeds, to more effectively market itself and to develop knowledge and understanding of local markets and businesses. This expansion took place despite 'grave reservations' from senior members of the Committee of London Clearing Bankers (Baker and Collins, 2010: 88). Baker and Collins discuss the record of a March 1955 meeting between David Robarts of the National Provincial Bank and ICFC Director Piercy in which Robarts criticised activities undertaken by the ICFC that he viewed as outside the scope of the Macmillan gap and therefore competing with the provision of finance by the market. Robarts explained that the banks 'wished to be assured, as shareholders and as lenders of money to the Company, that they were in future going to pursue their proper purpose of filling the Macmillan gap, and were not going into other fields' (p. 89).

The issue of finance and small firms was then taken up again, this time by the 1959 Radcliffe Committee (see the following discussion). Baker and Collins (p. 92) report a draft response from the Clearing Banks to the Committee stating that they could see no point in the ICFC. However, with the organisation praised by the Committee and an agreement to reduce its reliance on bank funding, 'it is clear that the clearers were glad to be shut of this historical aberration in financing the business sector' (ibid).

The subsequent development of the ICFC saw it align with the political focus of the mid-1960s, including focusing on spin outs and a 'technology gap,' as a result beginning to move away from the Macmillan gap. The ICFC underwent significant changes, leading to a 'loss of . . . overall identity and purpose' (Merlin-Jones, 2010: 14), and certainly a loss of focus on small businesses, following a merger with Finance Corporation for Industry in 1973 to become Finance for Industry. It continued to expand its base of activities, including overseas expansion, and to adapt and develop as the financial market changed in the 1980s. For example, it embraced the rise of the venture capital market as the organisation again 'regenerated itself, taking on a striking new identity, restructuring and rationalizing its activities and radically altering its corporate philosophy' (Coopey and Clarke, 1995: 135). This resulted in a 1983 rebrand as Investors in Industry (abbreviated as 3i), before the organisation was floated on the stock market in 1994 (Lonsdale, 1997).

Coopey and Clarke (1995: 74), in what stands as an official history of ICFC, claim that 'there seems little doubt that a fully funded ICFC using the investment strategies forged in the 1950s, would have made an even greater impact on the Macmillan gap.' However, while continuing to provide finance to small businesses as a part of its activities throughout the changes ICFC underwent, it became defined more through its long-termism than as a central force of enterprise policy. It is unclear the extent to which addressing the lack of finance for small businesses was always the key driving force behind the organisation or whether more funding would necessarily have extended its reach further for those firms unable to access finance through more traditional channels. As we will see throughout this book, the creation and long-term survival of ICFC was not an end to the policy question of supporting small businesses or entrepreneurs to access finance, as evidenced for example by the work of the Radcliffe Committee.

The Radcliffe Committee

The 1951 election saw Winston Churchill and the Conservatives return to power after six years in which Labour had significantly remade the country. The Conservatives stayed in power until 1964 yet, broadly speaking, they reinforced a post-war consensus in continuing macroeconomic interventionism with no concerted effort to reverse the majority of what Labour had achieved. They were unprepared to risk a return to high levels of unemployment amidst outstanding national debt, the Korean war and the threat of balance of trade deficits. The Conservatives denationalised iron and steel, but also pursued areas of what can be considered new forms of nationalisation, for example with the creation with the UK Atomic Energy Commission. The new consensus is sometimes referred to as 'Butskellism': a term, in part mockingly used by the *The Economist* newspaper to characterise the continuity from Labour's Hugh Gaitskell to the Conservative Chancellor of the Exchequer Rab Butler (who had argued for many for these policies prior to the end of the Labour government).

In the 1950s, restrictions on lending, the increases in requests for funding advances following the difficult economic conditions of the early part of the decade and political pressure on banks to limit lending led to further difficulties in access to finance for small firms. In 1955, these qualitative restrictions on bank lending were extended with quantitative controls imposed by the Bank of England (excluding loans supporting exports). Carnevali and Scott (1999: 60) quote a senior manager at Barclays who explained how small firms effectively gave up applying for financial support:

> . . . the small trader is certainly more liable to be hit than the larger or medium concern. This is not due so much to direct action as to the indirect effects of the squeeze, such as a general tightening and shortening of credit which has placed the more slender resources of the little man under greater strain. . . . *The banks are conscious that there is a very heavy suppressed demand for accommodation.*

As the decade continued, so too did the difficulties for small firms, limiting the availability of finance in the market as well as leading to further restriction of the activities of the ICFC. In many cases this led to business failure and the impacts were reported to the Bank of England by banks. Carnevali and Scott's (1999) archival research reveals that these effects were deliberately kept from being made public and that there 'is no mention in Bank of England files of possible measures that could be taken to avoid the credit restrictions forcing small firms into liquidation' (p. 60), demonstrating the significant limitations of enterprise policy at this time.

While the Macmillan Committee was held a decade after the First World War, another committee was appointed to consider similar monetary issues a decade after the second: the Radcliffe Committee (the Committee on the Working of the Monetary System). The Committee was again chaired by a Law Lord, in this case Cyril Radcliffe, and included academic members A. K. Cairncross and R. S. Sayers. It was established in a similar context of massive international debt, substantial devaluation of the pound and increasing cartelisation of the banking sector. Perhaps surprisingly given the advances of time and economic theory, there were many core similarities in the approach of the respective committees, for example in emphasising the use of discretion by central banks (Griffiths, 1974). Unusually, the report did not offer formal recommendations, seeking more to challenge ideas and offer ways of thinking about the challenges the country faced, focusing, for example, on issues of liquidity. While welcomed by government, the approach to monetary policy put forward was not well-received by economists, and Gordon (1972: 976) judged the report to be 'a dead document, of historical interest only.'

However, the Radcliffe report did call for greater availability of term loans for small businesses. It reinforced the idea of the Macmillan gap, in terms of a 'difficulty in borrowing' for small businesses, particularly in relation to its potentially restricting businesses' potential for growth. Nonetheless, this remained disputed by the banks, who continued to insist that any Macmillan gap resulted from a lack of creditworthy customers. However, Carnevali's (2005) in-depth analysis of a Midland Bank scheme suggests that the problem might have been more specifically related to the insufficient returns available.

Following the Radcliffe Report, Midland Bank launched a scheme that received significant press coverage, and was lauded by the bank's official historians and, 10 years later, was reviewed by the Bolton Committee (see Chapter 5 on this Committee and its work). The Bolton Committee found that the scheme was unsuccessful due to a lack of demand. However, Carnevali's research found that the scheme was 'little more than a public relations exercise' (p. 125) that it continued standard practices of focusing on short-term credit repayable on demand (i.e. insufficient for investment and small business growth). Carnevali's research identified instructions from the bank's head office instructing branch managers to discourage term loans. Nor did other banks respond to Radcliffe's call for help for small businesses in any meaningful way. The perceived difficulties of small businesses to access finance would continue to be a central, unresolved theme in UK enterprise policymaking.

Conclusion

As we have seen, small firm access to finance is a topic of debate that emerged from the changes in the economy and industrial makeup of the country following the First World War. This intensified after 1931 and the identification of the Macmillan gap, with the Macmillan report functioning as a convenient shorthand label, even if the work of the Committee did little to evidence or substantiate the problem. What this facilitated was the identification of small firms as a distinct interest group (albeit sometimes referred to as the 'small man' or 'small trader') with distinct problems resulting from a form of market failure. Discussions focused on the role of government in addressing the concerns of this interest group with general public and political acceptance of the market failure, even while this was persistently resisted by the banks (Baker and Collins, 2010). It is this debate focused on small firms as a distinct grouping that we identify as the birth of enterprise policy in the UK.

However, despite widespread adoption of the term 'Macmillan gap' and ongoing public and political debate, the perceived market failure was not challenged by regulators (e.g. the Bank of England also accepted the existing model of banking) and there was no attempt to address how the banks operated. Further, there was little consideration of demand-side problems and why small firms may be reluctant to apply for finance, especially in relation to equity finance but also more generally in terms of their perceptions and expectations of the finance sector. Instead, the policy approach pursued was to help provide additional forms of support for small firms. This tended to involve government supporting the establishment of limited companies in collaboration with the clearing banks (and involving investment from the latter) rather than direct government intervention. In this way, the early enterprise policy agenda reinforced and maintained the 'rules of the game' and privileged the interests of the existing financial institutions. This chapter has demonstrated how the existing financial institutions were very quick to defend their interests through significant dispute and debate, predominantly among clearing banks, the Bank of England and the Treasury. As a result, the fledgling attempts to support small firm finance were often restricted in their activities and limited in their successes, either through lack of funding (which relied on the existing financial institutions), political pressure or undermining of schemes through practices such as 'poaching' by the banks.

Nonetheless, small business financing problems such as those identified, albeit in passing, by the Macmillan Committee report remained a persistent area of enterprise policymaking. The Macmillan gap was considered by the Radcliffe Committee (1959), the Bolton Committee (1971, discussed in detail in Chapter 5) and the Wilson Committee (the Committee to Review the Functioning of Financial Institutions, 1979), which singled out small firms for special consideration. Where governments did intervene more directly in response to these debates this tended to be as part of a wider regional development agenda, and this is the focus for our next chapter.

4   Regional Enterprise Policy

In Chapter 3, we discussed how a range of factors including tough economic conditions and the growing dominance of large businesses during the interwar years created a challenging environment for smaller businesses. Further, there was the identification of a distinctive problem facing smaller businesses who sought to access long-term finance. In terms of how these challenges were addressed by government, a core feature of early enterprise policy emerged regarding the regional focus of many interventions, especially in relation to the mounting unemployment crisis of the early 1930s.

This policy agenda centred on a recognition of regional disparities and included the opening up of a second core area of enterprise policymaking, its support for regional development. As we will discuss in this chapter, regional policy was not primarily focused on small businesses, and the small business elements of regional initiatives tended to focus on providing alternative sources of finance akin to the national initiatives discussed in Chapter 3. There were some interesting innovations and moves towards deeper engagement with the businesses that we will highlight throughout the chapter but, as we will discuss, these tended to be limited in scope and often significantly underdeveloped. To explore these themes we will first discuss in detail the development of the 'Special Area' approach to regional policymaking and its implications for enterprise policies and then outline the years of relative neglect of enterprise policy in the 1950s and 1960s.

The Need for Regional Policy

The economic challenges arising from the doldrums of the 1920s and the subsequent great slump (outlined in Chapter 3) created significant regional disparities. Where previously, regional problems had been largely limited to rural areas of decline such as in the Scottish Highlands or Ireland, there were now large areas of the UK affected by the depressed state of the basic industries. Principally, this meant a difference between the South East and Midlands and areas in the North of England, Scotland and Wales. A common response to the decline of the staple industries was 'to seek the replacement of competition by co-ordination' (Page, 1976:

181), often through concentration (including mergers and the creation of cartels) to attempt to reorganise industry to reduce capacity, increase efficiency and maintain prices. As we will see throughout this chapter, these would be the predominant themes for several decades.

While the South East and Midlands in England, or 'inner Britain' (Foreman-Peck, 1985), was relatively prosperous and benefited from the job-creating power of new businesses, this was in stark contrast to the 'outer Britain' of the North and of South Wales, areas where the local economy depended on traditional industries. In this way, 'outer Britain' suffered from the concentration of the country's staple industries where depressed international trading and demand led to significant industrial decline and mass unemployment, while a short distance away the South East found 'a new industrial structure was being established which provided the real basis for the export boom and the rising prosperity of the second half of the twentieth century' (Stevenson and Cook, 1994: 12). These growth industries included motor vehicles, aircraft, chemicals and construction and building.

The areas that failed to benefit from these new industries became an issue of great social and political concern as unemployment in some areas of the UK rose as high as 70%. In the ironstone mining areas of Cleveland, the unemployment rate amongst adult males reached over 90%. Some argued that unemployment support helped to maintain this worklessness, where lowering this support would encourage labour mobility as people would then leave the deprived areas to find work elsewhere. Debate increased through 1930, with frequent, exaggerated stories in the press about benefit cheats and huge pay-outs to those judged to be undeserving (Skidelsky, 1967). George Orwell (2000: 125) nicely captured this attitude in an essay on unemployment written in 1928: '"idleness in luxury", as the Conservative newspapers say in righteous indignation, . . . [is] on closer inspection "a state of near starvation."'

Brockway (1932), a socialist and member of the Independent Labour Party (to the political left of the Labour Party, which he had previously represented as an MP) travelled around most of the UK, discussing the experience of unemployment (and the Means Test used to distribute relief payments). Brockway describes in detail several industrial regions (Lancashire, the Black Country and Birmingham, the Tyne and Tees, the Docks and Valleys of South Wales, Glasgow and the Clydeside) as well as agricultural areas suffering the impacts of persistent unemployment. For example, in Jarrow in the North East of England (which would, in 1936, see the famous Jarrow March of unemployed workers to London to deliver a petition to Parliament), where some areas had unemployment of 70%:

> I think the distinguishing feature is that the housing is so bad and the poverty so constant that the people have given up any attempt to make themselves or their homes look well.

There are no clean curtains in the windows, the pavements are dirty, the passages smell, the children are ragged, the women's hair is unkempt, the men are unshaven. There is one woman here—a very decent woman who, in other circumstances, would take pride in her home—who expresses it like this to me: "One hasn't the heart to try to keep the place clean."

(p. 100)

This is before taking account of the limited diets and poor health in such areas. In terms of our focus, there were also significant implications for local businesses:

One thing strikes me at once: the shop premises which are to let [observing that] one in four seems to be vacant. One gets here an insight into what an unemployed population, incapable of buying outside a narrow range, means in distress to the shopkeeping class. Every one of these little shops tells a tale of failure for some family.

(p. 88)

Unemployment was, then, an extremely serious, regional problem tied to the decline in traditional (exporting) industries. It led to mass protests and hunger marches (Miller, 1979) and required government to take action in response.

The Special Areas Act 1934

As early as the 1909 Development Act, there were also attempts (largely uncontested) to utilise public works (such as road improvements) to address unemployment. This involved the creation of a Development Commission and of Commissioners able to assess and report on the particular projects on behalf of the Treasury. However, the initial attempts to address regional unemployment in the late 1920s framed the problem as one of 'surplus population,' and this involved trying to get people to migrate away from the more deprived areas of the country, offering financial aid and training for those willing to do so.

Industrial Transference began in 1927 as coalminers were transferred between mines and into other industries, coordinated after 1928 by an Industrial Transference Board. The intention behind this policy, focused on labour, was to retrain workers whose skills were suited to declining industries and to facilitate movement to those areas in which industries were expanding (McCrone, 1969). Pitfield (1978: 429–430) records the recommendations made by this board:

. . . that the placing work of the employment exchanges be publicised; that grants of assistance towards projects in distressed areas be discontinued in favour of Transfer Relief Works in the prosperous areas; that the number of training centres be increased; and that advances of fares, advances towards removal expenses and certain maintenance allowances be paid to transferees.

These recommendations were taken forward, and policy focused on supporting the mobility of the labour force to tackle unemployment. Generally people moved from Scotland, Wales and Northern England to the South East of England, in some years (such as 1929) numbers exceeded over 43 000 people.

Understandably, there were some concerns that the high level of migration would do long-term damage to the regional economies outside the South East. Together with calls from the Liberals and Labour for a more interventionist approach, these concerns led to growing public pressure about regional disparity and unemployment (increased by a high-profile series of articles in *The Times*) and, eventually, to government taking action (see, for example, Booth, 1982). The mixed motivation, combined with a lack of clarity or new ideas on how to address the problems, meant that the policies introduced tended to be somewhat disjointed (e.g. in how they related to the transference schemes) and hamstrung by a lack of conviction and a range of caveats and limitations set on them.

For example, Chancellor of the Exchequer (and future Prime Minister) Neville Chamberlain, working with an anti-interventionist cabinet, sought more laissez-faire solutions. Booth (1978: 144) cites Chamberlain discussing the matter in 1934:

Has it been brought home to these people that prospects are hopeless if they stay where they are; can that be done by an authoritative pronouncement; would it accelerate the move away?

Nonetheless, Balchin (1990: 65) considers that '. . . regional policy subsequently was largely concerned with "taking work to the workers" [rather than transferring the workers] through measures aimed at generating capital mobility from areas of growth . . . to the depressed regions of the north.'

The 1934 Special Areas Act focused on areas of high unemployment also known as the 'derelict' or 'depressed' areas (the labelling of the areas moving to 'Special' as the Bill made its way through Parliament). Instead of the previous attempts to relocate labour, this Act utilised the ideas of Commissioners and sought to address economic deprivation by encouraging businesses to relocate to the deprived areas. However, it was still limited, and more ambitious ideas such as investing in local infrastructure were not taken up.

Pitfield (1978: 435) quotes Ramsay McDonald describing the government's approach:

> The Government are taking on an area, a specially defined and examined area; they are going to take an experimental area, and not to begin and end there, but, just as a scientist takes his test tube into his laboratory, works out his results and their reactions, so we begin with that area for the purposes of discovery from the experiments cures, methods of handling, ways of spending public and private money, approaches to unemployment, and, having got these things out from a limited area, which nevertheless is representative in its problems of the whole country, we are going to extend these results of our working . . . by experimenting in the concentrated area you can reach your universal cure.

The Act targeted areas in South Wales, North East England, West Cumberland and Clydeside/North Lanarkshire, excluding the major towns, with a Commissioner for England and Wales and a second for Scotland. Their funding was limited (£2m or 0.05% of GDP), and activities were engaged via local authorities and voluntary agencies and were to be strictly limited to non-profit organisations operating outside the existing activities of national or local government. The focus on organisations not operating for profit suggests some of the ways in which the approach may have been limited in terms of building regional development capacity and the funding predominantly focused on improvement schemes for water, sanitation and hospitals and for land resettlement schemes.

Unsurprisingly given the extent of the areas affected by high unemployment and deprivation, there were criticisms and complaints about the specific areas chosen and those excluded from this form of government support. Government files relating to the Special Areas include a range of newspaper clippings highlighting different regions lobbying for inclusion. For example, a news report from the *Daily Express* (24 November 1936) states that representatives of districts near Wigan (in North West England) were due to 'plead' with the minister of labour to designate them as a new distressed area. The account states that 'a few years ago' there were 17 coal mines in the district but now there was just 1 mine working and records that, in one district of 7000 inhabitants, unemployment had stood at 85% for the past seven years (TNA: MH61/1/3). However, despite frequent attempts by different regions to lobby for Special Area status or extension of the boundaries of existing Areas, the original designations were maintained (Dennison, 1939).

Financing the Special Areas

From 1935 (including in the Conservative Party manifesto), the Treasury began to relax the restrictions on the Commissioners, for example in relation to requests to establish an industrial estate in the North East of England (discussed later). This was part of a shift to a more interventionist approach, beginning to provide aid to private business in order to appease the public. Eventually this became support for Commissioners providing financial aid to support the establishment of new enterprises in the Special Areas as a result of the 1936 Special Areas Reconstruction Act. As Booth (1978) notes, this development of a more interventionist approach was *in spite of*, not because of the political beliefs of many of those involved.

A central element of the 1936 Act was an engagement with the Macmillan gap in finance for smaller businesses that had been highlighted in 1931 (discussed in Chapter 3). Three organisations were established to address finance for small firms: the Special Areas Reconstruction Association (SARA) set up in 1936 by the Bank Of England with £1m available to provide loans of up to £10 000 to small firms in the Special Areas; the Nuffield Trust (launched in 1936 with a £2m gift from Lord Nuffield); and another £2m available through the Treasury Fund (1938, aimed at firms with more than 10 employees). The latter two were particularly focused on supporting businesses that would create employment. Further limiting the scope of these organisations, Scott (2000) reports contemporary criticisms around the restrictive assessment criteria, including in SARA and the Treasury Fund, requirements for businesses to access at least half the required capital from other sources.

The situation, especially in the case of SARA, was made more complicated by the different agendas at play. McCrone (1969: 95) notes that, because SARA was focused on small firms, 'it was clearly insufficient to exert a major influence on the economic structure of the Special Areas.' Meanwhile, Heim (1986: 257) records that 'few in London financial circles thought the programmes necessary, or believed that finance was the main problem of the depressed areas' but they were keen to avoid criticism and to deter large-scale government intervention. Heim further explains the focus on small firms which arose from SARA's capital having been partially raised by large companies that were keen for this money to not be used to fund their competitors. Heim (p. 258) explains that, no doubt heightened by the challenging economic conditions, 'Sensitivity to the charge of selective subsidization generally was another force hampering the extension of interwar regional policy and especially the efforts of the Treasury Fund, the organization most closely identified with the government.'

Interestingly, SARA staff included technical experts such as accountants who vetted applications for both SARA and the Treasury Fund, including making inspection visits, especially for smaller applicants. Firms that failed were identified as tending to suffer management problems and the engagement with SARA (and then also Nuffield) experts expanded to include the provision of advice, for example in terms of improving administrative structures within the firm.

Trading Estates in the Special Areas

The 1936 Special Areas Reconstruction Act was followed by the Special Areas (Amendment) Act of 1937 which amended the Special Areas Act 1934. Building upon and consolidating some of the initial experiments, it increased significantly the powers of the Commissioners, most importantly in terms of supporting profit-making enterprises. The new Act introduced concessions on taxes (e.g. firms in the Areas could be exempted from the National Defence Tax) and rents to encourage businesses to set up in the locations which benefited from the 1934 Act. They therefore began to form an interesting precedent for later developments such as enterprise zones (see Chapter 9).

Another area pursued by the Commissioners was in the establishment of trading estates in the Special Areas. These estates were very large, publicly visible areas of dedicated industrial land where factories were built and rented to businesses by non-profitmaking government-financed companies. The Special Areas Commissioners were inspired by the perceived success of private trading estates that had proven attractive to businesses. In particular, they appealed to businesses keen to rent factory space rather than to invest capital in purchasing these facilities and saw the benefits of being sited within effective transport and utility networks and near to related businesses, developing external economies of scale (Scott, 1997).

This form of intervention began with the over 700-acre Team Valley estate in Gateshead in 1936. Scott (2000: 59) describes the undertaking:

> Its plan incorporated similar factory design and landscaping elements to those found in successful private sector estates in the South East. . . . A large administration building formed its centre, around which were grouped banks, a post office and other services. Factories were built to both standard design and to the special requirements of manufacturers, including 'nest' factories for small firms. The company provided a full range of utilities, including an estate railway.

Booth (1978: 151) quotes a Board of Trade note from the time that commented on the significance, politically, of this development in regional policymaking:

> This is the first Government trading estate and constitutes a most interesting experiment in practical state socialism respectably cloaked as loans to private enterprise. It is a complete breakaway from the orthodox laissez-faire attitude of Governments in relation to the location of private industry.

Scott (2000) reports that, at Team Valley, research and sales staff were also established to provide advice for tenants, for example on markets and sales methods and other estates also provided consultancy services to support small firms. In a paper on 'Government Sponsored Trading Estates,'. Colonel Kenelm C. Appleyard (Chairman, North-Eastern Trading Estates, Limited, and Northern Special Areas Reconstruction Association) describes the arrangements at Team Valley for those small businesses viewed as having the potential to become national success stories:

> With such men in view, the Estate Company conceived the idea of offering men of this type what it calls a "nest" factory. "Nest" factories are 45 feet by 33 feet 6 inches in size, their total area of 1,500 square feet forming a quarter of a 6,000 square foot building. As with their larger counterparts, "nest" factories are fitted with electric light and power, provided with office accommodation, given full road access, and share equally in the communal facilities of the Estate.
>
> In special circumstances such factories are available at the very moderate rental of £1 a week, which covers rent, rates, the consumption of light and heat, and insurance on the building. For example, if an industry is new to the area or if a man has an idea which he feels can be developed industrially on a commercial basis, the special offer may be made available. . . . It is an extremely satisfactory development that many men, who otherwise would never have had the opportunity of starting on their own, have taken up this scheme and that their businesses are already showing signs of expansion.
>
> (Appleyard, 1939: 854)

By 1939, three giant trading estates (Team Valley and its counterpart trading estates in Wales, Treforest Trading Estate, and Scotland, Hillington Trading Estate) and several small-scale factory projects had provided access to over 300 factories that were employing 12 000 people. However, the development of these industrial estates, and the wider programme of regional policy, was disrupted in its early stages of development by the more immediate concerns of war in 1939. The idea of 'nests' to support the early development and growth of small or new businesses did not, therefore, fully develop as an idea in enterprise policymaking.

Evaluative Overview

Even with the associated costs of establishment of facilities and infrastructure, the approach adopted in the Special Areas proved to be a very cost-effective means of generating employment. According to Scott (2000), the cost per job was around £81, significantly below competing approaches such as government works schemes (£400/job). However, such fledgling enterprise policies remained 'pitifully small' in their scope (Rubinstein, 2003: 190) and were described by Labour politician Aneurin Bevan as 'an idle and empty farce' (cited in Stevenson and Cook, 1994: 76). Stevenson and Cook (p. 85) agree, arguing that 'the initiatives of the National government were few in the direction of economic policy, and the Special Areas Act and transference schemes were carried with little conviction and slenderer means.' Overall, fewer than 50 000 new jobs were created under the Special Areas legislation. On such limited scale, the schemes were never going to redress the regional disparities and huge levels of unemployment and deprivation.

Unemployment and the problems facing the Special Areas were not solved by such government interventions and early forms of enterprise policymaking but by the rearmament boom of 1938. This produced a large-scale industrial effort including the traditional industries in the depressed areas of the country, radically reducing unemployment. This in turn was then overtaken by the needs of the Second World War by 1939 and the new problem of shortages of labour. As we will see, this increased government focus not on new enterprises or small businesses but on national industries and large firms.

Nonetheless, the Special Areas Acts did establish an important link between enterprise policy and regional policy, in part due to the localised nature of many start-ups and small businesses. These experiments in intervention laid some of the groundwork for what was to follow post war in terms of the development of industrial estates and the provision of loans and other capital (see Chapter 3 for a discussion of ICFC, for example). Unfortunately, the post-war development of industrial estates did not take up the ideas of developing a supportive environment for small firms and, as we will see, tended more to focus on larger businesses and staple industries.

Planning for Post-War Reconstruction

Established on 8 July 1937 under the Chairmanship of Sir Montague Barlow, *The Royal Commission on the Distribution of Industrial Population* was tasked:

> ... to inquire into the causes which have influenced the present geographical distribution of the industrial population of Great Britain and the probable direction of any change in that distribution in the future; to consider what social, economic or strategical disadvantages arise from the concentration of industries or of the industrial population in large towns or in particular areas of the country; and to report what remedial measures if any should be taken in the national interest.
>
> (Barlow, 1940: 1)

The resultant 1940 Barlow Commission Report had important implications for large urban areas and for the development of the New Towns movement (addressing for example concerns about congestion in the major cities). Between 1946 and 1950, 14 new towns had been initiated and, in particular for those surrounding London, there were stringent guidelines about what industries could be established in these areas (Scott, 1997).

Writing in *The Spectator* magazine shortly after the Committee's report was published, Barlow (1940: 10) explained how policy interventions to-date had '. . . suffered from one grave defect, it treated the problem not as national in character but as one limited to urban or regional areas.' The step forward made in appointing the Committee was, according to Barlow, the examination of the problem from a national perspective, not in relation to more localised interests.

Barlow saw a case for increasing the efforts already being made, including decentralising industries and the industrial population, dispersing people to garden cities and satellite towns. But he was also keen to highlight how the Committee's work broke new ground (divisions over implementation notwithstanding), identifying the regional disparities of the past two decades as a national problem requiring the national coordination of industry. The Committee recommended a 'central authority' to oversee industrial distribution, utilising financial incentives (and, to a degree, restrictions on expansion), but also to further diversify the industrial base in the depressed areas of the country.

The report was debated in parliament on 17 April 1940 (after the Prime Minister had several times deflected engaging with it, arguing for the more pressing demands of the ongoing war). An MP from the North East of England provided the following overview from his reading of the report:

> The report produces abundant evidence that there is no real control over industry, that the Departments as a rule do not know what is happening, and that the chief Department, the Ministry of Labour, which has to supply the labour, never knows until a decision has been taken. I cannot speak of the strategic questions, but they were so important in the view of the Commission that they had to take important evidence in secret. There was enough made known, however, to justify the misgivings of the House and the country about allowing this growth to continue because of strategic reasons. It has been ironic during the past nine months to see the evacuation of the very business people who have always held that they came down to this part of the country because of business interests, and to see Government Departments quickly evacuating themselves from London when for years they stood against proposals that have been made for stopping this growth of offices in London.
>
> (Hansard, HC Deb. 7 April 1940 vol.359 col.1033)

These debates had relatively little consideration of small businesses, either during or in the aftermath of the war. For example, a House of Commons debate on the position of small traders in late 1941 lacked a clear policy agenda:

SIR H. WILLIAMS asked the President of the Board of Trade whether, in view of the Location of Retail Businesses Order, 1941, he is prepared to take steps during the duration of that Order to prevent multiple shop organisations [i.e. large businesses] from buying up the businesses of independent retailers?

SIR A. DUNCAN: As at present advised, I do not propose to extend the scope of the Order on the lines which my hon. Friend suggests.

MR. SHINWELL: Is the right hon. Gentleman aware that there is throughout the country considerable discontent, particularly on the part of small retailers who have been thrown out of business as a result of the war, when they see the chain stores and multiple shop organisations flourishing? Is it not possible in some way to protect the interests of the smaller people and curb the activities of these octopuses in business?

MR. KIRKWOOD: Is it not the policy of our party, the Socialist party, to eliminate the small man?

MR. SHINWELL: Is my right hon. Friend aware that it is no part of the policy of any party in the House to eliminate the small business man in order to give advantage to the multiple shop organisations?

SIR A. DUNCAN: This is obviously a very controversial question, but with regard to the specific point put to me, I would remind hon. Members that the Retail Trades Committee, which made a report on this subject, advised that it would be very unhappy if anything was done to limit the possibilities of sale for the independent traders.

(Hansard, HC Deb. 18 November 1941 vol.376 cols.156–157)

Nonetheless, once the rearmament boom and then the necessities of war had ended, the challenges associated with the regional policy agenda of the 1930s would return. Scott (1997: 363) cites President of the Board of Trade Hugh Dalton's March 1944 diary entry, which gives an indication of where policy ideas were at this time:

[Distressed area policy] is a very simple problem. These areas had too few factories in them and too little variety of industry. The remedy is . . . more factories. . . . If this is persistently followed for several years, the problem will be solved . . .

Attlee's appointment of Dalton, over Bevin, to serve as Chancellor of the Exchequer following Labour's General Election victory in July 1945 was 'a tragedy for the conduct of economic policy' (Dell, 1997: 19). Still, Dalton's appointment as Chancellor came at a vital time for a country facing the challenges of not only recovering from war and from demobilisation but also addressing the economic weaknesses that had dogged the country before the war.

None of the previous problems of dependence on the industries of the past in particular areas of the country had been fundamentally altered during the war and, with a war time economy receding, the structural problems of unemployment looked set to return to where they had been in the 1930s. In response, politicians looked to the same set of solutions (utilising policies remained on the books, since the Special Areas legislation had not been repealed) albeit now 'intermingled' with administrative machinery that had developed during the war (Booth, 1982: 15). The new government built on the foundation of the Distribution of Industry Act with a large-scale interventionist, centralised approach to financing factory and infrastructure development, as well as seeking to support those firms that struggled to access finance, in order to achieve macroeconomic aims and reduce national unemployment. With the 1945 Distribution of Industry Act, the pre-war Special Areas (South Wales, Central Scotland, the North East, and West Cumberland) were renamed 'Development Areas' and extended, mainly to include adjacent urban centres. Wrexham and part of South Lancashire were then added in 1946 and Merseyside and part of the Scottish Highlands in 1949. These changes represented an increase from these areas covering 15.7% of the British population to 17.8% (Scott, 1997).

National Industrial Organisation

The biggest change of industrial policy with the advent of a post-war Labour government was the shifting of the boundary between public and private economic activities. Millward and Singleton (1995: 309) explain how 'By the end of the 1940s . . . one half of annual capital expenditure in the UK was undertaken in the public sector of which some 40 per cent was accounted for by the nationalised industries.' However, while some industries saw significant government intervention and areas of nationalisation, especially in what were seen as vital areas of the economy and where industries were related to export targets, in the remaining industries 'the Labour government [had] only a poorly articulated philosophy of how to cope with what remained in the private sector' (Millward and Singleton, 1995: 313).

The post-war reconstruction effort reflected the principles of cooperation that had been negotiated during the war. This was part of a process that started at the end of WWI where the government was looking to work with the emerging peak organisations to establish 'a national consultation and negotiating machinery for sector wages and working conditions' (Bennett, 2011: 39). Reconstruction would be planned, tripartism (state–industry–labour) would be retained and the institutions involved would have a greater part to play in the extended state, recognising a need to balance self-interest. In terms of government–industry relations, by late 1943, 'industry' (broadly grouped within representative bodies) had provided a relatively unified sense of how these relations could work in the post-war UK. Industry was willing to join a tripartite institutional arrangement that would provide assistance to the state, but which would also permit industry access to government and influence on policy. Middlemas (1986: 64) encapsulates the core of this deal:

> So long as government gave industry for the first time a substantive *generic* priority it would in return listen to what Ministers wanted; so long as it had a voice in the determination of that interest, at least as powerful as those of unions or the City of London, it would conform to the eventual national interest.

This had wider implications in terms of how problems such as unemployment in the depressed areas would now be addressed. For example, there was a shift of responsibility from the Ministry of Labour to the Board of Trade, whose remit involved the regulation of private industry. That is, the problem was addressed through a new focus on industrial coordination rather than the movement of labour. Scott (1997: 367) lists the criteria used by the Board of Trade when allocating government owned factories to the Development Areas in 1949, with an emphasis on employment rather than, for example, supporting small firms or business growth:

1. Employment
2. Availability of raw materials
3. Availability of essential machinery
4. Technical aspects re suitability of factory, etc.
5. Adaptations required
6. Foreign currency commitments
7. Status of applicant
8. Financial standing of applicant

A danger of this approach was that firms setting up additional capacity in the Development Areas were likely not to invest in this location (in contrast, the Board of Trade let firms set up R&D and more innovative functions in London) and, if the organisation was to experience difficulties, it was in these peripheral activities where layoffs were most likely to occur. Hague and Dunning (1954–1955: 211–213, cited in Scott, 1997: 372) explain:

> The suspicion arises that a number of branches were being exploited by their main factories, used to cope with demands beyond the capacity of the central factory and made to cut their output if any cutting had to be done.

A lot of this activity was therefore focused on large firms and industry-level negotiation that mostly excluded small businesses and enterprise policymaking. However, small businesses' access to finance did persist as an aspect of this regional policy activity.

The Development Areas Treasury Advisory Committee

Baker and Collins (2010: 73) quote a circular issued to branches of the Westminster Bank by its Chief General Manager in early 1945 that encouraged lending to small firms but not for long-term investment purposes:

> Given solvency and credit-worthiness the 'small man' is adequately catered for by the Bank; the provision of intermediate credits for periods ranging up to. . . *'five years' presents no problem to the Bank when commercial justification and reasonable safety can be demonstrated;* and, indeed, *except for the provision of long-term capital* the Bank affords adequate advance for all legitimate requirements. As a matter of principle a Deposit Bank should *not advance money on long term*; its lending policy should have as *its main object the temporary augmentation of a borrower's floating Capital* rather than the provision of funds to be invested in permanent assets. . . [italics in Baker and Collins]

Baker and Collins also discuss a similar memo from Lloyds Bank in July 1944 and an extensive review by Midland Bank in 1944. While banks, as we saw in Chapter 3, insisted that there were no problems with their practices, the difficulties for small businesses in accessing the types of finance needed to invest in significant, long-term growth continued to be perceived as an issue, especially in relation to the Development Areas where such business growth had the potential to create jobs.

The Development Areas Treasury Advisory Committee (DATAC) was established in 1945 to provide assessments for the Treasury on the commercial viability of a business and its inability to access funding elsewhere (superseding the similar structures that had supported the finance schemes under the earlier Special Areas Acts discussed previously). The financial assistance that these assessments could provide sought to target specific areas of the country or, after revisions in the 1958 Distribution of Industry (Industrial Finance) Act, where the Board of Trade identified that the finance provided would help address problems of persistently high rates of unemployment. Initially, it aimed to focus on grants rather than loans (c.f. the contemporaneous ICFC discussed in Chapter 3), although the specific remit and interpretation of the criteria developed over time, including becoming more restrictive during wider economic difficulties in 1947. It also saw the development of support and monitoring *after* finance had been provided, likely contributing to the relatively successful nature of the businesses supported (although this potentially innovative business support service was limited by an inability to gain treasury approval for additional staff).

There were also joint projects with ICFC, for example Coopey and Clarke (1995: 68–69) provide the example of 'Marchon Products, a subsidiary of Solway Chemicals in which DATAC had a major interest [and which] yielded a substantial profit for ICFC in the mid-1950s.' But, again, this potential development did not fully materialise beyond these initial projects and no formal arrangement was ever arrived at in terms of how the two organisations might continue to cooperate.

By July 1950, the DATAC scheme had committed finance of £2m and only 43 undertakings (Hansard, HC Deb. 4 July 1950 vol.477 WS). However, Carnevali and Scott (1999) present analysis from the Bank of England archives that demonstrates how the proactive offering of advice to businesses by DATAC, including appointing technical/managerial specialists, sometimes led to businesses taking their improved proposals and accessing finance elsewhere, similar to the poaching issues experienced by other schemes.

Carnevali and Scott (p. 62) provide an instructive example of the persistent limitation of such schemes considered as forms of enterprise policy with the potential to support smaller businesses:

> During May 1956, DATAC considered a supplementary loan application for £2,500 from A. L. Maugham & Co. Ltd, a chamois leather manufacturer. It was noted that 'it appeared that the company was handicapped by lack of funds which, before the "credit squeeze" could possibly have been raised without much difficulty'. The application was rejected despite the company being engaged in exports and having developed an innovative and more efficient manufacturing process. This was largely due to the undertaking being a small business, employing seven people, which could not therefore be regarded as of 'national importance'.

As we saw in Chapter 3, schemes aimed at supporting small firms to access long-term finance had certain strengths and often involved wider business support functions. The value of such schemes can be seen not only in the finance provided but also in the common theme of banks 'poaching' the businesses assessed. However, the schemes often remained small in scale, risk averse and focused on the larger of small businesses. They therefore failed to fully address the Macmillan gap.

The 1950s and the Conservatives

When the Conservatives returned to power following the 1951 election, they largely pursued an interventionist, Keynesian policy agenda. However, they did not continue to invest in any significant way in regional policymaking. While the legislation remained essentially unchanged, initiatives were no longer supported, 'with the partial exception of a few "blackspot" areas' (Scott, 1997: 41). There was a belief that regional unemployment was no longer a problem due to international demand and the reinvigoration of the staple industries on which many regions of the UK continued to depend. There were now concerns that encouraging new industries into the Development Areas would damage these staple industries, which were seen as more central and of greater importance to the economy.

Scott (1996: 50–51) quotes a 1956 Treasury memorandum:

> ... in North Lanarkshire, there is an unemployment figure of 3.5 per cent, but apart from this the realities with which the [Distribution of Industry] Act was originally designed to deal have disappeared. Indeed, I suspect the fluctuations of employment in the newer industries are likely to be greater than in the old-established ones.

Of course, this reinforced a lack of diversification in these regions, leading them to continue to be vulnerable to changes in the staple industries. In this way, the Conservative government had managed to 'achieve the worst of both worlds' (Scott, 1996: 55). Central planning and coordination continued for the major industries, but longer-term investments in the potential growth industries were denied support.

The end of the decade, 1959–1961, saw a period of collapse following a 1959 boom with economic restrictions in spring 1960 and, the following year, another currency crisis. This highlighted the fragility of the UK's recent prosperity and may have helped to encourage government, industry and trade unions to work together in the pursuit of economic growth through a sense of 'shared responsibility for economic policy decisions' (Blank, 1973: 221). This included negotiations around wage and price decisions as well as wider industrial planning.

Regional Policy but Little Room for Small Businesses?

In 1960, the Local Employment Act repealed and replaced the Distribution of Industry Acts. Regional development policy continued to target unemployment levels. In terms of enterprise policy, the ongoing focus on finance moved to the Board of Trade (although still with Treasury approval) and the DATAC was replaced with the Board of Trade Advisory Committee (BOTAC), but essentially with the same powers. However, the qualifying criteria were further restricted in an attempt to focus on those firms with a high chance of success rather than an inability to access finance elsewhere (Wren, 1996). The new 'Development Districts' were a lot smaller than previous focal points for regional policymaking, making the industrial estates approach less appropriate, although factory building and the provision of building grants continued.

The lack of focus on the concerns of small businesses may have contributed to Labour's slim 1964 electoral victory. The election followed the decision of Conservative Prime Minister Douglas-Home to push through the Resale Prices Act, abolishing resale price maintenance that had been in place to protect small traders from undercutting by large shops and chains. This may have cost the Conservatives valuable votes from the small business community.

The installation of a new Labour government saw an increased focus on regional policy, for example through the Industrial Development Act (1966). However, the new focus on economic growth rather than directly seeking to address unemployment soon faltered when, within a year, rising unemployment caused a reworking of this emphasis. The investment grants were now available to all firms, including new and small businesses that were not making taxable profits. That is, the changes continued the move away from targeted support seeking to address the Macmillan gap.

The Urban Programme, begun in 1968, represented a broad collection of policies targeting urban areas of 'special need,' that is, of disadvantage and discrimination. In part, this urban focus was shaped by increasing tensions around immigration. Within the programme of initiatives, there was expansion of local authority financial assistance for small businesses that would continue to play a significant role in this aspect of enterprise policy delivery, totalling around £26m per year by the mid-1980s (Wren, 1996). Nonetheless, while there was an opportunity for radical new approaches at this juncture, much policymaking was stuck within an established set of ideas, a set of dominant policy narratives that persisted (Atkinson, 2000). In terms of the economy and industrial policy, the focus continued to be on centralised negotiation among government, industry and labour bodies that tended to represent the interest of large businesses.

This emphasis was explicit with the Labour government's endeavours to support industrial development and economic growth through the Industrial Reorganisation Corporation, which focused on ensuring the 'optimum' size of firm. The IRC assisted the reorganisation and development of industries in terms of seeking to maximise efficiency and profitability, for example through the merger of GEC and Associated Electrical Industries. The guiding idea of this work was 'that production units in the UK were too small to be competitive in world markets' (Lonsdale, 1997: 46). In many ways, this was the very opposite of what we tend to consider forms of enterprise policy.

Negotiating the Post-War Consensus on Government and Industry

The tripartite means of organising the UK economy between the government, industry and labour continued to reinforce the consensus on centralised government intervention. In the early 1960s, it was under a Conservative government, rather than a socialist Labour administration, that the National Economic Development Council (NEDC) was established as the culmination of this tripartite approach.

The NEDC was a tripartite body comprising government and peak organisations representing collectively organised industrial and labour interests, acting as 'a national consultation and negotiating machinery for sector wages and working conditions' (Bennett, 2011: 39). It sought to coordinate economic activities and address the country's economic decline through a set of ambitious targets for national growth (Dell, 1997). This work was further extended through the 'little neddies,' the Economic Development Committees that focused on specific industries. Demonstrating consensus for this coordinated approach to government and industry, the incoming Labour administration of 1964 largely continued Conservative plans (Meadows, 1978; Dell, 1997). However, initially, negotiations involved three organisations representing industry.

The Federation of British Industries (FBI) was generally ineffective and lacked influence on government but had been well-placed to work with more interventionist governments after 1945 and was more united than, for example, the fractured Chambers of Commerce. The British Employers' Confederation (BEC) was more focused on labour issues and industrial relations, often overlapping and close to merging with the FBI. The third organisation was the National Union of Manufacturers (later National Association of British Manufacturers—NABM), predominantly an organisation of small firm members, and its approach was more tailored to the concerns of these members, with active local branches. The Devlin report (Devlin, 1972) recorded the membership of such organisations as dominated by small companies (those with fewer than 200 employees) and also including trade associations and employers' organisations which, in turn, represented many more small businesses. However, questions remained about the extent to which the actions of these organisations in tripartite negotiations with government were shaped by these businesses or the large- and medium-sized companies.

The Confederation of British Industry

The Confederation of British Industry (CBI) was formed in 1965 in response to the perceived need for effective representation of industry opinion via a merger of the three existing employers' organisations. This consolidation was supported by those seeking a counterweight to the Trades Union Congress (TUC) and from a Labour government seeking effective, clear means of discussion and planning with industry. However, NABM proved resistant to the merger, with significant concerns that the problems encountered by small firms would be ignored (leading to the creation of the Society of Independent Manufacturers, later to become the Smaller Businesses Association).

The CBI was generally focused on the large business concerns that were also the focus of government interventionist policy. Marsh and Grant (1977: 37) record the 1973 membership revenue of the CBI where over 50% came from large industrial companies (>1000 employees).

Nonetheless, NABM's inclusion in the merger meant that the new organisation had a substantial small business membership and these business owners began to demand more of a voice. In 1966, the CBI set up a Steering Group for Small Firms that later evolved into a fully fledged council and, ultimately, into today's Enterprise Forum. This growing small business lobby would come to have a significant influence on UK enterprise policymaking.

Conclusion

In the first half of the twentieth century, a second stream of policymaking relevant to enterprise gradually evolved in terms of addressing regional challenges. The elements of the regional policymaking agenda that addressed the challenges of small businesses tended to focus, almost exclusively, on access to finance, not on the development of new initiatives and not particularly responsive to local difficulties. However, it is notable that finance and regional development schemes, identifying what they saw as the key limitations facing smaller businesses, expanded to offer advice, for example in terms of improving administrative structures within the firm. These innovations point towards some of the key developments in enterprise policy that were to follow in the 1980s. However, at this time they lacked investment, time to develop or be rigorously evaluated and generally were very limited in scope and impact.

This regional policy agenda did establish a basis for the regional nature of later, more focused enterprise policy programmes such as Training and Enterprise Councils, Business Link and Local Enterprise Partnerships, including the emphasis on regional development but also the tensions between localisation and the ways in which this is constrained by centralised authority (through bidding processes, standards and funding). This would include the influence of European funding (and rules on subsidies), for example through the European Regional Development Fund as it related to the intertwining of regional policy and enterprise policy (see Chapter 7).

However, for the period discussed in this chapter, from 1931 until the end of the 1960s, there was a growing focus from government on large-scale businesses, especially in key industries. This played a central role in limiting the scope and potential effectiveness of enterprise policies. The centralised approach of government, focused on tripartite negotiations with industry and labour, also began to demonstrate the degree to which the owners of smaller businesses and the self-employed, and their potentially very different agendas, were excluded from such arrangements. The ways in which key groups attempted to raise the profile and influence of these interest groups provides the starting point for our next chapter.

5 Early Lobbying and Debating the Role of Government

In the 1960s, tensions grew between national strategies focused on large businesses and industries and the interests of smaller businesses. This represented the culmination of many years of growing prominence for large firms, their centrality for industrial policy and the wider economy and the beginnings of what would be a very long, drawn-out breakdown of the post-war consensus on industrial organisation, central planning and nationalisation.

Concerns over a decline in small manufacturing businesses and calls for greater acknowledgement and representation of the interests of small businesses led to the appointment of the Bolton Committee of Inquiry on Small Firms in 1969. The prominence given to this Committee in many accounts of UK enterprise policy in the years since leads us to focus on it in great detail in this chapter. We discuss the Bolton Committee in terms of its establishment as well as the processes of gathering and representing views on the role of government in relation to small businesses and the production of its influential report. As we will see throughout this and the upcoming chapters, the consolidation and promotion of a particular set of ideas and interests through the publication and influence of the Bolton Report was shaped by the wider political context and had important implications for the subsequent development of formal and informal institutions.

Economic Decline?

In the UK and elsewhere this was the age of the giant enterprise (Moran, 2009). Curran and Stanworth observe that 'big was still seen as beautiful and growth was seen as the key to the treasures of increased economies of scale' (1982: 3). More generally, Galbraith (1972: 50) asserted that 'by all but the pathologically romantic, it is now recognized that this is not the age of the small man.'

Through the 1950s and 1960s it was clear that British manufacturing was in trouble. Manufacturing output and productivity was growing at a slower rate than competitor nations, exports were suffering and, as

Matthews (2007: 775) records, profitability was falling such that 'by the late 1970s profits in British manufacturing were perhaps approaching zero.' This represented a general sense of national and economic decline. The degree to which the country was in decline is disputed, and the debate is outside the scope of this book. The decline narrative was used politically by whichever political group was in opposition to criticise the agenda of the government as resulting in the supposed decline (Tomlinson, 2016). However, what is clear is that the UK economy was changing. Services were growing, and represented a large part of the economy, but they were not yet the major export that they are today.

Falls in the number of manufacturing *establishments*, especially small establishments, were apparent in the Census of Production data collated 1924–1963 and provided to the Committee. In terms of small *enterprises*, the Bolton Committee's Report (1971: 59) notes that 'even in the period 1958–63, the population of small firms in manufacturing has declined by a thousand manufacturing firms a year, that is to say four firms per working day have gone out of business and have not been replaced by new firms.' As we will see later in the chapter, the Bolton Committee faced limitations in the available data and differences across industry sectors but it concluded that:

> . . . up to the middle 1960s the contribution of small firms to economic activity was declining in most industries with the possible exceptions of road transport and some of the miscellaneous service trades. Although there have again been exceptions we think it likely that in most industries this decline has been going on at least since before the war and there are indications that it has continued since the middle 1960s.
>
> (p. 67)

This sense of long-run decline in the economy in general and in the case of small businesses in particular was an important context as increasingly people began to question the post-war consensus.

Acorns to Oaks

Politically, small businesses became more prominent in the mid-1960s as part of a shift in position from the Conservative Party under its new leader, Edward Heath. In contrast with the broad consensus that existed in the first part of the decade between the major political parties (Labour and Conservative), the Conservative opposition now challenged the idea of detailed industrial planning and significant government involvement in industry. Setting out the Conservatives' position, Heath (1965: 9) charged that 'smaller enterprises may not fit into Socialist plans . . .' and promised action to support small businesses.

The contrast of small businesses with Labour's 'Socialist plans' by Heath and increasing frequency of references to small businesses in Parliament at this time (Beesley and Wilson, 1981; Dannreuther and Perren, 2013) gave indications of small firms' rise to greater political prominence. Beyond the overtly political debates, Geoffrey Ingham was publishing his study on the *Size of Organization and Worker Behaviour* (1970) and Jonathan Boswell was researching *The Rise and Decline of Small Firms* (1973) while E. F. Schumacher discussed 'a study of economics as if people mattered' in *Small Is Beautiful* (1973). In politics and current affairs magazine *The Spectator*, an article appeared criticising the main political parties for ignoring small businesses. The article, 'Mind the Acorns' asked:

> Who cares about small companies? Well, small companies do—passionately. But nobody else seems to give them a proper thought. The Government, when it notices them at all, sprays them with a kind of fiscal insect repellent: a disproportionate tax, an anomalous training levy, a restriction on their directors' earnings. The Opposition offers little present or prospective protection. And even the CBI is said (not altogether fairly) to show insufficient sorrow at their woes.
>
> (Michael, 1968)

The correspondent (a 'George Michael' who was rumoured to actually be part of the Confederation of British Industry's (CBI's) weekly magazine's editorial team writing under a nom de plume) goes on to make a case for the importance of small firms to the health of the national economy before recommending action. The article called for a survey of the challenges facing small businesses to inform government action to stop the decline of these businesses. The article adds: 'In the meantime, they could be given a kindly word or two about how good it is to have them around. After years of kicks and repression they would take heart even from that.' These words certainly seem to resonate with the position taken by the CBI at the time.

Continuing the acorns theme, the Conservative Political Centre published *Acorns to Oaks* (Weatherill and Cope, 1969) reinforcing calls for government to support small businesses. Bernard Weatherill MP was a Conservative MP with a background in running his family's tailoring business and who would go on to serve as Speaker of the House of Commons before his elevation to a life peerage. Weatherill had shared his views on small businesses in the House of Commons previously, including some of the ideas that informed *Acorns to Oaks*. Weatherill's co-author, John Cope, was a chartered accountant and former member of the Conservative Research Department, later being elected to Parliament in 1974 as an MP and then sitting in the House of Lords since his appointment in 1997.

Weatherill and Cope set out their case for government policy to account for small businesses, contrasting the small business agencies of Japan, the United States and Germany with the absence of such agencies in Britain. Arguing that simply removing the burdens of government leg-islation was insufficient, they appealed to the future Conservative gov-ernment to 'go further and give positive help to small businesses as their colleagues abroad have done' (p. 13). *Acorns to Oaks* is an outline for what the Small Business Development Bureau, previously signalled by Heath, could look like (Heath, 1965; Conservatives, 1966).

Weatherill and Cope (1969) foresee an organisation established as a government-funded body, with a minister responsible to Parliament for overseeing its success and use of public funds, but as independent of gov-ernment as possible. This new Bureau would 'exist to serve without fee or reward and it will be available to any firm qualified by size who wishes to use it' (p. 14). Once established,

> the aim of the Bureau should be to assist in the maintenance of a strong diversified foundation of healthy small firms and to develop constructive policies and programmes on behalf of such firms.
>
> It will do this by being ready with advice and help where necessary in the fields where small businesses tend to be weak, particularly finance, management and marketing. It could manage a programme for set-ting aside a proportion of government contracts for small businesses. It should act as the spokesman of small businesses to the Government and public, to ensure that the problems are understood and taken account of.
>
> (p. 15)

Making the Case for Small Firms

The CBI was also lobbying on behalf of small firms, asking the Board of Trade to take some positive action to address the grievances of its small business members (see BT360/4). Since the creation of the CBI in 1965, McHugh (1979) argues that there had been disquiet among some in small businesses that their voices were lost in an organisation oriented towards the interests of big business. Developments reflecting momentum build-ing behind small business advocacy, such as the launch of the Smaller Businesses Association, were thought to be increasing pressure on the CBI to demonstrate its role as an advocate for small businesses and their (owners') interests (TNA: BT360/4/1).

Amidst a tough economic environment, recent changes in legislation were perceived as making life especially difficult for small businesses (Boswell, 1973). Addressing the British Federation of Master Printers' Annual Congress, John Davies, the CBI's Director-General reflected that the small business owner might feel that their room for manoeuvre 'is being malevolently invaded' through burdens of estate duty, training levy, personal taxation, disclosure legislation, investment grants replac-ing tax breaks, plus administrative burdens from government. Davies concluded that government attacking the small firm 'seems to him [the small business owner] in accordance with all he has heard of government policies on re-structuring of British industry, mergers, concentrations and the like.' Although expressing some sympathy with the view that government was deliberately targeting small businesses, Davies felt this was incorrect and that, rather, '. . . all the additional burdens of which he [the small business owner] complains are the product of an excess of industrial theorising in government rather than of a pernicious and determined attack upon the small business' (CBI, 1968a). The CBI repeated this in its pamphlet *Britain's Small Firms—Their Vital Role in the Economy*, published three months later (CBI, 1968b).

At this time, however, the government was focused on industrial reorganisation to boost efficiency and the country's international competitiveness (Pass, 1971). Even if 'the "build it big" strategy' was losing its lustre within this environment (Gray, 1998: 9), attitudes towards granting small businesses particular attention were lukewarm. Records from July 1968 indicate that Board of Trade President Anthony Crosland's 'instinct in this case would have been to be laissez faire,' seeing little reason to take action supporting 'the less go-ahead firms which were making no effort to expand' (TNA: BT360/4/2). Nevertheless, Crosland did agree to seek views from other government departments on Davies' request for a survey of small businesses to ascertain whether treating small and large firms on the same basis was justified.

During the autumn of 1968, the CBI advanced its efforts for government action in the case of small businesses. Presenting its paper *The Problem of the Small Firm* to the National Economic Development Council (NEDC; Middlemas, 1983; TNA: BT360/4/15), the CBI reported on its own survey findings for *British Industry Week* indicating that three-quarters of respondent firms employing up to 250 people felt that the government was against them and that recent policies had hampered their development. The list of complaints featured the demands stemming from fiscal legislation, disclosure requirements, industrial training and the more general burden of government administration. The message that some action would need to be taken in response to the concerns raised by Conservative political figures and the largest employers' association in the country was not lost on the Board of Trade.

Establishing a Small Firms Inquiry

While the CBI urged the government to make some immediate changes as a sign of goodwill towards small firms (e.g. increasing the threshold for disclosures), it also repeated its call for the government to commission a study. The CBI outlined the following agenda for such a study, that it should consider:

> . . . the extent to which the small firm requires separate legislative provisions, of how existing legislation which penalises small firms

should be amended or differentially administered, and of whether any changes in Government machinery are needed to ensure that the needs of small firms are not overlooked.

(TNA: BT360/4/15)

By December 1968, Treasury officials noted that 'Ministers are pretty well committed to some activity in this field' (TNA: T328/235).

As the Board of Trade considered what form this activity should take, the CBI utilised its position within national industrial policy and government-industry negotiations to shape these decisions. The CBI opposed, for example, a study led by the National Economic Development Office (NEDO) as this would have permitted involvement from the Trades Union Congress (although in any event the TUC was seemingly not motivated to play a major role). The CBI also wanted to avoid an inquiry led by an academic on the grounds that this would not carry credibility with small business owners.

Despite the CBI's sustained push for some form of government investigation into the state of small firms, other stakeholders were less enthusiastic. Civil Servants were wary of a study becoming a platform for small businesses' complaints about government (see Dannreuther and Perren, 2013: 107) and the workers' representative body, the TUC, considered the proposal a matter of CBI 'propaganda' (TNA: BT360/5/1). This related to wider failures within the tripartite system of the NEDC at the time and a tendency towards bilateral discussions.

By mid-February 1969, Crosland was outlining to John Diamond (Chief Secretary to the Treasury) the impasse reached in respect of a small firms inquiry. The CBI wanted an independent, committee-led inquiry, sponsored by the Board of Trade, headed by a prominent businessman to study the problems of small businesses (TNA: BT360/5/33). Meanwhile, the Treasury and the Inland Revenue preferred an academic-led, single-person inquiry to gather the facts on small businesses' situation on the grounds that an academic would be less subject to political lobbying (TNA: BT360/5/11). Crosland asked whether the Treasury might come around to the CBI position if the parties were able to agree names of 'sensible people for the enquiry.'

Concluding his letter, Crosland re-emphasised the government's desire for harmony with the CBI, noting:

> The matter has been under discussion for several months—the small business members of the CBI are clearly getting restive—and if we could all register our agreement on the form of the enquiry at the NEDC meeting in early March we would avoid any possibility of a row at that meeting which might damage unnecessarily our relations with the CBI.

(TNA: BT360/5/39)

The Chief Secretary's reply of 31 March 1969 noted that, following the Chancellor's private discussions with Crosland and Davies, the Treasury was content with a small committee of inquiry. The Board of Trade's desire to avoid conflict with the CBI has been noted as a more general characteristic with Wilks (1999: 168) describing 'a sustained willingness to cater to FBI/CBI preferences.'

Finally, in July 1969, Crosland announced the founding of the Committee of Inquiry on Small Firms to be chaired by John Bolton. The terms of reference were as follows:

> To consider the role of small firms in the national economy, the facilities available to them and the problems confronting them; and to make recommendations. For the purpose of the study a small firm might be defined broadly as one with not more than 200 employees, but this should not be regarded as a rigid definition. In the course of the study it will be necessary to examine in particular the profitability of small firms and the availability of finance. Regard should also be paid to the special functions of small firms, for example as innovators and specialist suppliers.
>
> (Bolton Report, 1971: XV)

The Committee was chaired by John Bolton, who was credited with growing a successful small business, Solartron, and who had a history of public service through chairing the Rubber Economic Development Committee and serving as vice-chair of the Royal Commission on Local Government (Thomson, 2016). Bolton was joined by E.L.G. Robbins, an engineer and consultant, Professor J.H. Brian Tew, a highly respected economist from Nottingham University and L.V.D. Tindale, General Manager of the Industrial and Commercial Finance Corporation (ICFC, an organisation set up to address the lack of available long-term finance for small firms, discussed in Chapter 3). The Committee Secretary was David Hartridge and the Research Director, appointed several months into the Committee's work, was Graham Bannock.

What Was Known About Small Firms?

Despite the CBI's insistence that the facts on small businesses were already well-known, Boswell (1973), who had worked in the ICFC, decried 'a deplorable absence of facts' (1973: 14) holding that 'prejudice and mythology have reigned for far too long in this field' (1973: 18). The situation in respect of lacking data became apparent to the Committee members from the very start; the government possessed little in the way of suitable data on small businesses for the Committee to work with (Bolton Report, 1971). This realisation brought home the scale of challenges facing the Committee, even to gather the basic facts on small businesses in Britain, and the Committee postponed reporting dates several times as work extended beyond original and revised deadlines.

Over its two-year duration the Committee gathered and discussed a substantial body of information about small businesses and their relationships with government. There were some 95 recorded Committee meetings (TNA: BT262/20; BT262/21), plus numerous others to gather information and take soundings. The Committee members undertook visits to Canada, France, Germany, Japan and the US, alongside further references on practices internationally to understand the position of small businesses elsewhere as well as visiting regional groups in Britain. Contributions of opinion and evidence from individual firms of various sizes, government departments and industry groups were received in addition to several thousand survey responses and 18 official research reports. One of the things readily apparent from this mass of data was the complexity of the issues involved and the ways in which these were shaped by the fragmentation of views around government's role in industry, crystallised by the 1970 General Election and change of government.

The Bolton Committee and Its Wider Context

As observed, the Bolton Committee sat during a changing political time. Debates about the size of government and its role in industry were reshaping industrial policy (Blackaby, 1978) and the Conservative opposition was positioning small businesses as part of the economic and social alternative to the incumbent Labour government. The effects of these wider debates were not lost on the Committee, with Research Director Graham Bannock (1989: 17) later reflecting on how the Committee '. . . agonized at some length on the issue of whether positive discrimination in favour of small firms would be justified.'

Giving evidence to the Committee, Conservative spokesperson for industry and trade and later Thatcherite adviser Keith Joseph argued against government subsidies in areas such as finance and government services (TNA: BT360/11/33). One particular scheme considered by the Committee was an ongoing pilot for subsidised consultancy services in Bristol and Glasgow. Bolton himself, counter to the view of other Committee members, was in favour of expanding this scheme nationwide. In his meeting with the Committee, Joseph argued against expanding the scheme. He argued that, instead of using subsidies to mitigate the effects of harm caused by government policies, the government should avoid such damage in the first place through small businesses having a stronger voice outside and inside government. Such evidence highlights a key tension in the government-appointed, civil-service managed Committee's work: whether the answer to disproportionate burdens imposed on small businesses by government lay in further, remedial, government action; whether it pointed to a need for smaller government and less intervention or whether alternative options were available.

As Joseph's comments suggest, the Conservative Party of the time was coming down firmly on the side of addressing government failures. A famous meeting of the leading party figures took place at the Selsdon Park hotel at the end of January 1970 in order to work out the party's platform ahead of the 1970 general election. After this meeting, 'word went out that the party leadership had come down firmly on the side of the free market rather than on that of the interventionist economy' (Halcrow, 1989: 43).

The subsequent Conservative Party campaign emphasised making reductions in the size and cost of government. In the sphere of industrial policy, the party promised to withdraw government involvement from the nationalised industries. It focused on promoting competition and free enterprise, as presented in its manifesto (Conservative Party, 1970):

> We reject the detailed intervention of Socialism which usurps the functions of management and seeks to dictate prices and earnings in industry. We much prefer a system of general pressures, creating an economic climate which favours, and rewards, enterprise and efficiency. Our aim is to identify and remove obstacles that prevent effective competition and restrict initiative.

With particular reference to small businesses, the manifesto targeted many of the well-established complaints of business owners:

> Small businesses have had a raw deal from Labour. They have had to suffer higher and more complicated taxes, and waste more time filling up forms. Our policies for reducing taxation and reducing government interference in industry will reduce the heavy burdens on the small firm. We will decide the best method of providing advice and encouragement for small businesses in the light of the Bolton Report.
> (ibid)

The implications for the Bolton Committee were therefore clear: there was a changing political context, with the likely future party of government establishing a clear preference for small government and less intervention, whilst also promising to engage with the Committee's recommendations.

Following the Conservatives' General Election victory in June 1970, the new government signalled its intention to 'reduce and rationalise the functions of government' (Cmnd. 4506: 15). The 'wide range of advisory services notably for small and medium-sized firms' (Cmnd. 4506: 8) were announced to be included amidst these broader aims of reducing increases in total public expenditure (see Cmnd. 4515).

John Davies, the former CBI Director General who was now a Conservative MP and leading the Secretary of State for Trade and Industry, addressed the House of Commons in November 1970 explaining that '. . . the vast majority lives and thrives in a bracing climate and not in a soft, sodden morass of subsidised incompetence. . . . We believe that the essential need of the country is to gear the policies to the great majority of people, who are not lame ducks, or do not need a helping hand . . .' (cited in Blackaby, 1978: 55). Moreover, Davies continued the theme in his speech to the Industrial and Commercial Finance Corporation explaining the government's attitude towards 'disengagement,' signalling that government would be much less involved in industry and the affairs of the City (TNA: T342/115b).

The change in direction marked by the Conservatives replacing Labour in government was not lost on the Committee. It is noted in Committee minutes from November 1970 that, in view of the change of government, Chairperson John Bolton was no longer inclined to recommend a national system of subsidised consultancy grants to support small businesses' access to these services (TNA: BT262/21/CSF273).

As the Bolton Committee continued to work on interpreting its data and developing recommendations for how government should engage with small businesses, this direction of political travel was abundantly clear. For example, a draft speech for the Minister for Industry, Sir John Eden, for the dinner with the Southern Region Branch of the Engineering Industries' Association on 13 January 1971 was shared with the Committee:

> Our industrial policy starts from the conviction that prosperity is generated by industries' own efforts—by the efforts of people working at all levels in industrial companies. The design of a product, the organisation of production, decisions on R and D, on new investment or to go for a particular export order—all these are matters for industry alone, not decisions for Government to seek to take on industries' behalf or even to try to take part in.
>
> Where Government does have a role to play is in ensuring that industry operates within the right general framework. This means that there must be proper incentives for enterprise and efficiency both for companies and for individuals. The reduction in income tax, corporation tax and the new system of investment incentives we have announced are designed to encourage more profitable and hence more efficient use of industries' resources. Our new regional incentives are similarly intended to attract the right kind of profitable industry to invest in the development areas.
>
> (TNA: BT361/15)

By the time it delivered its report, the Committee had been somewhat overtaken by events. The Committee's major recommendation, to create a Small Firms Division, was already a long-standing commitment of the party now in power. Leaving aside the apparent contradiction with the government's own reorganisation plans, politically the Committee was reporting into an environment broadly in favour of small businesses as a sector. In light of this, it appears that the 'broadly held notion that small firms policy began in the UK in 1971 with the publication of the report of the Bolton Committee . . .' (Dannreuther and Perren, 2013: 98; Beesley and Wilson, 1981) potentially over-emphasises the significance of the Bolton Committee alone. Rather, the Bolton Committee and Report might be viewed as reflecting and forming a wider shift in political attitudes towards small businesses that had been apparent since the mid-1960s as part of more fundamental debates concerning the size of government and its relation to industry.

Report and Its Findings

The Committee's work concluded in autumn 1971 with the circulation of the report to government departments. The report featured almost 60 recommendations and spanned over 400 pages, not including the 18 research reports that had been conducted on behalf of the Committee. The report found that small firms '. . . suffer from a number of inequitable and unnecessary disabilities, mostly imposed by Government, which amount to discrimination against them. The fact that this is unintentional is irrelevant.' However, the report added that despite this unsatisfactory situation there was insufficient cause to justify positive discrimination in favour of small firms (Bolton Report, 1971: 91).

The report, perhaps reflecting the mood of the time, concluded that small businesses provided valuable social and economic functions. Although Committee members discussed the extent to which their report could highlight these perceived social benefits when tasked with understanding small businesses' role in the *economy* (TNA: BT262/21/CSF357), this tension was neatly avoided in the final report:

> If they were unable to survive as entrepreneurs this social contribution would be greatly missed, and thought would have to be given to means whereby it could be preserved or replaced. The difficulty here would be that the spirit of the sturdy independence which is the special quality of the small businessman would not survive dependence on Government patronage. Happily, we believe that the sector is economically viable, so that this dilemma does not arise.
>
> (Bolton Report, 1971: 343)

In terms of the economic function served by small businesses, the Committee identified many of the attributes that have subsequently been used to characterise these firms, such as providing a productive outlet for those who might not fit typical employee roles and offering sources of competition to large multi-product firms. They identified one of the most important contributions of small firms as being to 'provide the means of entry into business for new entrepreneurial talent and the seedbed from which new large companies will grow to challenge and stimulate the established leaders of industry' (Bolton Report, 1971: 343). This recasting of small businesses as entrepreneurial with the potential to grow is an important emphasis, which we will return to, but it is important to note that positioning small businesses as dynamic in this way might have helped provide a base for the Committee's main recommendation.

Contrary to the view expressed by small businesses' representative groups on how their members were feeling, and submissions from small businesses themselves, the Committee concluded that there was no deliberate discrimination by government against small firms. The report explained:

> Our complaint against Government is simply that the interests of small firms are neglected because it is nobody's job to consider them . . . and the fact that we have made so many recommendations shows that in our view this absence of effective concern and true understanding is widespread in Government.
>
> (Bolton Report, 1971: 345)

In the US things were different. Mills (1951) had perceived that, while espousing the rhetoric of business, owners of small businesses often looked towards government for protection from the worst of the effects of competition. He summed up the complicated relationship between small businesses and government by noting that '. . . while he looks to government for economic aid and political comfort, the independent businessman is, at the same time, resentful of its regulations and taxation, and he has vague feelings that larger powers are using government against him' (p. 52). In its report, the Bolton Committee noted the power of the small firms' lobby to which Mills referred and this was seen as having been important for the creation of the Small Business Administration (in 1953), an independent agency of government tasked with fighting for the interests of small businesses.

Although proposed by some witnesses to the Bolton Committee, it was concluded that such an arrangement would not fit with the UK's system of government. As opposed to the US, where it was seen that departments compete for the sympathy of Congress and funds using public campaigns and lobbying techniques, in the UK the role of public pressure was seen as less important than gaining the support of a powerful Cabinet Minister who could influence the government's agenda. Such debates did, therefore, shape the Committee's main proposal, that a new division should be established within the Department of Trade and Industry to represent the interests of small firms. Such a division would 'ensure that the interests of the small firm sector and the maintenance of its ability to fulfil its proper role in the industrial structure are never again allowed to go by default' (Bolton Report, 1971: 345).

Small Firm Finance

The questions of finance for small firms, and especially whether those businesses could access the external finance they needed from existing provision, had been the dominant theme in enterprise policy since the identification of the Macmillan gap in 1931. However, in addressing this question, the Bolton Committee could have been clearer in presenting its thoughts.

Introducing the chapter on Sources of Finance, the Committee report observes that there were a substantial number of submissions made to the effect that the Macmillan gap continued to be a problem. A paper prepared by the Secretariat (TNA: BT360/10/CSF124) had emphasised difficulties faced by small firms in retention of profits for internal financing, highlighting the Macmillan gap and subsequent work by the Radcliffe Committee (see Chapter 3). In the 23rd Committee Meeting (Minutes) John Bolton raised the examples of the US and France (from a Secretariat paper) where there was provision for insuring the risks involved in certain types of loans to small firms through credit guarantee funds financed by a charge on the borrowers. The Committee had also engaged the Economists Advisory Group to conduct a separate analysis to inform their debates on the issue.

Finally, the Committee determined that, notwithstanding the very real difficulties experienced by small firms, the Macmillan gap had been filled 'by the development of institutions such as ICFC, Charterhouse and others, and by the rise of Finance Companies such as United Dominions Trust' (Bolton Report, 1971: 187). It is perhaps worth noting here that a member of the Committee was the General Manager of the ICFC, presenting significant expertise and necessarily a viewpoint on the issue. Consequently, the Committee came out against creating a new institution to address problems around access to finance by small firms or the provision of finance at subsidised rates. The report concluded on this point: 'We believe that small firms in general should be and are capable of paying the economic or going rate for the finance they need, provided they make full use of the resources, including net trade credit, available to them' (1971: 192).

Regions and Unemployment

In terms of the regional aspect of enterprise policymaking, the Committee addressed the effects of development and planning controls on small businesses. Among the issues examined were the reported difficulties caused by control of industrial development. Powers under the Town and Country Planning Act 1962, and subsequent legislation, provided that industrial developments above a threshold of square feet required an industrial development certificate, or IDC. Recognising the disparity between the relative prosperity of the Midlands and the South East, in comparison with other areas of the country, the IDC regime was intended to both encourage expansion of firms to the Development and Intermediate Areas and to limit demand on existing resources in already thriving areas of the country.

Small firms had complained that the policy, and its administration, was hampering their operations and expansion plans although the Hunt Committee (1969) on *The Intermediate Areas* (to which the Bolton Committee referred) had already recommended relaxing the rules as they applied to small firms, citing four grounds:

> 486. . . . We do so, first, because we wish to minimise the loss of growth to the economy caused by the control, marginal though this appears to be. Second, we recognise the importance for small firms of their existing close network of relationships with suppliers and sub-contractors. Third, we recognise that small firms are often less used to dealing with officials and less well equipped to do so, and may find the procedure burden-some. Although the majority of such firms are not refused i.d.c.s, since their limited mobility is recognised by the Board of Trade, we would like to see them given greater freedom from the i.d.c. procedure. Fourth, we consider that the development of completely new infant industries should not be discouraged.
>
> (Hunt Committee, Cmnd. 3998)

The Hunt Committee went on to recommend raising the threshold to 10 000 square feet as a compromise position that would support the smaller businesses while limiting any negative impacts on the Development Areas. Although the government had recently accepted this recommendation in part, taking the exemption limits from 5000 to 10 000 square feet generally (apart from in the Midlands and South East where the increase was from 3000 to 5000 square feet), the Bolton Committee called for full implementation of the Hunt recommendation. In its own report, the Bolton Committee found that the revised limits had not resolved the problems experienced by small firms, not least in the Midlands and South East where it considered that small firms were experiencing the greatest problems. Consequently, the Bolton Committee recommended that 'small firms throughout the country be relieved of the need to apply for an IDC when their plans involve the creation of less than 10,000 square feet of industrial floor space' (p. 326).

Support and Advisory Services

An area of enterprise policy that we saw beginning to emerge but largely remain underdeveloped in Chapter 4 concerned support and advisory services. Through its own research efforts (such as Golby and Johns' research report for the Committee) and evidence submitted by other interests, the Committee noted both a concern with the standard of management in small businesses and a reluctance, or hostility, among small business owners towards outside interference. Certainly there appeared to be no shortage of advice on offer to businesses that were aware of its existence and willing to engage. As the Committee noted in its report, government involvement in seeking to improve management in businesses had been marked by subsidies to the industrial Research Association since 1918 and the founding of the British Productivity Council (1952). The Committee also noted a substantial increase in government intervention with industry under the recent Labour government.

In submissions to the Committee there was discussion of firms not recognising, or being unaware of, the value of the advice or services available. There were therefore suggestions for more effective signposting or developing the skills to make effective use of advice (although not necessarily via government; TNA: BT360/9/79).

An internal paper on advisory services was prepared by Hartridge and suggested it was not clear that small firms wanted advisory services (even if they were free). The rationale for the provision of advice was a perceived lack of financial and management expertise. There had also been consultancy grants piloted in Bristol and Glasgow (subsidising 50% of costs for firms with fewer than 500 employees), although with concerns reported about some dubious methods adopted by consultants in Glasgow (TNA: BT360/9/79). There was already a lot of activity (the paper notes that the NEDC listed 247 bodies), but perhaps these were poorly coordinated and there were plans to look into rationalising provision (possibly through local organisation, e.g. TNA: BT262/20/CSF60). The paper discussed a range of alternatives including 'a computer-linked information service like those in America and Japan' (p. 6). Tew had also suggested universities and colleges could have a role to play (apparently with scepticism from some quarters about the ability of the more 'academic' institutions to engage effectively with small businesses). Many of these ideas and discussions prefigure significant enterprise policy initiatives of the future that will be discussed throughout the remainder of this book. However, the Hartridge paper argued against subsidising such services: 'We have to answer the question why those businesses which cannot meet the time cost of efficient operation (which includes the cost of necessary services) should not be allowed to go to the wall' (TNA: BT360/9/79). It was perceived there were risks in such schemes propping up failing firms and, if government were to intervene, of damaging the existing market for these services.

The final report takes on a negative tone in respect of government support for advisory services. Setting out hurdles for justifying services to be provided at tax payers' expense, the Committee required firstly that the service was needed and private enterprises did not, or would not, provide it. Further conditions were set for services that were to be made available freely or with subsidy, namely that 'the economic benefit to the nation deriving from the services is greater than their cost' and 'that users of the services cannot or should not be expected to pay their full cost' (Bolton Report, 1971: 136). Applying this test to existing provision, the Committee concluded that none of the services they had reviewed met their criteria to justify subsidy. Rather, they proposed a signposting and referral service to be provided by government via a network of Small Firms Advisory Bureaux in major industrial locations. The bureaux were envisaged as reporting to the DTI and responding to business queries by highlighting, and making introductions to, the most appropriate advice available. Although being promoted as focusing on small firms, the Committee recommended that the service should not be strictly limited to small firms exclusively.

Conclusion

The Bolton Committee was established during a period of divergence in views between the two major political parties in Britain over the role of government in industry. The post-war consensus had begun to fracture in the 1960s and, although no decisive moves on this question were made until Thatcher's governments at the end of the 1970s and of the 1980s (Gray, 1998), the foundations had been established for what was to come (Glynn and Booth, 1996; Hall, 1992; Pemberton, 2004; Wilks, 1999). An element of this fracturing of consensus can be related to the increased interest in small businesses.

As demonstrated through Committee witnesses, speeches, press cuttings included in the Committee files and John Bolton's own change of view on recommending subsidised consultancy services, the wider political environment has to be taken into account when analysing the forces and interests influencing the Committee and its work. In reconnecting the Committee and its report with its wider context however, we are not questioning the significance of the Committee's work. It is apparent that the Committee was 'path-breaking' (Bennett, 2014: 77) in how small firms came to be viewed and treated in government, research and policy circles (Wapshott and Mallett, 2018).

Examining the processes of forming the Bolton Committee reveals the influence exerted by the CBI and wider political debates in getting a Committee established and the shape that it took. This understanding is especially helpful when considering criticisms made of the Committee that, for example, it adopted too-positive a view on the state of industrial relations in small firms: 'In many respects a small firm provides a better environment for the employee than is possible in most large firms' (Bolton Report, 1971: 21; for criticisms of this view see, for example, Holliday, 1995; MacMahon, 1996; Baines and Wheelock, 1998; Dundon et al., 1999). The limited TUC involvement left the Committee largely reliant on employers' responses and, although Committee members treated some claims with scepticism, an overall positive view was retained (Curran and Stanworth, 1981).

The Committee also framed small businesses as being entrepreneurial and providing the seedbed for future growth ventures. In this guise, today's small businesses would become tomorrow's giants or otherwise challengers to incumbents. The shift in terminology, effectively re-framing small businesses and their function in the economy, is significant in two related ways. Firstly, it signals the potential for a repositioning of small businesses from industrial backwaters and a bygone era. Carrying echoes of the *Acorns to Oaks* analogy, small businesses are recast as the seedbed of future prosperity and dynamism; a characterisation that, as we will see, would spread in subsequent years.

Secondly, with small businesses cast in this new, dynamic light, the case for government intervention becomes stronger, if not compelling when weighed against other priorities. The debate is switched from whether governments should prop up a declining group of businesses, to one whereby governments should consider the fate of small businesses as tied closely to the future of the economy more widely: 'We therefore believe that in the absence of an active and vital small firm sector the economy would slowly ossify and decay' (Bolton Report, 1971: XIX).

6 Taxation, Lobbying and a Voice for Small Business

The publication of the Bolton Report was not the stimulus for a raft of new ideas in enterprise policymaking. In the early 1970s, the Conservative government attempted to reduce regional spending and subsidies, pursuing a small government agenda. This was clearly at odds with any calls for a substantial increase in government intervention to support small firms. However, the first half of the 1970s was a time of high unemployment, economic crises and recession (as well as debates about membership of the European Community, as will be discussed in Chapter 7). These crises prompted the government to move away from its focus on unemployment and away from Keynesianism; it also provoked debates about the place and contribution of small businesses and entrepreneurship in the economy.

It is in this context that the Bolton Report was received and the Small Firms Division established. The crises accompanied a growth in small firm numbers and a nuanced change in their collective voice and platforms for political influence. While this was formally recognised with the creation of the Small Firms Division, it also began to grow outside the mechanisms of government–industry relations. This chapter will outline the enterprise policies of the early 1970s in relation to small business voice, culminating in angry debates about taxation and the emergence of new organisations seeking to challenge the political establishment and change the way governments engaged with small businesses.

The Conservatives' New Political Agenda

Arriving into government in 1970 promising reforms to reduce the activities and scale of the state, the Conservative administration under Edward Heath was initially guided by its policy of disengagement (see Chapter 5). Addressing his party's conference at Blackpool in October, when setting out the government's domestic agenda, Heath (1970) placed emphasis on reforms to the state:

> I shall shortly be announcing the reconstruction of the Whitehall Departments. This will be of major importance and wide-ranging.

My object is to produce as far as possible a rational structure of Government which will enable us to streamline the Departments and reduce the demands which are made on money and manpower. My objective is also to produce a better way of taking decisions and to provide the Cabinet with the means for doing so. I hope that this reconstruction when it is achieved will provide Whitehall with a period of stability which it badly needs. I hope it will provide a structure which will be effective and which will last for many years to come. . . .

These, then will be the first fruits of our first few months in office. They are of major consequence, but I repeat that this is but the first stage to create room for us to manoeuvre as we move on to our new course. To follow this, I have now asked each Minister to organise an examination of every function carried out in his department, to examine personally the consequences, and then to recommend whether it is essential for each of these functions to continue. The purpose of my request is to ensure that Government withdraws from all those activities no longer necessary either because of the passage of time or because they are better done outside government, or because they should rightly he carried on, if wanted at all, by individual or by voluntary effort.

The ethos underlying these changes in the early days of the Heath administration stressed the importance of personal freedom and personal responsibility, and bears comparison with the Thatcherite agenda of the following decade (see Chapter 8):

Our purpose is to bring our fellow citizens to recognise that they must be responsible for the consequences of their own actions and to learn that no one will stand between them and the results of their own free choice. Until this is made clear up and down the country, not only will men and women themselves, but their fellow citizens in the community as well, suffer from the feckless behaviour of irresponsible groups within our community.

As applied to industrial policy, this new agenda placed emphasis on disengagement and, for example, the Industrial Reorganisation Corporation was to be wound up. Nevertheless, to avoid creating the impression that this was a simple rejection of government–industry relations, it is important to note that this agenda was not all-encompassing. The aircraft industry was exempted from this general policy approach and, within months, the government had effectively nationalised the strategically important Rolls Royce by supporting the company through its struggles to develop the RB211 engine (Mottershead, 1978).

Faced with rising inflation and the threat of significant levels of unemployment, it was not long before there was a wider 'rejection of the liberal individualism expressed in the early days of the Heath Government'

(Wilks, 1999: 182). Middlemas (1990) reveals how Heath instructed a Cabinet Office Committee under Sir William Armstrong to review the government's position. The review led to the 1972 budget, a tripartite deal on wages and prices, and the Industry Act of 1972, which 'contained some of the most interventionist powers to direct and subsidise industry ever taken outside wartime' (Wilks, 1999: 182). This has been described as 'probably the government's greatest u-turn and most palpable rejection of economic neoliberalism' (Rubinstein, 2003: 299).

The Industry Act included the reintroduction of investment grants (Regional Development Grants) for industry in assisted areas and via general powers where this was deemed necessary, under a broad range of possible circumstances. This provision of funds for deprived areas and industries was viewed by some as a move towards socialism. That such claims could be made about this Conservative government so soon after it had launched an aggressive plan for smaller government and free markets suggests the continuing pull of the post-war consensus, even after it had become significantly fractured.

The ways in which this political shift were discussed at the time is suggested by a Conservative Party pamphlet written by newly appointed Minister for Industrial Development, Christopher Chataway (1972: 15):

> To say that government should not in any of these areas ever assist private enterprise would be urging us, if I may adapt a phrase of George Brown's, to run the economy in a way that no other capitalist country attempts to do. If taken literally the advice could only lead to a substantial extension of nationalisation because it would mean that private industry would be debarred from meeting a number of essential national needs. So let us put an end to the somewhat curious line of criticism, which says that a Conservative Government is necessarily betraying its principles by acting in support of private industry.

It was in the context of this shift of emphasis that the Bolton Report was received and its recommendations were considered.

The Response to the Bolton Report

Organisations representing small business owners responded with a mix of disappointment and cautious welcome. The Smaller Businesses Association was reportedly disappointed by the 'complacency' shown towards small firms in the report given the situation facing those businesses. The CBI and Association of British Chambers of Commerce welcomed the report in broad terms and took the opportunity to comment on how the report was consistent with the views they had been expressing (Bolter, 1971).

Despite the report representing a major contribution to knowledge on small firms and subsequent recognition of its importance and influence, initial reactions to the report in academia and the media were muted. Writing in 1976, Bannock was disappointed by the 'limited and short duration of the interest aroused by the report in academic circles' (p. 6) observing that Boswell's (1973) notable academic study into small firms had commenced before the Committee was formed. In the press, *The Economist* (1971) described the report as 'a disappointment,' especially in regard to the limited criticism of government and the limited scope and ambition of the recommendations. Writing in *The Sunday Times*, Philip Clarke, author of a forthcoming book of entrepreneurial biographical sketches, was somewhat dismissive. He commented, reflecting the ways in which events had somewhat overtaken the Committee's work (see Chapter 5), that the report:

> . . . may well stand as a historical monument—a study which ana-
> lysed in great detail a situation that had started to change even before
> the ink was dry on its 436 pages. Inevitably, therefore, the report—
> and its recommendations—have an anachronistic flavour.

Bolton himself (Bolton, 1982), suggested that the report had failed to sufficiently establish the importance of the small firm to a balanced economy, both in terms of regions and particular industries. Further, that it had not drawn sufficient attention to 'the unique role of small firms in providing "wealth-creating" employment in the new technology, high added-value economy' (p. 308). He now saw small firms as vital to tackling unemployment (citing the work of Birch, see Chapter 8).

The Bolton Report was received in government accompanied by pressure from the Prime Minister for actions that could be announced alongside the report's release in November 1971 (TNA: FV62/45). Significant difficulties were encountered given the size of the report, the number of recommendations and, perhaps, the limited specific focus on small businesses to-date in the machinery of government. However, in opposition, the Conservatives had spoken since 1965 of creating a small business function in government, *Acorns to Oaks* had presented a case for supporting small businesses and the Conservatives' manifesto for the 1970 General Election campaign pledged, however vaguely, to consider the Bolton Committee's recommendations.

The Small Firms Division

The recommendation to create a part of government dedicated to the interests of small businesses went against the spirit of the Conservative's wider message about disengagement and its plans for reorganising central government (Civil Service, 1970b: 4). There was the charge that establishing '. . . official bureaux to teach people how to mind their own business' was a symptom of the 'Socialist disease' (Daily Telegraph, 1969).

The Central Policy Review Staff, created by Heath to advise on strategy and policy (James, 1986), challenged the creation of a small firms lobby within government, arguing that 'there was and should be no such animal as "small firms policy"' (TNA: T342/116, Qg/0226).

Despite such internal scepticism and opposition, the Committee's main proposal for the creation of a Small Firms Division was accepted. John Davies, formerly of the CBI and subsequently elected to Parliament and appointed Secretary of State for Trade and Industry, told the House of Commons on publication of the report:

> First, in order that the place of small firms in the economy should be continuously watched and their interests be taken into account in the formulation of policies, the Committee recommends that in my Department a Minister should be designated as responsible for small firms and that a small firms division should be set up. I accept both these recommendations. I propose to give the ministerial responsibility to my hon. Friend the Under-Secretary of State for Industry, and a division will be set up whose primary function will be to support him in this work.
>
> (Hansard, HC Deb. 3 November 1971 vol.825 col.188)

The Small Firms Division was to be 'responsible for the development, inter-departmental co-ordination and implementation of policy towards small firms and for the administration of such official services as are provided for them,' to be overseen by a Department for Trade Minister and with liaisons in all other relevant departments (Hansard, HC Deb. 15 May 1972 vol.837 col.17).

In 1973, the role of the Small Firms Division was extended to include further research, for example 'to form a view of the present and future role of small firms in all industries in which they are important' (Hansard, HC Deb. 8 March 1973 vol.852 cols.204–205). The Division would also consider important factors such as competition policy, government procurement (another perennial issue) and the potential impact of joining the European Economic Community (see Chapter 7). By November 1983, there were still 10 research projects ongoing (Hansard, HC Deb. 16 November 1983 vol.48 col.468).

Small Firms Information Centres

In responding to the Bolton Report's recommendations there were also commitments for departments to consider the impact on small firms of surveys and other form-filling, some relatively minor details on tax and finance and an exemption for 'small firms' from the levy mandated by the Industrial Training Act (definition to be decided by each relevant board). It was suggested that the Training Boards could offer fee-based training to small firms as an alternative that would be more suited to the needs of these businesses. In suggesting this, the non-committal, small-scale nature of the government's response to Bolton is evident. The underlying assumption of small firms as distinctive is accepted but without any significant policymaking or interventions to address the challenges that might face these businesses. In the case of form filling, this would remain a perennial issue (for example, a review into the problem was conducted in 1980).

In 1977, Bob Cryer, Secretary of State for Industry, set out the general provision that had been established as a result of the post-Bolton activity:

> Small firms in England are eligible for a wide range of Government assistance, which is generally available throughout the United Kingdom to encourage the growth and expansion of firms of every size. In particular, most of the sectoral schemes in operation under Section 8 of the Industry Act 1972 contain special provisions for assistance towards the cost of consultancy studies for small firms; in two schemes, the minimum size for investment projects has been reduced; and 108 individual terrace or nursery units for occupation by small firms are being built. Small firms can also call on the services of the small firms information centres at any stage of their development.
>
> (Hansard, HC Deb. 22 March 1977 vol.928 col.496)

The small firms information centres constituted a second major response to the recommendations of the Bolton Report, in particular to calls for better signposting of the array of services available to support small businesses. This represented a significant step forward in the development of ideas around advisory and support services in UK enterprise policy and provided a foundation (at least in terms of ideas) of large-scale schemes that were to follow and will be discussed later in the book:

> (A)—9. Among the management advisory services we have considered we recognise none which meets our criteria for continuing subsidy. There is, however, a need for a pure "signposting" or referral service which could not, we believe, be made to pay for itself, and this the Government should provide. This could best be done by setting up a network of small firms advisory bureaux in important industrial centres.
>
> (Hansard, HC Deb. 8 March 1973 vol.852 cols.204–205)

These bureaux, reporting directly to the Small Firms Division, would provide answers to queries relating to technical, financial and management problems by introducing small business owners or employees to the appropriate sources of available advice within different industries. They operated as a regional information service for small businesses, offering a telephone helpline and centres in Birmingham, Bristol, Leeds, London, Luton, Manchester, Newcastle and Nottingham, each staffed by three experienced civil servants (Hansard, HC Deb. 28 July 1976 vol.916 col.277).

However, there were concerns that existing sources of management consultancy and advice may not have been effectively tailored for small firms. For example, in a paper to be presented at the Association of Special Libraries and Information Bureaux (the event was cancelled), Wood (1974: 76) explained:

> . . . many of the Industrial Training Boards have insisted, for grant purposes, that small firms should follow the recommendations of the Central Training Council with its emphasis on job specifications, training records, etc. The CTC's recommendations were based on research carried out in big firms. Fortunately, some of the ITB's have recognized that running a small firm is a very different process from management in a big firm.

Wood (p. 77) made the case for the protection of small businesses 'from both the charlatans, selling new clothes to emperors, and also the well-intentioned experts who do not recognize their own limitations.'

These types of concern provided support, once the bureaux framework was in place, for it to begin to extend its service provision. A further 80 Area Counselling Centres were added in 1978, expanding the service and appointing people with relevant industry experience as self-employed contractors to respond to more detailed enquiries and offer specialised guidance. These advisors would provide up to 10 days of advice for free within a year. At this time, about a fifth of queries were from those starting up a new business (Hansard, HC Deb. 3 August 1978 vol.955 col.645), approximately a third relating to management advice and a third to issues broadly related to regulation and government (Hansard, HC Deb. 12 July 1977 vol.935 col.117). The service was then further expanded in 1983 to support the delivery of the new Enterprise Allowance Scheme (see Chapter 8). By 1984, it 'handled around 300 000 inquiries and nearly 25 000 new counselling cases . . . [and] the government came increasingly to rely on these services to provide support and to screen small-firm applicants for its assistance schemes' (Wren, 1996: 168).

Courting the Small Firm Vote

Despite managing Britain's entry into the European Community (in 1973, see Chapter 7), the Heath government had not been a great success and Heath himself had become a divisive figure. The right wing of the Conservative Party was unhappy with the focus on a tripartite approach and an accommodating attitude towards unions. While the plans implemented following the Conservative u-turn had reduced unemployment, they had also increased the balance of payments deficit and inflation (Denver and Garnett, 2014). This left the economy vulnerable to the first OPEC shock and rising international fuel prices. This led, in turn, to widespread industrial unrest, the miners' strike through the winter of 1973–1974 resulting in restrictions imposed on the electricity supply and limiting electricity for industry to just three days per week.

Early in 1974, Heath called an emergency election to gain a mandate for his conflict with the trade unions. However, by the time Heath called the election, people's mood had changed from rallying around the government to just being irritated at the state of affairs. While the Conservatives won more votes than Labour, they lost seats and were unable to form a government. Labour formed a minority government and then, in September 1974, Labour leader Harold Wilson called a second election to strengthen his position.

It was in the 1974 elections that small firms started to appear more prominently in political manifestoes and the language of these documents repeatedly associates SMEs with economic growth (Wapshott and Mallett, 2018). The Conservatives in October 1974 argued that 'Small businesses often face the problem of long-term finance' and committed to setting up an enquiry to investigate. Their manifesto featured a section dedicated to *Small Businesses* in which this 'backbone of British enterprise' is described as 'immensely important to the economic life of Britain and to future industrial growth.' It is unclear the extent to which this direct pitch to small business interests was trying to recall the early days of the Heath administration or a late play to pacify small business interests who felt ignored. Nevertheless, some small business owners would soon be starting to consider fresh avenues for representing their interests.

Owners of small businesses had experienced mixed fortunes in terms of having their interests recognised in mainstream politics. As we have seen (Chapter 5), the effective influence of small firms was more pronounced during the 1960s, not least in creating leverage through the CBI for the Bolton Committee to be formed. Yet, there remained a sense that small businesses were being overlooked by government (Middlemas, 1990). The Bolton Report (1971: 93) commented on 'the relative insignificance of the small firm lobby as a political factor.' It was suggested that the traditionally Conservative leaning of small business owners meant that 'unqualified loyalty to one party may result in the small firm vote being taken for granted by one side and written off by the other.' Gamble (1974) comments that small business owners disliked the consensus politics that appeared to see their interests overlooked even by the Conservative Party leadership. While Enoch Powell's right-wing political faction offered a radical agenda that found favour with elements of the small business community, Heath's more managerial approach earned few fans. Consequently, as we will see later in this chapter, the sense of estrangement from mainstream party politics led many small business owners to the new associations and lobby groups that emerged in the mid-1970s (Bechhofer and Elliott, 1981).

The National Enterprise Board

In 1974, the Labour government was limited in its ambitions by both its small majority in Parliament and the ongoing challenges facing the country. Nonetheless, with the 1975 Industry Act, it established the National Enterprise Board (NEB, with 'enterprise' here being used much more broadly than we are using it in terms of enterprise policy). This organisation meant that the Secretary of State, when providing financial assistance to industry, would now no longer take equity finance only as a last resort or be prevented from acquiring or holding onto a majority of shares (i.e. increasing the scope for forms of nationalisation). This was primarily focused on supporting larger businesses like British Leyland.

The NEB also had a similar industrial reorganisation role to the former Industrial Reorganisation Corporation. It was 'to be an instrument through which the Government would operate directly to create employment in areas of high unemployment' (Dept of Industry, 1977: 8). This agenda was intended to develop as a result of the NEB's own initiatives but would be incentivised by government. However, this regional policy agenda did not, in the NEB guidelines, explicitly address small firms or self-employment.

The area of NEB activity that was of relevance to enterprise policy involved the latest attempt to address the difficulties small firms were perceived to experience in accessing long-term finance. However, Lonsdale (1997) records that this role was relatively neglected, with the majority of the organisation's focus on large businesses and that 'Between 1975 and 1979 the NEB made 22 investments under £200,000' (p. 51). Lonsdale reviewed the various investments, including interviewing company directors, and attempted to unpick any (additional) impact made by NEB. He concludes that, overall, the performance of the NEB was mixed but that there were more failures than successes. As with many schemes and initiatives before it, the NEB did not overcome the gap in finance for small businesses: the activities were far too narrow in scope and limited in ambition to make even a dent in the perceived problem. Further, for those investments the NEB did make, only 7 out of 37 were disposed of at a profit. However, Lonsdale emphasises there were successes, especially in biotechnology (where a strategic focus managed to stimulate this industry in the UK), and that 'the claim that the Board made little contribution to its successful investments was largely rebutted by the companies concerned' (p. 120). It is also helpful to note that, unlike some other schemes, the NEB had made high-risk investments, especially where there was political pressure to do so (e.g. in deprived regions), so a high failure rate was perhaps to be expected.

Council of Small Industries in Rural Areas

Another element of the attempt to stimulate regional development in the mid-1970s that did include important areas of enterprise policy was the work of the Council of Small Industries in Rural Areas (CoSIRA). Together with other initiatives under the new Development Commission, this organisation had 'a general duty to preserve village life and prevent depopulation of rural areas' (Mitchell and Cattermole, 1979: 56).

CoSIRA included three core areas of activity: development of small factories outside the Assisted Areas; financial and technical advice and training; loans (up to £50 000 per firm) to rural businesses with 20 or less employees who were skilled (no limit on total employees). Mitchell and Cattermole (p. 54) record that 'more than half the loans outstanding in summer 1978 were for buildings, rather over a quarter for equipment and one eight for working capital.' Potential borrowers received advice and support around management and finances at a price designed to cover the costs of delivery, with the latter area perceived as being particularly important. This work was supported by County Committees made up of volunteers with business, banking or accountancy backgrounds. The provision of advice and support, beyond any signposting role, had now become a standard part of the enterprise policy package for both Conservative and Labour governments.

The Ongoing Political Exclusion of Small Businesses?

Despite the existence of the Small Firms Division and quite small-scale initiatives such as those outlined previously, Labour's focus on large businesses risked maintaining a difficult environment for small firms. For example, the Employment Protection Act 1975 sought to make substantial gains in terms of worker rights, introducing new regulations around areas such as maternity pay and creating Acas as a statutory body to improve industrial relations. This improvement of worker rights was seen as a significant challenge for small firms and was strongly opposed by the Association of Self-employed People. For example, the leaflet 'Slow to Fire—Quick to Hire' gave advice to small firms on dealing with the Act, including recommending taking on employees as self-employed (cited in McHugh, 1979). However, the biggest challenge to small firms was widely represented as changes to the system of taxation.

Although it had been the case for some time that Ministers attributed complaints about government attitudes towards small firms as stemming from dissatisfaction with taxation, there had been little desire for the Bolton Committee to engage with the topic in detail (BT360/4/61; BT360/6/

GD/3725/6/G). The terms of reference agreed for the Committee's work did not include taxation and these matters were already subject to regular discussions between the Inland Revenue and the CBI. Nevertheless, the Committee received a large number of complaints about the taxation system and its effects on small businesses. Consequently, while acknowledging that the Committee was not engaged to focus on taxation, and that supporting tax cuts for relatively prosperous business owners was politically unfeasible, its report had included a substantial chapter generating thirteen recommendations. Moreover, the Committee went out of its way to:

> . . . emphasise again that what is needed is a taxation policy which will restore initiative, encourage entrepreneurial activity and improve the liquidity position of small businesses. We believe that continued reduction in taxation of personal incomes and of estates would be most likely to achieve this result. The point is not specific to small firms, however, and we therefore merely state our view for the record.
> (Bolton Report, 1971: 349)

Nonetheless, Labour introduced 8% Type 4 National Insurance on the taxable profits of the self-employed. Additionally, after joining the EEC in 1973 (discussed in Chapter 7), the UK introduced a Value Added Tax (VAT). These changes were met with widespread anger among the self-employed, an opposition that was crucial for the emergence of various groups claiming to speak for and to organise these businesses and small firms more generally.

The Voice of Enterprise

Shortly before the Bolton Committee reported in late 1971, the CBI and the Association of British Chambers of Commerce (ABCC) had jointly established the Commission of Inquiry into Industrial and Commercial Representation, chaired by the Right Hon. Lord Devlin, a Law Lord. For small businesses, Devlin identified the key means of exerting their interests as residing with the CBI, the Chambers of Commerce and relevant trade associations (although the report (Devlin, 1972) had important gaps such as limited attention paid to small retailers, McHugh, 1979). What was recognised by both Devlin and Bolton was a need for more effective representation of small businesses at a national level. This was, in part, what the Small Firms Division was supposed to have addressed.

Nonetheless, the anger at the political and economic environment of the mid-1970s led to new organisations being created to represent the interests of small businesses and the self-employed as an alternative to the establishment CBI or National Chamber of Trade. As McHugh's (1979) colourful account of these organisations presents, they were typically more radical (and in many ways more ragged) than the existing organisations. The National Federation of the Self-Employed (NFSE, which would go on to move from an outsider to an insider position of influence as the Federation of Small Businesses, the UK's largest dedicated small business representative organisation, Jordan and Halpin, 2003) enjoyed rapid growth in its early membership owing to opposition to changes in the National Insurance regime.

The NFSE developed from an existing organisation of small shopkeepers and in the context of other campaigning groups such as the Middle Class Association or the National Association for Freedom (who disseminated the economic ideas of Hayek and Friedman that were also helping to reshape the ideas of the Conservative Party). As now, a key focus of its activities was to lobby government and lead public campaigns, organising to challenge what they saw as problems with the political system. The NFSE had recruited 10 000 members by the end of 1974 and, a year later, the organisation claimed that this had risen to 50 000.

Membership was bolstered further, according to McHugh, by the difficulties encountered by small businesses and the self-employed in administering the VAT system. Drawing disapproval from the NCT, the NFSE proposed that its members withhold VAT payments due to the government (1000 members paid their money instead into a shared fund). In September 1975, there was a march to Downing Street to deliver a 250 000-signature petition. The landscape of small business representative groups would diversify further as alternative groups were founded, such as the National Association of the Self-Employed (NASE) and the Association of Self-employed People (ASP). Although, in the latter part of the 1970s, as small firms had regained some ground in mainstream political agenda, the futures for these more radical representative groups looked uncertain.

As we saw previously, by the second 1974 election, the opposition Conservative Party were focused more on winning the votes of small business owners. The apparent unionisation of the self-employed worried Conservatives who had traditionally tended to assume support from this constituency (McHugh, 1979). Conservative backbenchers had set up a small firms backbench committee in 1973 (officially recognised by the party's influential 1922 Committee in 1974) and, partly in response to organised activity, the party then went further by setting up a Small Business Bureau in 1976 to improve contacts with small businesses and the self-employed. The greater focus on small businesses might also have owed something to small businesses representing a cause to defend against 'the depredations of a Socialist administration' (King, 1979: 162) amid wider criticisms of the new Labour government's legislative agenda. Small businesses, and their owners, also offered an opportunity to identify values aligned with Conservative thinking apparent in the early days of Heath's government and which would later be further advanced under

Thatcher. In such re-engagement with small businesses, Bechhofer and Elliott (1981: 192) see an ideological appeal to 'a simpler, freer, more competitive economy . . . in which the invisible hand steers individual competition along paths of efficiency, prosperity and freedom.'

Conclusion

In the immediate years following publication of the Bolton Report, for both Conservative and Labour governments, enterprise policy did not take centre stage, especially as successive governments faced mounting inflation, balance of payment deficits, high unemployment and industrial relations crises. As we will describe further in the next chapter, this decade saw a fundamental shift away from the Keynesian, Butskellite consensus and towards monetarism. Such crises and political changes overshadowed the gradual development of an enterprise policy agenda.

The recommendations from the Bolton Report were implemented, at least in part, and this saw the creation of the Small Firms Division, which cemented a place for small firms as a distinct interest group within government. It also saw the creation of a small firm advisory service, placing the emerging area of advice and support on a more formal footing with the potential to grow in scope and service provision. This was now part of the standard enterprise policy package, together with attempts to address local unemployment and deprivation and to support small business access to finance.

As in other periods, economic crises along with regional inequality and deprivation saw attempts to provide finance to small firms, but these fell well short of anything that could fill the perceived Macmillan gap. The tough conditions facing small firms, and a sense that they were not being listened to in government, led to a much greater voice and the lobbying for political change. The movements developing this small business voice were also being influenced by ideas about the role of enterprise in free markets that, despite Heath's historic u-turn, were also continuing to shape the Conservative Party and that would come to form a crucial part of the future of UK enterprise policy. We discuss this is Chapter 8 but, first, it is important to consider the remainder of the 1970s and the additional influence of membership of the European Community and the UK's record IMF bailout.

7 The Europeanisation of Enterprise Policy

As a focused enterprise agenda gradually developed in UK politics and small business organisations promoted their voices, the 1970s also saw the UK debating and then joining the European Economic Community (EEC) in 1973. As we discuss, this would come to have significant implications for UK enterprise policy that would very likely not have been previously apparent (for example to the Bolton Committee). We focus on these implications in terms of discussing the European Regional Development Fund.

The latter half of the 1970s saw political, economic and social turmoil, the rejection of Keynesianism and experiments with monetarism, especially as the country applied for an IMF bailout in 1976. This chapter will explore the implications of this turbulent context for small firms and the place of enterprise policy in the government's response to ongoing crises. In particular, we highlight the increasing calls from both ends of the political spectrum for an expansion in the ambition and scope of enterprise policymaking in the UK.

Joining the EEC

Following the conclusion of the Second World War, the European Coal and Steel Community was founded and then developed during the 1950s. Its founders, Belgium, France, Germany, Italy, Luxembourg and the Netherlands, hoped that, through close economic and political ties, a lasting peace could be secured. In 1957, the European Economic Community was created from this foundation, eventually leading to a common market and customs union among its members.

The UK was not a founding member, though membership had been discussed for some time before it did eventually join. The OECD, in its 1962 economic survey of the United Kingdom, noted that, relative to the EEC members, UK economic growth had been slow during the 1950s. Although recognising that the underlying problems in the UK economy were complex, the OECD (1962) considered that, among various remedial steps being taken, 'membership should materially help the United

Kingdom economy in the task of maintaining cost and price stability by the introduction of a more competitive atmosphere in British industry' (p. 31).

In the UK, the idea of EEC entry had already been accepted by Cabinet in April 1961 and built into policy planning. Middlemas (1990: 34) considers that entry, while not taken for granted, 'would henceforward justify state intervention on a novel scale, aimed at wholesale modernisation.' Nevertheless, the question of UK membership was not a given and, in 1963, French President de Gaulle vetoed Britain's entry with debate still continuing on the other side of the channel and arguments cutting across party lines (Davis, 2017; Middlemas, 1990). Nevertheless, following another unsuccessful attempt in 1967, the UK (along with Ireland and Denmark) eventually joined the Community on 1 January 1973. Joining the European Economic Community meant more than embracing its approach to free trade, it also meant a process of 'Europeanisation.'

Europeanisation refers to 'the impact of EU [European Union, as the EEC would become] level decisions on national level policies and institutions' (Schmidt, 2002: 894). This involves complicated processes of adjustment rather than a simple means of dictating policy from Brussels. Bache and Jordan (2006: 30, italics in original) describe Europeanisation as involving '*the reorientation or reshaping of politics in the domestic arena in ways that reflect policies, practices and preferences advanced through the EU system of governance.*' It involves a two-way interaction between the Commission and member states, with indirect as well as direct forms of influence.

The growth, range and complexity of EEC, later EU, policymaking lends itself to increasing unanticipated consequences (Pierson, 1996). Agenda-setting and 'soft' or cultural influence also involves the EU acting as a means of spreading ideas and policy learning. This applies to enterprise policy as much as it does to other areas of government action, for example through activities such as the European Year of SMEs (1983) or the Small Business Act (2010), which proposed a general framework for improving the approach to entrepreneurship across Europe, including the active promotion of self-employment and small business.

In late 1972, the Small Firms Division produced a report 'Entry Into the EEC and Small Firms: The Immediate Impact' (TNA: FV80/20). There was uncertainty at the time about how significant the impact on small firms would be, especially around regulatory changes. First impressions were that the changes would be difficult for small firms to incorporate, but this view appears to have softened. Nonetheless, the common view was expressed that most small firms lacked appropriate expertise, in this case that they were unaware of the consequences of joining the EEC and that few had reconsidered their business strategy. Further, it was recorded that it was difficult to communicate with small firms. This general conception of small firms as lacking expertise and as 'difficult' would come to form a recurrent theme in debates around the developing enterprise policy agenda.

State Aid and the EEC

In order to join the EEC, the Heath government introduced the European Communities Act in 1972, which accepted the Treaty of Rome. This was designed to encourage industrial free trade but with protections for agriculture. For our purposes, a particular point of interest was the prohibitions against subsidies and state aid for industry, although the Single Market programme ultimately sought more to redirect state aids than to abolish them, especially in relation to regional policy (Lord, 1996).

Part Three of the Treaty of Rome set out the common rules on competition including a section focused on Aids Granted by States. Article 92.1, with exceptions also detailed in Article 92, set out that:

> Save as otherwise provided in this Treaty, any aid granted by a Member State or through State resources in any form whatsoever which distorts or threatens to distort competition by favouring certain undertakings or the production of certain goods shall, in so far as it affects trade between Member States, be incompatible with the common market.

However, the EEC, and later EU, has not only acted in coercive ways but has also lent support to particular agendas or interests, including areas of relevance to enterprise policymaking. For example, Schmidt (2002: 907) has argued that 'the EU's suggested rules provided the British government with extra legitimation for its radical privatization programme, thereby enhancing its political institutional capacity to reform.' This was alongside other support for a change in political direction that developed in the second half of the 1970s.

Aid for Enterprise Policy

Although the provisions limiting state aid and intervention designed to facilitate competitive markets were not to have significant enforcement or influence until the mid-1980s, the Treaty of Rome did allow that certain uses of state resources would be considered compatible with the common market. Article 92.3 provided that the 'aid to promote the economic development of areas where the standard of living is abnormally low or where there is serious underemployment' would be compatible. These provisions not only encouraged an emphasis on regional policy agendas, it also appeared to allow significant scope for discretion, and more specific guidelines and precedents developed over time. For example, Bennett (1983: 30) cites the following from the Commission's 1981 Eleventh Report on Competition:

> Of special importance . . . it regards measures to promote the development of small and medium-sized enterprises which some studies have shown to be an efficient means of encouraging the growth of new industries and technologies as well as of employment.

This report highlighted SMEs as the cornerstone of the industrial and commercial structure of the EEC and the difficult economic context in which many SMEs operated (with 'SME' defined as those businesses with annual turnover less than 100 million ECU, the European Currency Unit). The report expressed the importance of supporting SMEs, not only in access to finance but also in access to new markets, stating that representative organisations had expressed frustration with the administrative and tax burdens of doing so (Commission of the European Communities, 1981). In this way, the European project would shift the emphasis and prominence of state aid and intervention further towards smaller businesses.

The UK, as one of the poorer member states, was particularly receptive to this type of activity, concerned as it was with gaining some form of budget rebate. This approach to membership viewed forms of aid (e.g. the European Regional Development Fund, discussed further in the next section) as a form of reimbursement for the money paid into the EEC. In the search to capture funds, and to demonstrate the value of membership, UK policy therefore adapted to EU rules and criteria (Conzelmann, 2006).

The Treaty of Rome had established the European Investment Bank (EIB) which provided nearly £500m in loans to the UK in 1979 (Wren, 1996). These loans mainly funded infrastructure and large-scale industry projects, but they also provided finance to support the creation of new businesses that, it was hoped, would help to offset structural changes in certain industrial sectors. Bennett (1983: 35) concludes a review of early EEC support for small firms by highlighting that 'it is now recognised that the inadequacy or unavailability of suitable forms of finance is a significant factor impeding the growth of investment' and that this had led to the development of a range of Community lending instruments.

This was part of an emerging compromise that allowed (partial) exemptions for SMEs from member states not subsidising industries, especially in particular (deprived) regions and to support particular areas of development, such as training, consultancy and technology. The exemptions for SMEs were justified by a belief that these firms were key to competition and so supporting them helped to achieve the wider aims of developing competitive markets. These exemptions were likely influential in shaping subsequent UK enterprise policy, although this in part reflected a reinforcement of existing policy agendas. In addition to the types of financial assistance previously discussed, there were also 'global' loans made to organisations that, through the intervention of the Department of Industry, could then provide loans to SMEs (Wren, 1996). For example, Wren (1996) records how funds were made available to SMEs via the Industrial and Commercial Finance Corporation (see Chapter 3). However, the 'partial' nature of the exemptions for SMEs is also important. For example, Wren also notes the example of a proposed £20m investment for small firms in textile and clothing industries that was rejected by the European Commission.

The Commission increasingly acted against industrial subsidies as damaging competition but it did maintain the exemptions for areas it saw as relevant to its economic objectives, including support for SMEs. For example, the Strategic Programme for Innovation and Technology Transfer (SPRINT) initiative was begun in 1983 by the Commission and increased in scale after five years of piloting. SPRINT sought to support technology transfer to improve SME competitiveness across the European Communities (EC) through greater cooperation. It provided financial assistance for technology diffusion projects and network building, including conferences and workshops as well as sponsored competitions. Evaluation of the project was positive but raised a common concern with such enterprise policies, which is that, while they can be effective, there is often not an effective plan in place for ending the subsidy in order for the project or initiative to continue without government finance (Quince, 1994).

The European Regional Development Fund

The exemptions for government subsidies also extended to other of the EEC's own interventions. What would come to form the basis of the EU structural funds are composed of five funds: the ERDF, European Social Fund (ESF), Cohesion Fund, European Agricultural Fund for Rural Development, and the European Maritime and Fisheries Fund (EMFF). We will focus here on the ERDF as a key example of the allocation of resources driving wider policy implications. The ERDF was established in 1975 and sought to address regional inequalities within the EC. It required local match funding with an expectation that it would not replace existing funding or initiatives (i.e. it sought to ensure 'additionality').

Regulation (EEC) No.724/75 of 18 March 1975 records the creation of the ERDF:

> A European Regional Development Fund is hereby established, hereinafter referred to as 'the Fund', intended to correct the principal regional imbalances within the Community resulting in particular from agricultural preponderance, industrial change and structural under-employment.

Its aims of providing additionality in tackling regional imbalances through this funding were explicit, for example the preface to the regulation stated that 'the Fund's assistance should not lead Member States to reduce their own regional developmental efforts but should complement those efforts.' However, these aims were largely frustrated by the approach taken by certain states, including the UK government. As McAleavey (1995: 249) records: 'The ERDF has primarily been regarded in UK central government departments as a partial reimbursement on the UK's net contribution to the European Union (EU) budgets.' As a result, it did not tend to result in increased expenditure or support in those regions of the UK eligible for this assistance. Significant amounts of the funds were, for example, utilised by local authorities to fund infrastructure projects.

In its early years, the ERDF faced significant criticisms about its limited size, inflexibility and poor organisation (Croxford et al., 1987). It was revised to try and address some of these challenges, such as the process of allocation and identification of worthwhile expenditure, together with an increase from 4.8% of the EEC budget in 1975 to 9.1% in 1986, remaining a relatively marginal activity and, for some, a token exercise unlikely to make a significant impact on regional inequalities (Wise and Croxford, 1988). The wider Structural Funds budget was then doubled in 1988, providing the opportunity to tighten the rules around its operation, in particular attempting to ensure additionality which 'now required demonstration of increased aid to target regions' (McAleavey, 1995: 250), with strong opposition from the UK government. This led to greater transparency, but it is unclear if it achieved the core aim of providing additional assistance to areas of deprivation.

Bache (1999: 31) cites a 1981 House of Lords Select Committee: 'the Regional Fund caused very little to happen that would not have happened anyway.' This additionality problem is a potential issue for our understanding of UK enterprise policy where those policies pursuing regional development or seeking to support areas of relative deprivation and high unemployment may not have been pursued because of the availability of European funding. In fact, the greater problem for local authorities was financing the match funding in the context of control from central government.

In practice, according to McAleavey (1995: 252), the UK Government engaged in a practice of 'subtractionality' whereby local authority funds were top-sliced to create the ERDF 'pot' to which authorities then needed to apply for 'additional' funds. Success in applying for these additional funds would then return them to the baseline expenditure levels in line with original forecasts. This added element of uncertainty, in bidding to win the funding required, created additional problems for local authorities without any commensurate additionality in funding or support.

Since the 1980s, ERDF has particularly targeted support for small businesses and their environments. In the period 1981–1984, for example, the UK received an average allocation of 485.2m ECU assistance from the ERDF (Croxford et al., 1987). This included funds to convert disused buildings and to provide services for SMEs in areas of the UK that had been reliant on steel and shipbuilding industries (Wren, 1996). This led to a tension with the Thatcher government's move away from regionally focused support and around schemes such as enterprise zones (see Chapter 9) and, at least in part, resulted in the more EU-aligned Enterprise Grants introduced by the Labour government in 1998. EU membership has therefore been a critical influence in shaping the relationships between the UK government and small business and entrepreneurship.

The Move Away From Keynesian Interventionism

By the mid-1970s, there was increasingly widespread concern that Keynesian approaches were not suitable for the crises at hand (see Chapter 6). Although the second half of the decade saw the growing influence from the left of the Labour Party (shaping, for example, aspects of the National Enterprise Board discussed in Chapter 6), it also saw Labour Chancellor Denis Healey considering letting unemployment increase in order to fight skyrocketing inflation. This was part of the early move towards monetarism that would come to reshape UK economic policymaking.

The market system had developed with inherent links to monetarist policymaking and related institutions (Polanyi, 2001). However, the focus on trying to fight unemployment that had characterised a lot of political debate since unemployment had reached dismal levels in the 1930s (see Chapter 3) was at odds with making cuts in line with monetary targets that would mean accepting high levels of unemployment. As we have seen, the post-war, Butskellite consensus had supported a range of government interventions, including important aspects of the enterprise policy agenda of the time (albeit with a limited scale, especially if this focus on smaller businesses were to have made any impact on the unemployment numbers).

The Heath Conservatives had performed a significant u-turn in the early 1970s, retreating from monetarist talk to the embedded assumptions of Keynesianism in the face of rising unemployment. However, the party had then, in opposition, begun the move back to the small government right when, in 1975, Thatcher, with the help of key allies such as Keith Joseph, had challenged and replaced Heath as leader of the Conservatives. For their part, the Labour government's move towards monetarism was not taken in refutation of Keynesianism but, as described by Hall (1992), accompanied a shift in interests from the working class, trade union support for Keynesianism to the finance industry support for monetarism. This was shaped by the increasing influence of financial interests through financial markets (and as a result of an indebted economy and changing gilt market) and the diminishing of trade union influence from 1976 onwards. These changes were then accelerated by the terms of an IMF bailout.

By the end of 1976, by-election losses meant that Labour had lost its overall majority, constraining its ability to take bold measures or to follow a socialist route out of the troubles the country faced. James Callaghan took over as Labour PM when Wilson retired. He faced rising inflation and substantial cuts to public expenditure from Chancellor of the Exchequer Healey as the value of the pound began to plummet, declining by nearly 25% against the dollar (see, for example, UK Government, 1976, a leaflet explaining government policy on tackling inflation). As inflation and unemployment continued to grow and the country faced a mounting balance-of-payments crisis, the government requested a loan from the International Monetary Fund (IMF), at £3bn the largest the organisation had made at that time.

In return, the Labour government was committed to £2.5bn in spending cuts and the selling off of British Petroleum for the remaining £0.5bn. At this point, under the terms and restrictions of the bailout agreement that were fully implemented (and in repaying the loan before the end of the decade), Labour took the monetarist, free market approach to battling the country's problems, limiting the influence from the left wing of the party that argued for a more protectionist approach to economic recovery. However, it is important to note that many of the cuts to expenditure and monetarist policies were already in place. This reflected, as Rogers (2009) identifies in the archival records, a pre-existing preference amongst key figures in the Labour Party for a monetarist direction and the use of IMF conditionality to provide a useful justification for consolidating this choice of policy.

Enterprise Policy Responses to the Crises

In 1976, the Conservative Political Centre published a booklet making the case for the crucial role of small businesses as employers (6 million jobs, including the self-employed), economic contributors (20% of GNP) and providers of consumer choice and market competition. The booklet offered several recommendations to support the survival of this vital part of UK industry developed from a survey conducted of 225 small firms (including sole traders) that collected a range of enterprise policymaking ideas that would be central to the ongoing development of this agenda. The survey suggested that small firms were being 'victimised' and, in response to the issues raised, the booklet's authors recommended relief from bureaucracy (reduced form-filling) and from taxation, including raising the VAT threshold, a lower rate of corporation tax for small firms and 'justice for self-employed regarding pensions and National Insurance contributions' (Brown et al., 1976: 14).

A key focus for the booklet was on developing financial support for small firms, which included a Small Business Loan Guarantee scheme.

Other recommendations made included support and finance to encourage exports; the establishment of a Small Businesses Training Board in addition to vouchers to access other forms of support and training; and the creation of a Small Businesses Commission to help organise and deliver these interventions. A final recommendation that prefigured what would become a major line of enterprise policymaking was the review of new regulations in relation to the 'small business angle' (p. 14).

The Labour response, as the party of government, was less comprehensive but still included new endeavours in enterprise policymaking to try to address the unemployment problems stemming from the crises facing the country. The government's 'Urban Programme' created a degree of decentralisation by granting the power for local authorities to make loans at commercial rates, which Wren (1996) notes would go on to become an important source of funds for many small firms in urban areas, amounting to around £26m per year by the mid-1980s.

Labour also introduced the Small Firm Employment Subsidy Scheme in the budget of March 1977. It was to be one of a set of employment measures that sought to tackle unemployment and was initially run as an experiment:

> . . . there will be an experimental scheme for six months from 1st July applying only to manufacturing firms in special development areas employing fewer than fifty workers. They will be given a weekly subsidy of £20 for six months for each additional worker taken on.
>
> (Hansard, HC Deb. 29 March 1977 vol.929 col.270)

The scheme was therefore, especially in this 'experiment' phase, quite limited in terms of industry and regional focus. Nonetheless, it received 2476 applications by the end of June 1978, 2228 of which were approved at a cost of £2.6m (Hansard, HC Deb. 4 July 1978 vol.953 col.59W). As a result of initial, positive evaluations of the experiment, it was then extended in both scope and duration (Wren, 1996). Secretary of State, Albert Booth, announced in late 1978 that:

> From 1st January 1979, the present scheme will be extended to small manufacturing firms throughout Great Britain. Furthermore, the subsidy will be available to small non-manufacturing firms in the special development areas, development areas and inner city partnership areas. The new scheme will be open for applications to 31st March 1980. The changes have been notified to the EEC Commission. I estimate that these changes will more than treble the number of new jobs created by the scheme.
>
> (Hansard, HC Deb. 9 November 1978 vol.957 col.1197)

On the other side of the House, however, James Prior, Conservative MP for Lowestoft, was critical of the government's handling of the economy. Prior suggested that 'we are becoming a subsidised society, constantly propping up small firms by subsidies' rather than, for example, reforming the Employment Protection Act, reforms which he believed would deliver employment through free markets (ibid). The emphasis on removing burdens rather than subsidising solutions, echoed a position expressed by Keith Joseph almost 10 years earlier. By the conclusion of the scheme in March 1980, its precise impact was unclear in terms of new jobs that would otherwise not have been created (Wren, 1996).

The Wilson Committee and Small Firm Finance

In January 1977, amid the economic struggles and concerns about key industries, Labour set up the *Committee to Review the Functioning of Financial Institutions* chaired by former Prime Minister Harold Wilson. The Committee was composed of a varied membership (in terms of their backgrounds and views) of 18 members and, over the next three years, it held 55 meetings at a cost of £334 000 (Hansard, HC Deb. 30 June 1980 vol.987 col.372). As well as several interim reports (including an important one on small firms discussed further later), the Committee produced a substantial final report (not published until June 1980) and 13 volumes of evidence.

The terms of reference for the Committee were:

> To enquire into the role and functioning, at home and abroad, of financial institutions in the United Kingdom and their value to the economy; to review in particular the provision of funds for industry and trade; to consider what changes are required in the existing arrangements for the supervision of these institutions, including the possible extension of the public sector, and to make recommendations.

This included institutions such as the Bank of England, other banks, finance houses, life insurance companies, pension funds, building societies and the Stock Exchange, together with the arrangements in place for export credit.

The Committee produced an interim report in 1979 on *The Financing of Small Firms*. This report, and the wider work of the Committee, attempted to weigh the contrasting views and complex nature of small firm access to finance and whether the Macmillan gap still existed. The authors of the report explained their rationale for focusing on small firms:

> The main reason for singling out small firms for special treatment in this way is the virtual consensus in the submissions we have received

that there are problems with the arrangements for financing smaller businesses, whatever the availability of funds to industry and trade as a whole. There appeared to us to be a case for closer examination of these claims, both because of their importance in their own right and because of the general lessons which might be expected from the scrutiny of the financial system at what is so widely believed to be one of its weakest points. Moreover, the Government has specifically asked for our views on the subject so that they can take them into account in deciding about further action to help small businesses.

(p. 1)

This work was informed by several relevant research projects the Committee commissioned. For example, Jones (1979) conducted research for the Committee on 296 incorporated companies with less than £4m capital employed (from a population of nearly 0.25m companies), analysing accounts submitted to Companies House. Jones found that small companies predominantly relied on retained funds within the business, but were also more dependent on bank finance than were large companies. Other studies also confirmed the importance of retained profits and overdraft facilities, but that banks were generally perceived as indifferent to small businesses.

A commissioned study by Mitchell and Clay (1979) looked at ICFC through interviews with area managers and controllers in two ICFC area offices and with 18 successful small firm owners recommended by the managers. Mitchell and Clay found that ICFC staff felt themselves operating in a competitive environment but that small firms did not perceive this and believed there to be no practical alternative. Those firms with criticisms of ICFC felt they were given poor advice and that the terms were too high.

However, access to finance, despite its ongoing prominence in enterprise policymaking, was perceived as less of a problem than the economic environment in which businesses were operating. Nor was lack of external finance regarded as a major constraint on business growth. What did exacerbate the challenges faced in the tough conditions of the 1970s was what was perceived as excessively high and overly complicated taxation and by legislation and restrictions concerning employment (which, for example, made it difficult to deal with staffing problems by laying off employees).

Overall, the Committee identified some supply side problems in SME finance, alongside the information asymmetry problems in assessing the risks involved for all parties. There was also an important highlighting of the reluctance on the part of small firms to give up equity. The report acknowledged that many of the relative difficulties in accessing finance relate to the higher costs and risks of providing loans to these businesses

(Wilson, 1979). Ultimately, in terms of the Macmillan gap, the interim report on small firms concluded:

> There can be little doubt that at the time of this report there are deficiencies in the availability of equity finance for small businesses and that this is putting undesirable constraints on their rate of creation and growth. The present equity gap is now seen as having two consequences—a shortage of initial capital for new start-ups and a deficiency in the provision of development capital to finance the expansion of established enterprises.
>
> (p. 9)

On this basis the report recommended, for example, the creation of a Small Firm Investment Company; a publicly underwritten loan guarantee scheme; and that the Department of Industry review their schemes to ensure small firms were not excluded. They also noted (p. 35) that 'what is required now is not any further increase in the volume of information and advice but improvements in its quality and effectiveness.' They recommended, for example, that accountants and banks become better equipped to offer advice to small firms. Some of these themes will be taken up in terms of the policies discussed in the following chapters.

Conclusion

The 1970s saw significant external influences shaping industrial policy in the UK. In addition to the types of crises and unemployment shocks that had encouraged previous interventions to provide small firms with financial aid, support and guidance, the government was now also negotiating with international bodies, principally the EEC and IMF. Both these bodies encouraged the UK in the more free trade, less interventionist direction that both Conservatives and, to some degree, Labour had already been experimenting with while in government. The EEC, and later the EU, also provided additional funding for regional policy activity, including support for small firms. Wider exemptions for SMEs from rules relating to state subsidies may have shaped the focus of future industrial policy, although it is difficult to ascertain the degree to which this was impactful in the types of intervention undertaken. Ultimately, the degree to which additional support or exemptions were used by the UK to create a form of rebate casts doubt on the enterprise policy impact this funding may have actually supported.

While we have not focused on it here, there was an emphasis on support for exports (unsurprising given the balance of payments challenge the country faced) and the government continued to look to small businesses to create jobs and help tackle unemployment, especially in areas of deprivation and where the traditional industries were in retreat. However, these schemes still tended to lack the scope and the ambition to make a significant impact, and questions persisted about the degree to which the jobs created were 'new' jobs that would not have existed without the subsidies provided.

Unpredictability, a fluctuating economy and significant labour unrest marked a turbulent decade in the 1970s. This created a very different operating environment for the large businesses that had come to dominate the economy and that relied on economies of scale that left them potentially vulnerable to the types of challenge that were becoming increasingly frequent. In response, these businesses began to look for new ways to organise in order to manage the risks and uncertainties they were facing. As we will see, this had important implications for enterprise policy and for small firms.

Further, with work conducted both by the opposition Conservative Party and the Labour-appointed Wilson Committee, there were calls for the expansion of enterprise policy, including some form of loan guarantee scheme; greater consideration of small firms in government (including in relation to the development of new regulations); and the improvement of advice and support, with considerations about the most effective way to provide this to small firms.

8 Neoliberalism and Enterprise Culture

The shift from Keynesianism to monetarism, which had begun in the 1970s under both Conservative and Labour governments, in the 1980s accompanied a broader development of free market, small government policies commonly characterised as neoliberal. While there were limits to the extent monetarism was pursued in this period, the wider political context is important for understanding the development and growing prominence of enterprise policy from the 1980s onwards. This chapter will focus on the development and general influence of neoliberalism and market-based reforms, in particular in relation to the emergence of a new form of political discourse promoting entrepreneurship.

To unpick the political context of the 1980s and its shaping of enterprise policymaking, we explore two major themes. Firstly, we examine the new ideology overtaking Keynesianism and the associated centralised, interventionist approach to the economy (variously referred to as Thatcherism, neoliberalism or free markets). Secondly, to fully understand enterprise policy in this era, we also explore the changing makeup of the economy and the rise of small firms. In policy terms, these two themes shaped the new enterprise policy banner of an 'enterprise culture' and a range of government actions that will be discussed here and in the following chapters. In this chapter, we focus on the Enterprise Allowance Scheme and new initiatives aimed at supporting finance for small firms, though now with a new focus on this support being delivered in relation to the investor rather than the business owner. In Chapter 9, we will focus on deregulation and then, in Chapter 10, business support services, in particular the development of the Business Link service.

Thatcher's Election

Late in 1978, the Labour government's relations with the TUC began to breakdown (primarily around a proposed maximum wage increase) and a series of high-profile industrial actions took place throughout the winter. As Rubinstein (2003: 315) notes, this action meant 'suddenly bringing Britain to the point of chaos.' The strikes through this 'winter of discontent' ultimately led to public dismay and a vote of confidence lost by the Labour government (by one vote) to bring about a General Election.

Callaghan's Labour Party faced the electorate with a message built on the optimism that lay in the decade ahead. Identifying its priorities as being to curb inflation; reform the relations between government, unions and industry leaders; aim for full employment; enlarge people's freedom at the expense of bureaucracy; and to work towards the achievement of world peace and the elimination of poverty. To achieve these objectives:

> The Government's industrial strategy is about how to create more wealth and more jobs through a constructive national partnership with unions and management. The Conservatives will not admit that nowadays governments must step in to help create employment, to limit price rises, to assist industry to modernize itself. They are ready to gamble the people's future on a return to the nineteenth century free market—despite its pitiless social consequences. They are as dangerously out of their time as a penny farthing on the motorway.
>
> (Labour Party, 1979)

Kavanagh (1990) reports analysis of Thatcher's speeches during the 1979 election campaign and identifies two key themes: the negatives of socialism and the positives of 'freedom,' or a free society. These themes echoed the influential work of economist Friedrich Hayek and his book, *The Road to Serfdom*, which argued for only a limited role for government in supporting the effective working of free markets and competition.

Introducing the Conservative Party (1979) manifesto, Thatcher highlighted 'how the balance of our society has been increasingly tilted in favour of the State at the expense of individual freedom' and associated this with the country's recent woes. In response, Thatcher explained, the party would tackle the nation's problems:

> . . . *not* because we think we have all the answers but because we think we have the one answer that matters most. We want to work *with the grain* of human nature, helping people to help themselves—and others. This is the way to restore that self-reliance and self-confidence which are the basis of personal responsibility and national success.

The manifesto argued that recently politicians had, in attempting too much, failed to fulfil the necessary tasks of government. The Conservatives set out the tasks they saw as important for the next government: controlling inflation; 'striking a fair balance between the rights and duties of the trade union movement'; incentivising work and creating jobs; upholding Parliament and the rule of law; supporting family life (including helping people to become homeowners); and strengthening the country's defences and its military allegiances. The Conservative campaign focused on economic discipline, anti-union measures and some 'denationalisation.' They won the election with a sufficient majority to enact many of their proposed changes.

The Shift in Ideology to 'Neoliberalism'

The election of Thatcher's Conservative government in 1979 saw the rise of a particular set of ideas that we will consider as 'neoliberal.' Neoliberalism can be effectively used to group together a number of policies related to monetarism, deregulation and market-based reforms that developed and reshaped key areas of enterprise policy. More broadly, it can also be considered 'as the set of discourses, practices and apparatuses that determine a new mode of government of human beings in accordance with the universal principle of competition' (Dardot and Laval, 2014: 4). Hall (1986: 290) argues that the key to this policy agenda was 'to reinforce the operation of market mechanisms in the hope that they will rejuvenate the economy with a minimum of state intervention.' As Hall makes clear, and as we will see in this and the following chapters, this nonetheless meant quite significant state intervention in order to reshape many longstanding practices and institutions within the UK economy.

Many of these ideas had featured in the Heath government nearly 10 years earlier. The experience of this government, and the significance of Heath's u-turn in the face of mounting unemployment (see Chapter 6), was a formative experience for many of those (such as Keith Joseph) who were now back in government. Joseph (1976) had subsequently proposed that *Monetarism Is Not Enough* (a pamphlet including a foreword by Thatcher). He argued that the trade unions, and the wider labour market, were in need of reform for markets to work effectively. Stedman Jones (2012: 177) records that it was Joseph, 'as the philosopher-king of the new Conservatism of the 1970s,' who reintroduced Thatcher to the work of Hayek and Milton Friedman.

Hall (1992) highlights how, where Heath had faced a deeply entrenched belief in Keynesianism, Thatcher pursued the monetarist alternative at a time when the ideas had already been implemented by the previous Labour government, were more clearly elaborated and articulated and had received institutional support from economists, the City and the media. This was strengthened by the loss of the Treasury's monopoly on economic forecasting and the emergence of new economic voices in university centres and think tanks. Indeed, think tanks such as the Institute of Economic Affairs (IEA) and the Centre for Policy Studies (CPS) were 'unquestionably the two most important channels for Thatcherite ideas' (Desai, 1994: 28). The ideas were also established more widely through the journalism of writers such as Peter Jay in *The Times* or Sam Brittan in the *Financial Times* (Stedman Jones, 2012). The ideas resonated with some of the wider changes underway in the economy.

Small Business Revivalism

Piore and Sabel (1984: 182) argue that, amongst many developed economies, including the UK, the social and economic crises of the 1960s and 1970s and deregulation seeking to increase market influence on wages and unemployment increased uncertainty and meant 'pushing industry toward more flexible production and marketing strategies.' Corporate responses included conglomeration and multinationalisation, essentially aimed at hedging risk from the uncertainty of the socioeconomic climate. Large businesses also responded to crises by moving from employees to subcontractors, and therefore from fixed to variable costs, meaning that 'former employees now had to bear the risks—as dependent subcontractors—that the firm would otherwise have borne' (Piore and Sabel, 1984: 214). This created an important context for the development of enterprise policy from the late 1970s onwards: a significant growth in numbers of small firms and their utilisation by large businesses through subcontracting arrangements and increasingly complex supply chains.

Smaller businesses therefore became more prominent as a result of significant economic restructuring (Mallett and Wapshott, 2017). As large firms decreased the size of their operations they created more opportunities for small businesses as they fragmented their operations through decentralisation (e.g. more small plants), devolvement (e.g. franchising) and disintegration (e.g. subcontracting). Shutt and Whittington (1987) argue that this enabled large firms to introduce greater control of labour (and potentially weaken trade union power through limits to collectivism), better manage the risk of innovation (encouraging highly competitive small firm innovation and then buying the successes) and to manage fluctuations in demand (limiting the number of employees and giving flexibility in capacity through subcontracting and supply chain arrangements). In these ways, large firm 'fragmentation strategies serve to shift responsibility and employment from large firms and plants to small firms and plants' (Shutt and Whittington, 1987: 18; also see Bechhofer and Elliott, 1981).

The government set out its own analysis of these processes in the context of structural changes (a shift from manufacturing to services) and technological changes (e.g. PCs, fax machines) and described how they were:

> . . . encouraged by cultural and organisational change (enterprise culture, self-employment, contracting out, franchising, management buy out). Economies of scale are diminishing in some industries, as the emphasis shifts towards quality and meeting customer needs, and as flexible production methods become more widespread.
>
> (DTI, 1995a: 28)

These processes of change in the economy were partly responsible for the substantial increases in the number of small businesses that had begun as early as the late 1960s (before the publication of the Bolton Report) and by the early 1980s 'new registration levels of "non-nominal" companies rose by 43%' (Shutt and Whittington, 1987: 14). Thus, a core tenet of the Bolton Report, that small firms were in decline, was inaccurate at the time of writing and became even more so, such that 'the reversal [in the decline of small business] started before governments in this country had a small business policy' (Bannock, 1989: 17).

While small firm numbers were at record levels, they increasingly faced tough, highly competitive conditions where they absorbed many of the risks large firms now sought to avoid. As Piore and Sabel (1984: 263) highlight, 'firms come under increasing pressure from mass producers or lower-wage flexible specialists, they cut production costs by sweating labor and using inferior materials' (see also Shutt and Whittington, 1987; Rainnie, 1989). This is important because the changing structure of the economy and the types of small firms that represent the significant growth in the 'sector' have central implications for the types of challenges they face and the forms of government intervention that develop, including potentially to support large firms and their supply chain management.

The Department of Trade and Industry (1995a) White Paper *Competitiveness: Forging Ahead* highlighted these changes in terms of 'an economy-wide shift in favour of the smaller business' (p. 28). The White Paper explained how small firms had created twice as many jobs as large businesses (although it did acknowledge that 'some of these jobs will have been associated with a transfer of work from larger firms, rather than newly generated work,' [ibid]). On this basis, government policy focus was set out in terms of supporting those firms with the potential and the will to grow.

Enterprise Culture

During the economic difficulties experienced in the 1970s, a cultural explanation had emerged for how the UK had fallen from its once-dominant position relative to other nations. Raven (1989: 188, our italics) identifies that 'the idea of the decline of the *industrial spirit*, of a British cultural "Luddism", enjoyed powerful influence' across a wide span of academic, social and political fields. Such ideas, in Raven's analysis, gained particular traction in the political arena, with both Conservative and Labour parties making efforts to promote the values of industry, signalling that the people of the UK had somehow lost admiration for business and the people engaged in business. Such critique carried with it echoes of the negative evaluations of the late-Victorian entrepreneurs that had circulated some decades prior (see, for example, Chapter 2).

Thatcher (1984) explicitly related her political agenda to reverse this decline to small business and to the creation of an 'enterprise culture':

> I came to office with one deliberate intent: to change Britain from a dependent to a self-reliant society—from a give-it-to-me, to a do-it-yourself nation.
>
> A get-up-and-go, instead of a sit-back-and-wait-for-it Britain.
>
> This means creating a new culture—an enterprise culture—which accords a new status to the entrepreneur and offers him the rewards to match; which breeds a new generation of men and women who create jobs for others instead of waiting for others to create jobs for them.
>
> That is why this Government has given so much attention to the promotion of the small business.
>
> It is not simply that tall oaks from little acorns grow. Small businesses are the very embodiment of a free society—the mechanism by which the individual can turn his leadership and talents to the benefit of both himself and the nation.
>
> The freer the society, the more small businesses there will be. And the more small businesses there are, the freer and more enterprising that society is bound to be.
>
> So my message to you today is quite simple: we will do our best for you, so that you can do your best for Britain.

Leyshon (1982: 59) captures the key themes underlying the approach to small firm policymaking at this time (also noting that it tended to focus on manufacturing):

- small firms act as a mopper-up of declining manufacturing employment;
- increasing the small firm sector is a desirable corrective to excessive big company dominance in the UK;
- small firms are innovative;
- small firms are market responsive, dynamic and flexible; and
- small firms are profit seekers and growth orientated.

Whether or not the Bolton Report explicitly shaped these themes, they are largely apparent in the Bolton Report and had grown out of the 1970s debates around enterprise policymaking that were discussed in Chapters 6 and 7. Leyshon (ibid) notes that these ideas represent more of a 'lament for the lost virtues of the competitive large firm model . . . rather than a list of explicit characteristics which can explain satisfactorily the growth and development of small business activity.' Many of the assumptions underpinning enterprise policy appeared to be shaped by ideology and a sense of market competitiveness rather than arising from evidence-based policymaking.

The impact of neoliberalism's influence can be seen clearly in the specific promotion of an 'enterprise culture' at the heart of this agenda, with the government seeking to encourage a particular set of social values based on self-reliance and self-help (and in opposition to a 'dependency culture,' see, for example, through the Enterprise Allowance Scheme, discussed further in a following section). This set of values was seen as embodied in the independent entrepreneur and the government set out to influence public attitudes towards small business and entrepreneurship. Here, enterprise was claimed to capture espoused values of 'thrift, hard work, independence, self-responsibility, wealth-creation, family-orientation: living examples of Victorian capitalist principles' (Anderson et al., 2000: 11). The policy agenda sought to reshape informal institutions alongside government attempts to reshape the formal institutional environment, for example through deregulation (see Chapter 9).

The moral dimension of the enterprise culture has been associated with a way of 'remoralising capitalism' (Bechhofer and Elliott, 1981: 192). Small businesses were cast as offering an embodiment of desirable attributes. These were attributes associated with a particular vision of a Victorian entrepreneurial golden age of market competition and government laissez-faire, albeit a set of ideas that were being actively challenged during that Victorian era (Perkin, 1992). 'Specifically, this involved the promotion of 'individualism; independence; "flexibility"; anti-collectivism; privatism; self-help; and so on' (Burrows, 1991: 28). The enterprise culture often lacked clarity or a rigorous elaboration in policy terms, but it nonetheless provided a way to make sense of the changes many people were experiencing, for example as they moved into self-employment (perhaps now as a sub-contractor rather than employee) or as a member of a small firm (perhaps rather than as part of a unionised workforce in a large company or nationalised industry).

An important part of this meaning-making was the recasting of entrepreneurship and small businesses through Thatcher's own Christianity and the ways in which this was enmeshed with the ideas of freedom and economic choice (Anderson et al., 2000; see also Roberts, 1992). This sense of freedom and choice was as opposed to, for example, Christian notions of charity, and was a focus that continued, in broad terms, into the New Labour governments of Tony Blair (see Chapter 11). In Thatcher's famous 'Sermon on the Mound' to the General Assembly of the Church of Scotland in 1988, she stated, 'What is certain, however, is that any set of social and economic arrangements which is not founded on the acceptance of individual responsibility will do nothing but harm.' This idea of individual responsibility (and therefore a very different role for the state) was therefore at the heart of the Conservative's enterprise culture agenda.

For Thatcher and some commentators (Morris, 1991; Anderson et al., 2000), this discourse of enterprise was heightened through the use of religious symbolism and language. For example, Anderson et al. (2000: 14) cite Thatcher as referring to a 'crusade for freedom' and 'the cause,' emphasising the religious justification and legitimisation underpinning a lot of this discourse and the resulting policy agenda.

The Department for Enterprise

David Young was a 'devotee' of the enterprise culture policy agenda (Ritchie, 1991: 19). Following the 1979 election, Young was an advisor to Keith Joseph, then Secretary of State for Industry, and later was himself a cabinet minister in Margaret Thatcher's government, responsible for shaping the development of the enterprise culture agenda in the mid-1980s (Young, 1992). We will also meet Young again in Chapter 11, acting as the coalition government's 'Prime Minister's adviser on enterprise and SMEs.' Morris (1991) highlights Young's view that ideas such as profit had become dirty words and that the British education system was dulling enterprising instincts along with other cultural institutions of class, welfarism and trade unions.

Young (cited in Coffield, 1990) saw four key factors as responsible for the problems in the UK economy, which ultimately related to a lack of 'enterprise': the education system (and its having little regard for industry); the financial system (and its poor support for small firms); protectionism in industry; and confrontational industrial relations. This informed the approach to the enterprise culture policy agenda, for example Young wanted to introduce 'enterprise' into the education system as a means of tackling youth unemployment. This would involve schemes such as the Mini Enterprise in Schools Project (school children encouraged to explore starting a business) or the Enterprise in Higher Education initiative (following the idea that graduates should have developed competencies of relevance to enterprise) as well as wider changes with the introduction of new forms of vocational training (such as National Vocational Qualifications, NVQs).

Perhaps reflecting both Young's passion for the enterprise culture and the increasing emphasis on job creation through enterprise (see the following section), the Small Firms Division was transferred from the Department of Trade and Industry to the Department of Employment under Young in the September 1985 Cabinet reshuffle. Young himself then moved to the DTI in 1987, where he attempted to rebrand it the Department for Enterprise (see, for example, DTI, 1988) on launching the 'Enterprise Initiative' (see Chapter 10). Young's tenure illustrates how the focus on enterprise was, as in this ministerial rebranding exercise, partly a focus on language as much as concrete policy ideas. In Fairclough's seminal analysis (1992:

131–132) of Young's speeches and associated government documents, it is identified how 'the word "enterprise" is subjected to a process of semantic engineering . . ., which involves articulating around the word a set of qualities associated with entrepreneurship as understood by proponents of enterprise culture, including self-reliance and self-help.' Promotional items were found to intertwine these 'ideologies of enterprise' with the political strategies of the New Right Conservatives' (p. 133).

Casting Britain's problems in a cultural frame (Selden, 1991) opened up questions about how exactly this cultural problem could be addressed. It was in seeking to change economic, political and cultural institutions that a new focus developed for enterprise policymaking in this era of the 'enterprise culture.' For example, this involved both a changing approach to welfare and the promotion of individualism shaping policies such as the Enterprise Allowance Scheme.

Enterprise Allowance Scheme

The Enterprise Allowance Scheme (EAS) was introduced in 1982, and it has been described as 'radical and innovative' (Greene et al., 2008: 63). The scheme ensured that unemployed people who set up their own business could receive a payment of £40 a week for a year. To qualify, participants had to have been unemployed for a certain period (this changed as the scheme evolved) and to have £1000 capital. These businesses were intended for industries deemed to be 'socially desirable': retailing; services to building and construction; car maintenance services; agricultural services; and manufacturing (Hansard, HC Deb. 17 May 1982 vol.24 cols.167–168).

It was initially piloted in five areas of the UK between January 1982 and July 1983, funding 3300 individuals with 90% of those in the pilot staying in the scheme for the full 12 months (Hansard, HC Deb. 1 February 1984 vol.53 col.240). The estimated cost of the scheme run across the five pilot areas, including administrative costs, was £5.5m (Hansard, HC Deb. 1 February 1983 vol.36 col.69). However, it is worth noting that all participants were already receiving welfare payments such that the actual additional costs were negligible (and, in theory, possibly negative). Additional advice was provided to applicants in the pilot through the self-employed counsellors contracted through the Small Firms Advice Bureau (now the Small Firms Service) at a rate of £25/day (for a total cost of all advice through this service for 1983–1984 totalling over £1.1m, Hansard, HC Deb. 25 May 1984 vol.60 col.526).

The scheme was then extended nationwide in 1983, with increased take-up until reaching a height of 106 000 individuals in 1987–1988 (the popularity of the scheme causing problems of waiting lists in some areas) with only 15% of those who completed the scheme having returned to unemployment 6 months later (Hansard, HC Deb. 20 July 1989 vol.157 col.329). However, it is difficult to identify the deadweight effects with the scheme—how many of the participants (those with £1000) would have remained unemployed after 18 months?

The principal motivation of the scheme was to encourage those who may be deterred from entering self-employment because of the risk of losing their welfare entitlements. In this way it represented the Conservative's idea of moving from a 'dependency culture' (with people dependent upon welfare) to an 'enterprise culture' (with people pursuing self-employment as an individualistic response to their unemployment, albeit with a welfare safety net). The downside of this approach may well have been experienced by those whose new businesses failed and who found themselves back on welfare, potentially with additional debts (Wren, 1996). Nonetheless, the use of the scheme to encourage people from unemployment to self-employment appeared a success. This was bolstered further by the idea that the new businesses created might go on to create further jobs.

Small Businesses as Job Creators

In the economic crises that set the scene for the 1979 General Election, with the country facing increasing unemployment and 'economic decay' (Liberal Party, 1979), the link between SME growth and job creation became increasingly important. The incumbent Labour Government had promised the continuation of the small firms employment subsidy (paying small manufacturing firms for jobs created, see Chapter 7) and proposed returning jobs to the inner-cities by stimulating the development of SMEs. The soon-to-be-elected Conservatives asserted explicitly that 'the creation of new jobs depends to a great extent on the success of smaller businesses' (Conservative Party, 1979). For the Liberals, the link was more implicit, but SMEs, and positive discrimination in their favour, was still associated with job creation.

In a letter to Francis Maude setting out key lines of argument for the forthcoming election manifesto, Joseph (1978) set out the need for small businesses in job creation:

> We can, perhaps, put even more emphasis on the discouraging implications of the Employment Protection Act and the extra employment potential of the 800,000 small firms if only the majority of them were given sufficient encouragement and confidence to take on one extra employee.
>
> (p. 1)

The idea that SMEs were responsible for creating a disproportionately high number of jobs had gained increased attention with the 1979 publication of Birch's influential study. Birch (1981) reported that two-thirds of net new jobs created, in a sample of 5.6 million US businesses (1969–1976), were in firms employing 20 or fewer people. In 1984, Birch was invited to a job generation conference sponsored by the Department of Trade and Industry. The conference reflected the contrary evidence that had begun to emerge around the role of SMEs in creating new jobs and an increasing questioning of Birch's findings (Ganguly, 1985; Hirschberg, 1999). Exploring the impact of SMEs as job creators in the UK, Storey and Johnson (1987: 41) conclude that '. . . over a decade half the jobs created in every 100 small firms occur in the four firms which grow fastest.' Nonetheless, the idea of SMEs as job creators was a powerful one with a persistent hold over enterprise policymaking, with politicians increasingly looking to start-ups and small businesses as potential job creators (a powerful, if unrealistic, refrain being that, if every self-employed person and small business in the UK created a single job each, there would be x million new jobs created).

While a few policies targeted key sectors such as manufacturing, the focus on 'More Small Firms' (Conservative Party, 1983) or 'Backing Small Business' (Liberal Party, 1987) continued to propose measures relating to removing general obstacles affecting all SMEs rather than attempts to target the small proportion of firms responsible for a disproportionate amount of net job creation. For example, while Labour has generally had less to propose in this area, both Conservatives and Liberals have frequently suggested SME job creation could be supported through reductions in taxation, access to public procurement and the areas of access to finance and burdens of regulation (Wapshott and Mallett, 2018). These types of proposal tend not to discriminate amongst SMEs nor address how to support the limited number of potentially high growth firms, but we will see them influencing several of the policies developed over the coming chapters.

Finance for Small Firms in the Enterprise Culture

When the Conservatives came to power, new guidelines were introduced for the National Enterprise Board (NEB), for example introducing a greater emphasis on the need for potential future profitability and an expectation that it would sell off its portfolio as soon as possible. The general approach to the NEB is perhaps suggested by the title of a book written by Conservatives Grylls and Redwood (1980) and published by one of the new, influential think tanks: *The National Enterprise Board: A Case for Euthanasia*. However, the Conservatives did not radically change or limit the NEB in the short term and it is also worth noting that several regions began to set up their own local Enterprise Boards. The NEB was also the partial basis for the development of a range of new organisations and initiatives delivering enterprise policies focused on financial assistance for small businesses that included: the British Technology Group; Oakwood Loan Finance Ltd; Small Firms Loan Guarantee Scheme; and the Business Start-Up Scheme.

The NEB maintained an investment role, focused on high technology companies and investment, particularly in the North of England. This was developed through the formation of the British Technology Group (BTG) in 1981 by amalgamating the National Research Development Corporation and the National Enterprise Board to support the translation of research into commercial products, seeking to promote industrial competitiveness. It offered five-year, unsecured low-interest loans to small firms, predominantly in what were now termed the Assisted Areas in England. There were also calls to extend its engagement further, for example 'to establish a patenting advisory and assistance service for small firms' (Hansard, HC Deb. 16 December 1982 vol.34 col.214). Operating at a fairly large scale, by 1982 the BTG sought to invest £20m and was obliged to dispose of all holdings at the earliest opportunity. It came to focus on technology transfer and in 1992 was privatised (via the British Technology Group Bill) and subject to a management buyout to a consortium including BTG management, financial institutions and universities (it is today focused on the healthcare industry).

Oakwood Loan Finance Ltd was set up as a subsidiary of the NEB to offer loans to small companies, in its nine-year history making about 70 investments, for example 'in 1982, 29 offers of finance were made involving £1.15 million' (Lonsdale, 1997: 57). Other schemes focused on specific industries such as Small Engineering Firms Investment Scheme focused on engineering companies with fewer than 200 (later extended to 500) employees, seeking to support investment in advanced capital equipment to improve their manufacturing ability and productivity. The scheme received 1748 applications during its eight-and-a-half weeks of operation, 1355 applicants receiving offers of a grant from the £30m investment (the number of applications necessitating this as an increase from the originally planned £20m), the majority of firms in the South East of England and West Midlands (Hansard, HC Deb. 15 June 1982 vol.25 col.234).

Other schemes saw a shift in approach for the provision of finance to small businesses, focusing more on supporting the lenders than offering alternative sources of finance as enterprise policies had often tended to do since the identification of the Macmillan gap in 1931 (see Chapter 3).

The Small Firms Loan Guarantee Scheme

The Small Firms Loan Guarantee Scheme also started in 1981, with a relatively high profile. This scheme involved the government underwriting approved bank loans to those small firms unable to access finance. Such schemes 'seek to redress perceived capital market imperfections by providing collateral to the lender on behalf of the firm' (Cowling and

Mitchell, 2003: 64). A loan guarantee scheme had been recommended by the Wilson Committee (see Chapter 7) and organisations such as the Union of Independent Companies and had been proposed by a minister within the previous Labour government. A similar scheme had also existed in Germany since the 1950s. The new scheme initially involved London and Scottish Clearing Banks and the ICFC before being extended to a range of other financial institutions after what was viewed as a successful operation in its first three 'pilot' years. It was extended to involve a wider range of industries and, in some form, continued until it was replaced by the Enterprise Finance Guarantee scheme in 2009 (see Chapter 11).

By 31 March 1986, a total of 16 642 guaranteed loans had been issued under the scheme. Only 68 applications had been rejected (Hansard, HC Deb. 22 April 1986 vol.96 cols.107–108). At 30 November 1985, 4950 guarantees had been called under the loan guarantee scheme, the government paying when the lender informed them of default, with no follow-up or exploration of the causes (Hansard, HC Deb. 3 December 1985 vol.88 col.192). An evaluation of the scheme, which we will return to, conducted by private consultants for the Department of Employment (TNA: T430/470, para. 2.7) found that '1981–84 was the "high tide" of the scheme.'

The refinement of the scheme over time through negotiation with the banks (TNA: T390/742) demonstrated where its perceived value may lie. The original guarantee was for 80% of the loan with a premium charged of 3% of the guaranteed amount. However, following a high early failure rate of guaranteed loans (around 40% of the loans in 1981 had gone into default within three years), the government reduced the guarantee to 70% and increased the premium to 5%. This resulted in a plummeting level of demand (from a monthly average of 385 guaranteed loans to just 35 in 1986), necessitating an increase in the guarantee to 85% and a reduction in the premium to 2.5% and then 1.5%. Demand then increased again, to 248 guarantees per month (TNA: T430/470, para. 2.3; Wren, 1996; Harrison and Mason, 1986).

Concerns about the rates of default have subsequently been examined by Cowling and Mitchell (2003) who conducted a detailed analysis of the scheme and found that 'a rise in the cost of borrowing (induced by the presence of the SFLGS) does in fact increase default' (pp. 65–66). This supported an interpretation of credit rationing in the market for small business finance, with credit rationing becoming even more important an issue in the 1990s than the 1980s. The reasons for default were found to be various, although other reports (DTI personal communication, cited in Harrison and Mason, 1986) suggest that defaults were mostly likely to occur in the first year.

Importantly, early analysis of the scheme in 1984 (Robson Rhodes, cited in Harrison and Mason, 1986) suggested that only half of the loans guaranteed were genuinely additional. That is, the government was guaranteeing a lot of loans that would have been made anyway. Worse, an article in *The Times* in August 1982 recorded allegations that banks had been using the scheme to transfer the worst risks in their lending port-folio to the government scheme as the government would then cover the bill for up to 80% of any losses incurred (TNA: PJ6/10/97).

Reflecting the political focus on small firms as job creators, a question in the Commons requested the cost per job for the loans this scheme was guaranteeing:

> The net Exchequer cost of the loan guarantee scheme per person leaving the unemployment count is estimated to be of the order of £450. This figure is derived from the costs of a typical loan adjusted by the benefit, tax and national insurance savings relating to those leaving the count in the first year of a loan as a direct result of the scheme.
>
> (Hansard, HC Deb. 19 February 1990 vol.167 col.497)

An evaluation of the scheme for the period 1981–1991 (TNA/T430/470, para. 10.8), found that each £1m of LGS loan resulted in 57 new jobs when accounting for deadweight effects (i.e. attempting to identify job creation that would not have happened without the intervention). This £1m in loans does not represent the direct cost to government but high-lights the significance of defaults representing a failure rate of up to a third of the loans. The evaluation identified that 88% of the economic activity generated was displaced from other UK businesses. It is acknowl-edged that this may still represent an overall benefit (e.g. dynamic firms displacing less dynamic firms), but it nonetheless raises significant ques-tions about the ultimate value of the scheme.

The Business Start-Up Scheme

In the 1981 budget, the Business Start-Up Scheme was established to provide tax relief for private investors who would contribute not only capital to small firms but also their 'direct personal business expe-rience' (Hansard, HC Deb. 10 March 1981 vol.1000 cols.781–782). For private investors looking to invest in small companies less than five years old, they could claim up to £10 000 income tax relief per year. Lonsdale (1997: 70) comments that the scheme, representing a significant shift in focus from the business owner to an outside inves-tor, 'was therefore significant as it represented further evidence that the Government was willing to retreat publically from its reliance on market forces.'

Lonsdale provides the example of Electra Investment Trust Ltd which, in order to operate within the scheme, set up a subsidiary, Electra Risk Capital (ERC). ERC invested £8m in 32 companies, losing up to 75% of their money. This was a high-profile example for others in the finance industry of the limits of venture capitalist insight and the high-risk nature of small start-ups. Lonsdale (p. 141) records, 'Many venture capitalists who began their operations in the 1980s refer to the Electra Risk Capital fund when discussing how they decided on their position in the market. The fund reinforced the doubts many had over high-risk venture capital.'

Possibly as a result, many of the investments the scheme supported tended to be focused on low risk industries such as farming and property (as well as others such as thoroughbred horses), both of which were excluded when the scheme was redesigned and relaunched as the Business Expansion Scheme (BES). The redesign also sought to return to the original ambitions of the scheme and to ensure that investment was going to genuinely new businesses and not to more established businesses. It was also suggested that the Small Firms Advisory Service could help 'identify, and certainly evaluate, venture capital opportunities' (Hansard, HC Deb. 10 May 1984 vol.59 cols.1196–1202). Ultimately, as Lonsdale (1997: 71) records, 'the greatest problem for the Government at that time was that the scheme was not attracting sufficient investment,' only raising £15m against an expected £100m. This was the key problem BES needed to address when it was expanded to mean that 'an individual and spouse [could] claim tax relief up to the marginal rate on full risk equity investments in qualifying unquoted and unrelated trading businesses up to £40,000 per annum' in addition to other avenues such as ideas for a small firms investment company (Hansard, HC Deb. 10 May 1984 vol.59 cols.1196–1202).

In 1988, the government opened the scheme to companies letting residential property in an attempt to stimulate this sector. This type of investment came to dominate the scheme, and it subsequently never accounted for less than 75% of the overall finance (Lonsdale, 1997), moving BES away from supporting small businesses and making it more attractive as a tax shelter. By the end of the decade it had become perceived as predominantly a tax avoidance scheme (Tomlinson, 1994; Wren, 1996). There were also significant potential issues with limited additionality where, despite the scheme's best efforts, investment funds went to firms that could have raised it anyway (Lonsdale, 1997).

Conclusion

The election of the Thatcher government in 1979 signalled a significant change in direction for the UK. While monetarism had been experimented with by both Conservative and Labour governments in the 1970s, a revised, neoliberal focus on the economy through free markets and (in theory) limited state intervention was being actively pursued. For policymakers, this shift presented a change in policy paradigm, structuring how they viewed the world and responded to challenges (Hall, 1992). This accompanied a substantial increase in the number of small firms and self-employed as large businesses sought to externalise the forms of uncertainty and risk they had been subject to during recent crises. These changes framed the new 'enterprise culture' that promoted individualism and personal responsibility and saw this as represented in small businesses and the 'entrepreneur.' This saw a new prominence for enterprise policy in the UK.

However, it was not always clear how such a 'cultural' framing of problems would translate into policy action. A range of new enterprise policies were produced, including in the areas of deregulation and consultancy services that we explore in the next two chapters. In this chapter, we have seen how a new emphasis on small businesses as job creators and the ideas of personal responsibility led to a significant encouragement for those in unemployment to move into self-employment. Further, there were substantial new schemes designed to aid small start-ups in particular to access investment, now by targeting investors through guarantees and tax relief. This was a period of relative innovation in enterprise policymaking, and the new schemes undoubtedly had an impact, albeit they may seem odd for a government pledging to limit the role of the state.

Across many of these schemes there were significant concerns about the degree to which they really made a difference or whether they simply displaced jobs or economic activity from one area to another, or whether they simply provided additional guarantees or tax relief for investments that were likely to have happened anyway. Of course, many of the new businesses started by the unemployed or investments made into new business ideas were significant and represent genuine impact for these enterprise policies. Nonetheless, concerns about deadweight, displacement and a lack of additionality would persist and raise important questions about enterprise policymaking.

9 Market Liberalisation and Deregulation

The UK government's shift towards small government and market liberalisation led to significant changes in the development and delivery of enterprise policies. This chapter will explore two areas in which the government sought to tackle rising unemployment and to spur new and growing small businesses for wider job creation and economic growth. Firstly, we discuss the development of new approaches to regional policy in relation to the retreat of government, both in terms of regeneration areas with low regulation and taxation (enterprise zones) and new, private sector–led regional bodies (Local Enterprise Agencies).

The second focus in this chapter is the national-level attempts to remove regulation to support a free market economy. Business start-up and small business growth in particular have been highlighted as important rationales for deregulation, and this chapter will discuss these policy initiatives in relation to enterprise policy. The chapter will analyse high-profile commitments from the Conservative governments of the 1980s and 1990s to remove the 'burdens' of regulation and to improve the institutional environment in which to start-up and grow a small business.

The Conservative Government

The newly elected Thatcher government, with an emphasis on reducing inflation and cutting taxes to 'incentivise' work, quickly saw unemployment rise to levels of 3 million people, numbers not seen since the interwar years. Contemporary commentators highlighted the impacts of 'de-industrialisation' (with significant decreases in manufacturing investment and productivity) that were occurring as a result together with, in the first nine months of 1980, 5000 company liquidations, the majority of which were small businesses (Coutts et al., 1981: 86). There was disquiet in Cabinet that Thatcher was too right wing, perhaps reflecting some of the same concerns that had led Heath to perform his famous u-turn. However, unlike under Heath, this time there was no return to the post-war consensus (albeit there was, for example, increased government spending).

At the same time, Labour had internal tensions and lacked a clear direction. Further, the breakaway Social Democratic Party quickly linked up with the Liberals to become the Alliance (later the Liberal Democrats). The future Liberal Democrats were popular in terms of national voting and reshaped many local races, splitting the vote of those opposed to the government. However, without regional concentrations of voters (as with the Conservatives and Labour), the Liberals were not able to convert this into a large number of seats in the UK's 'first past the post' voting system.

With the main opposition parties ill-placed to mount a serious challenge, the successful Falklands military campaign of 1982 and signs of an economic turnaround, the Conservatives won the 1983 General Election with a substantial parliamentary majority.

New Approaches to Regional Policy

The areas of the UK suffering potentially catastrophic economic challenges as a result of struggling staple industries continued to be a matter requiring the attention of policymakers. However, rather than deliver such policies through local authorities, the government now sought to work with nationalised (or formerly nationalised) industries, generally where these industries had been the source of large-scale redundancies, for example supporting the coal industry through rent subsidies and loans, including premises converted from previous mining industry use. Organisations such as the British Steel Corporation (Industry) Ltd (BSC) or the British Shipbuilders Enterprise Ltd were formed (or re-formed in the case of BSC, which had originally formed in 1974), utilising packages of assistance from local, national and supranational bodies, supporting the provision of retraining. This included financial assistance and advice on training to individuals wishing to start up in business (Wren, 1996). More broadly, the mass unemployment facing the country led to new approaches such as encouraging the unemployed into self-employment (see Chapter 8). It also led to innovations in regional policymaking, with new and small businesses a key element in the search for job creation.

Enterprise Zones

The Conservative government that had been elected in 1979 considered a range of ways of rolling back the state and liberalising markets. One of the more innovative ideas pursued was the creation of enterprise zones. Enterprise zones sought to reinvent often derelict inner city areas by recreating them as places with reduced regulation and costs for businesses, in order to stimulate entrepreneurial activity.

In execution, this was not perhaps radically different from some of the early attempts to support Special Areas discussed in Chapter 4 where there was some experimentation with different ways of making particular areas attractive for business. However, the fundamental idea for enterprise zones was more radical. The original idea for enterprise zones specifically, as an apparent laissez-faire jumpstart for inner city deprivation and decay, came not from within the neoliberal grouping of academics and politicians that developed the new Conservative agenda but from a social democrat, Peter Hall. As Hall (1991) describes it, the idea was first raised in 1969 of the 'nonplan,' creating spaces in regional development that would be free of bureaucracy (including, for example, planning controls) and open to the immigration of entrepreneurs and capital. This was in contrast to being (centrally) planned and controlled, as much previous regional development initiatives had been.

The idea received wider attention after a planning conference in 1977 and was taken up in a subsequent conference organised by the Adam Smith Institute by prominent architect of Thatcherism, Keith Joseph. The idea of areas where 'the Queen's writ shall not run' (Joseph, quoted in Hall, 1991: 183) thus became part of the agenda for the incoming Conservative government in 1979. Enterprise zones were announced in the 1980 budget and enacted in subsequent legislation. For businesses, this provided incentives (especially exemption from property taxes) to locate in these new zones. Eleven initial zones were created in 1981–1982, with a further 13 in 1983–1984 (before any meaningful evaluation of the initial tranche). While there was a lot of variation in the sites, in general they focused on areas of industrial, urban dereliction.

Regions would apply for the siting of the zones, and then authority for the zones lay with the relevant local authority. As with other forms of regional development investment and support, there was competition for allocation of the sites, even from Labour-controlled councils (perhaps driven by the reduction in local resources and the promises of job creation). The processes by which sites were allocated was somewhat obscured and with the potential for political decision making ahead of an upcoming election (Hoare, 1985). The zones that resulted were varied, although generally targeting areas in need of regeneration.

A lot of what was radical in the idea (e.g. openness to immigration) was dropped, and there were significant limitations in the extent to which these areas represented regulation-free opportunities for business (e.g. particular local authorities instituted additional rules such as banning video arcades). Also, contrary to the laissez-faire ideas behind enterprise zones, they often required significant investment of public funds for infrastructure to make the derelict area attractive (in addition to, for example, marketing costs), creating a substantial burden on the Treasury and effectively acting as state subsidies for business (Shutt, 1984; Jones, 2006). The more successful of the early enterprise zones tended to be those with services already in place, such as Team Valley (discussed in Chapter 4; see Jones, 2006).

Evaluation of the enterprise zones has been mixed and often overshadowed by the scale of the zone in the London Docklands, where Canary

Wharf was developed. This was a large development but one that may have happened anyway, raising the familiar additionality challenges (especially in the creation of genuinely new jobs). Crucially, the zones risked simply encouraging businesses to make small-scale moves from one area to another with few additional benefits, similar to many previous regional policy initiatives, in addition to damaging local competition, with detrimental effects for local small businesses (Shutt, 1984). Jones (2006) concludes that the most significant legacy of the enterprise zones is not in terms of laissez-faire planning but in the use of tax incentives. Nonetheless, the idea of enterprise zones was one that was exported around the world.

Local Enterprise Agencies

Another key area of regional policy activity was in the creation of Local Enterprise Agencies (LEAs). LEAs were private sector–led, independent bodies. They were typically non-profit, run by a management team reporting to a board that included local authority members, large and small business representatives, lawyers, accountants, academics and clergy as volunteers. They therefore involved partnerships between local interests, local authorities and Chambers of Commerce, influenced by US Community Development Co-operations (Bennett, 1995). By 1991 there were 421 such agencies (Hansard, HC Deb. 3 July 1991 vol.194 col.156).

The 1982 Finance Act (s48) instructed that LEAs would have as their primary objective:

> . . . the promotion or encouragement of industrial and commercial activity or enterprise in a particular area in the United Kingdom with particular reference to encouraging the formation and development of small businesses.
>
> (cited in Maville, 2012: 200)

Maville (2012) suggests the first business support agencies of this type emerged in 1976 in response to major job losses after the closure of local employers in Somerset and Merseyside. Smallbone (1991) dates the first LEA to St Helens, Lancashire, in 1978, and the London Enterprise Agency was established by the London Chamber of Commerce in 1978.

Fazey's (1987) detailed account of the origins of the enterprise agency highlights the role of the private sector through the importance of Pilkington Brothers plc as a supporter of the scheme. The major local employer in St Helens, Pilkington's was concerned about the problems of unemployment in the St Helens community, problems they would contribute to through efficiency gains reducing their demand for workers. A team of managers (GAP9) were tasked with tackling a problem entitled simply 'The development of products and services in St Helens' as part of their management training. The work of the GAP9 team, taken up by Bill Humphrey, described as 'the patron saint of enterprise agencies' by David Trippier (Parliamentary Under-Secretary of State for Trade and Industry and later for Employment, and the minister responsible for small businesses) laid the groundwork for the Community of St Helens Trust in support of new and small businesses (see Fazey, 1987).

The LEAs engaged in forms of enterprise policy activity, including provision of advice and support for local businesses, and were encouraged to engage with the Small Firms Service to develop this provision. LEAs also helped to link small businesses with potential investors and many established loan funds. These loan funds had high conversion rates, which Irwin (2006: 23) suggests was due to the role of LEA advisors in filtering initial propositions such that 'the propositions unlikely to be supported have already been weeded out.'

Illustrating the new emphasis on the private sector in this policy area, the LEAs received financial support from a range of sources including local authorities as well as large businesses and banks (e.g. significant contributions from Shell and Barclays Bank), later with tax relief on the contributions. This necessitated LEAs competing to secure funds from these large, often national (rather than locally oriented) organisations as well as placing greater emphasis on the need to charge for services. There was also a grant of £75 000 provided to Business in the Community (a business-led charity of the Prince of Wales) to support its work of establishing and sponsoring LEAs. However, the initiative was still dependent on substantial funds from central government; early forms of financial assistance provided totalled around £3m a year through which the government argued it was 'encouraging the private sector in this role' of financing the LEAs in the long term (Hansard, HC Deb. 16 December 1986 vol.107 col.524). By 1989, these funds exceeded £8.3m (Hansard, HC Deb. 16 May 1989 vol.153 col.175).

From 1987, funds included £25 000 a year for individual LEAs 'dependent on a pound for pound matching contribution from the private sector, and on the submission of an acceptable three year business plan and five-year financial strategy' (Hansard, HC Deb. 26 June 1986 vol.100 cols.262–263). This is an important element in the development of private sector involvement in the regional enterprise policy agenda. While such initiatives are promoted as being about decentralisation, local responsiveness and the importance of being led by the private sector, there are significant ways in which central government controls and shapes bodies such as the LEAs. The conditionality of government financial support, alongside restrictions in local authority finance or scope to develop their own regional development initiatives meant moving from local authorities to private sector–led organisations shaped by central government imperatives. The factors determining income-generation for these organisations therefore had potentially important implications for the particular services and support provided to small firms and questions were also raised about the levels of accountability in place (Smallbone, 1991).

Inner Cities

Inner City Task Forces were set up in 1986, partly in response to inner city riots and evidence of deprivation and disadvantage. They represented another effort on the part of the Conservative government to take power away from local authorities and to develop partnerships and forms of private investment. Ultimately, however, the overall approach in terms of inner cities, and regional policy more generally, was not radically different to the policies of the 1930s discussed in Chapter 4.

Kenneth Clark (Minister of State for Employment and then Trade and Industry) set out the objectives of the scheme as being to generate jobs and encourage local enterprise, including the provision of 'enterprise training, financial and managerial assistance to new businesses' (Hansard, HC Deb. 2 December 1987 vol.123 col.602). As well as seeking to tackle crime and improve coordination of government programmes, it also sought to 'strengthen the capability of local organisations to undertake long term economic and enterprise development activity' (ibid). It did so, in part, by exploring how to make effective use of other schemes such as the Enterprise Allowance Scheme (see Chapter 8). The elements of enterprise policy within this agenda involved testing training and employment initiatives with annual funds for each task force (16 by May 1987), which enabled them, amongst other activities and forms of advice, to offer grants of up to £4000 towards the cost of business plan preparation, business research, training and start up costs (Wren, 1996).

By June 1989, the task forces had spent £33m supporting nearly 1100 projects, from which it was claimed to 'generate, or safeguard, nearly 4,000 jobs, facilitate over 23,500 training places and provide support for over 2,600 businesses' (Hansard, HC Deb. 21 June 1989 vol.155 cols.174–175). The idea was that, once task forces in particular areas had achieved their goals, they could share this learning and move on to new areas. However, the amount of money and projects continued to grow, reflecting a demand for assistance but perhaps also reflecting the difficulty in resolving activities and moving on. Overall, these interventions lacked the scope or depth of engagement with the underlying challenges to make a meaningful impact, for example by engaging more fully with, and empowering, local communities (Deakin and Edwards, 2005).

Regional Funding

There were also additional sources of funding that sought to address areas of deprivation more generally. From 1988, Regional Enterprise Grants were available for firms with fewer than 25 employees in the

Development Areas (later extended to include European Regional Development Fund programme areas). There were two forms: Regional Investment Grants (RIG), which provided a 15% grant towards new machinery, buildings and similar, up to £15 000; and Regional Innovation Grants (RIN), which provided a 50% grant towards projects leading to new, innovative products and processes involving novelty and technical risk to improve product range or efficiency, up to £25 000. This was partly a replacement for the Regional Development Grant and was influenced by the perceived success of the Business Improvement Scheme. It was more in line with EC regional policy, removing some of the tensions between previous government initiatives and EC rules around state subsidies (Conzelmann, 2006).

Initially there was low take-up of the grants, with just 64 applications for a total value of £710 000 by mid-1988 (Hansard, HC Deb. 27 July 1988 vol.138 cols.273–274). This led to marketing campaigns, including TV and newspapers but also mailshots and leaflets via organisations such as the Chambers of Commerce (Leslie Hays Consultants, 1990). There were also changes to the qualifying criteria, including extending the RIN to firms with less than 50 employees. Wren (1996) notes that the scheme eventually attracted about 3000 applications a year, with around £18m total funds offered.

Leslie Hays Consultants (1990) conducted interviews with a sample of 74 participating firms selected by government departments. They found benefits of the scheme in terms of improved efficiency, job creation and increased turnover. However, this was an early evaluation, partly based on expectations and with challenges identifying additionality. They estimated that 'total deadweight [i.e. not additional] consequently amount to 42% of the gross exchequer total cost of the REG investment grant' (p. 31). Interestingly, they identified a reluctance among small businesses to engage with consultants, even when subsidised, due to expectations around cost and the perceptions of consultants as too far removed from the concerns of their business (see further discussion around consultancy in Chapter 10).

Segal Quince Wicksteed (1991) re-interviewed the original 74 cases, plus 100 RIG cases and 45 RIN, and then in 1992 followed up on the 55 remaining cases (those missing including 6 business failures). While they found RIG to have had little impact on the businesses that were unambitious, it was noted that the scheme was fairly cost effective as a job creation measure, with a yearly cost per net job of £1240. RIN had also had more significant impact on those firms with growth potential, acting as a trigger for innovation and overcoming funding difficulties, and it was suggested this should be strengthened. However, additionality results by number of cases was lower than the original evaluation, with an estimate of 56% gross cost deadweight. Overall, the firms engaged with the schemes were generally performing acceptably well with the aggregate figures pulled up by a few dynamic, high-growth firms.

In addition to this type of relatively targeted and often regionally focused enterprise policy, the Conservative government also sought to change the general operating environment for all small businesses in the UK. They did this by attempting to tackle what were perceived as the burdens of regulation.

Deregulation

Calls to address the 'burden' of regulation on small businesses had formed a persistent part of recent discussions on small businesses prior to Thatcher's election. In the late 1960s, Keith Joseph, in his Foreword to *Acorns to Oaks*, had emphasised the detrimental effects of 'a torrent of new laws and regulations' from a Labour government hostile to small businesses. A subsequent Conservative Political Centre publication, *Small Businesses: Strategy for Survival* (Brown et al., 1976: 12), further complained that 'small firms are being crucified by the burdens that are being imposed on them. Burdens that include penal taxation, stifling bureaucracy, the complexity of ever-changing legislation and the ravages of inflation.' The 1979 Conservative manifesto (Conservative Party, 1979) had provided a clear example of how this agenda developed to address perceived barriers, detailing the need to reduce taxation, form-filling and 'amend laws such as the Employment Protection Act where they damage smaller businesses—and larger ones too—and actually prevent the creation of jobs.'

The debates around deregulation were not solely focused on small businesses and used the term 'enterprise' broadly. However, small businesses were a significant part of the debate. As the Conservatives continued reshaping the economy and government's relation to industry, there were ongoing discussions around tax with small business lobby groups. For example, in early 1984, a proposal was made by NFSE that small firms with fewer than 20 employees have a new tax code with self-assessed employees, treating their employees as though they were self-employed as far as tax purposes (TNA: FV96/62). It was suggested that this would support removal of these firms from other legislation. However, within government this was seen as at odds with Inland Revenue attempts to tighten definitions of employee status.

NFSE also provided a paper to the Small Firm Division titled 'Death by Red Tape.' This paper provided a lengthy list of regulations, establishing the quantity of rules facing small businesses. The introduction to the paper concludes:

> The wonder is that businesses survive at all. The cost of first finding out what legislation says, then complying with it, is heavy. How many would-be entrepreneurs are deterred by obstacles that the State places in their way? How many jobs are still-born?

When the British economy finally gives up the ghost, the coroner's verdict will be: 'Death by red tape.'

(TNA: FV96/62, p. 2)

In 1985, Chair of the Alliance of Small Firms and Self-employed People (ASP), future Conservative MP and proposer of the Small Firms (Liberation) Bill (Hansard, HC Deb. 20 April 1988 vol.1131 cols.833–835), Teresa Gorman wrote *Business Still Burdened: More Regulations for the Scrapheap*. Published by influential think tank the Centre for Policy Studies, and with a Foreword by Michael Grylls MP, Chairman of the Small Business Bureau, Gorman's (1985: 11) paper argues that too many 'regulations have been drawn up without a proper understanding of what their consequences will be, and without adequate consultation with the spokesmen of small business.'

Welcoming the appointment of David Young to head up an Enterprise Unit tasked with identifying opportunities for deregulation, Gorman works on three themes: the exemption of small firms from 'as much vexatious legislation as possible'; replacing regulation with insurance, for example mandatory business insurance should replace government regulation and inspection regimes, while Statutory Sick Pay should be abolished with employees taking out sickness insurance cover; and the right to elect for self-employed status. Through processes of deregulation, it was argued, small businesses would prosper and grow, contributing to the national economy. There was significant scepticism within the DTI about Gorman's arguments and, for example, her claims about a small business boom in Italy and its causes (TNA: FV96/64). However, Gorman's ideas appear to have been popular with Thatcher, had the imprimatur of a key think tank and were regularly part of the debate.

Reviews of regulation generally, and in relation to small firms specifically, were ongoing within the DTI, for example with The Administrative and Legislative Burdens Exercise in 1983. The focus on small firms, which sought to identify and remove burdens placed on these businesses by government, still made explicit use of the Bolton Report and its list of recommendations (e.g. on form filling, see Chapter 5). The White Paper *Burdens on Business, a Report of a Scrutiny of Administrative and Legislative Requirements* (DTI, 1985a) included extensive discussion of the impacts of regulations on small firms. The paper argued that the cumulative burden of regulation weighed heavily on enterprise and employment. Government requirements were represented to add significantly to business costs, especially in relation to management time; they therefore deterred start-ups and business expansion.

In his Foreword, Norman Tebbit (Secretary of State for Trade and Industry) suggested that:

Cutting the burden of regulation is one important way Government can act to help business prosper—and create the soundly-based new jobs we need. Small businesses have a vital role to play. They provide millions of jobs already and will be a major source of new employment.

(p. III)

The paper went on to argue that:

2.4.1 Regulatory burdens bear most heavily on the very smallest businesses where managers lack the staff support, the time and sometimes the expertise to cope with the work involved and to handle central and local government bureaucracies effectively. The larger businesses with specialised management capacities tend to be less vulnerable. (p. 3)

. . . exemptions [for small firms] would distort the market by putting larger firms at an unjustified competitive disadvantage; and would create 'threshold' problems at the point of transition from exempt to non-exempt status.

(p. 5)

The research underpinning these assertions found that small businesses tended to simply accept regulatory requirements, and associated costs, as part of the environment and as less pressing than finance or sales pressures. Yet, it suggests that compliance costs, both those that are real and those that are perceived, 'may limit market entry by inhibiting start-ups and expansion of small enterprises; especially those involving first-time recruitment of full time labour' owing to employment-related regulations featuring significantly in overall regulatory burdens (p. 3). The paper argues, therefore, that reducing regulatory burdens could deliver economic benefits in terms of jobs and curtailing informal economic activities through boosting enterprise in small businesses.

This provided support for an exemption approach that distinguished small businesses within the economy and in terms their responsibilities. For example, Smith (1985) identifies five key areas of exemption from employment regulation that applied to small firms at the time: sex discrimination; maternity leave; making a health and safety statement; extended trial periods (unfair dismissal); and exemption from supporting workplace balloting. However, the exemptions applied to different sizes of firm (some small, others only to micro businesses), risking greater confusion and uncertainty. In the fluctuating position of small businesses, uncertainty could be created since exemptions related to employee numbers, and several of the exemptions relate to the classification of these employees.

The 1985 White Paper also recommended the establishing of a deregulation task force. The Enterprise and Deregulation Unit (EDU) was created in the Department for Employment in 1986 (though it followed Young to the DTI a year later). The White Paper *Building Businesses . . . Not*

Barriers, presented in May 1986, explained the ongoing work that sought to make change happen across was government departments:

> 1.18 Existing regulations are being reviewed to identify whether they can be changed or abolished. The means of enforcing regulations through licensing are being reviewed. And the way in which Departments communicate with business and train their officials is also under review.
>
> 1.19 These assessments and reviews are carried out by Deregulation Units in individual Departments and by the central task force—the Enterprise and Deregulation Unit includes secondees from the private sector. The central task force reports direct to the Secretary of State for Employment and the departmental Deregulation Units report to Ministers in their Departments. The allocation of specific responsibility to units supervised by Ministers emphasises the Government's commitment to better regulation.
>
> (DTI, 1986: 4)

A deregulation task force has continued in some form ever since, albeit with several subsequent name changes, from the Deregulation Unit, to the Better Regulation Unit, 1997, then to the Regulatory Impact Unit, 1999, and, in 2010, to the Better Regulation Executive. The persistent need for such a task force leaves unclear the extent to which the EDU can be considered to have been successful in overcoming the challenges facing this deregulation agenda.

Obstacles to Deregulation

A Prime Ministerial reply to an update on progress of these initiatives suggests some of the dynamics of the debates around deregulation, with an expectation to be bolder (perhaps in line with some of the suggestions by Gorman):

> The Prime Minister . . . is extremely disappointed at the lack of progress in this area. Many of the items reported on represent not achievements but questions still to be settled. She believes Departments must give greater commitment to this initiative. She proposes to hold a meeting herself in about a fortnight to consider what more needs to be done . . .
>
> The Prime Minister believes the idea of an Enabling Bill to exempt small firms from large areas of legislation should not be ruled out at this stage and would welcome a fuller report on its implications.
>
> (TNA: FV96/62, p. 1)

There were a range of factors making consideration of a deregulation agenda problematic. A central issue, hinted at in the previous quotes, was that the initiative seems to have run into problems when engaging with other departments. A June 1984 draft minute to the Secretary of State, written to inform a report to the Prime Minister on key challenges for reducing burdens on small firms, highlighted the main 'sticking points' (TNA: FV96/62, p. 1). These included planning and local authority regulations (including bureaucratic complexity), tax collection (if unable to change tax requirements, could improve guidance and support) and Statutory Sick Pay (the relevant department stating there were no problems for small firms, the Small Firms Service disagreed). Crucially, the minute argues that support at a higher level was needed to bring other departments on board and to overcome these challenges.

The minute to the Secretary of State also highlights the importance of wider debates:

> We are, as you know, coming under increasing pressure—from lobbyists, and from within the Party—to introduce an Enabling Bill to exempt small firms from large areas of legislation. The best way of resisting such calls will be demonstrating that we have made further reductions in burdens, specifically targeted to relieve the pressure on the most vulnerable parts of the sector.
>
> (ibid, p. 4)

The draft report to the Prime Minister recommends a regional 'one stop shop' (p. 2) to help overcome bureaucratic complexity. This idea had been developing at least over recent months and appeared to have the potential support of Thatcher. It can be seen in the later development of Local Business Partnerships (see the following discussion; see also Chapter 10 for the development of this idea more generally).

A second major challenge was the impact of EC membership. For example, attempts to create an exemption for small firms from the 1975 Sex Discrimination Act was prevented by the EC. The EC also objected to plans to amend a VAT exemption limit:

> The European Commission has written to the Foreign Secretary arguing that the revalorisation of the VAT exemption limit over the past six years has been pressed beyond the level necessary to maintain its value in real terms; that we have failed to respect the requirements of the Sixth Directive and that the UK has therefore not fulfilled its obligations under the EEC treaty.
>
> (TNA: FV96/63, p. 1)

EC stipulations were resisted and, in many of these instances, legal advice sought on how to pursue the deregulation agenda and to expand the scope for small firm exemptions. However, it was clear that EC membership presented a substantial obstacle to the deregulation agenda, something Gorman attributed to 'the influence of socialist and corporatist traditions' in the EC (1985: 37).

A further issue was an awareness within the DTI of the benefits of regulation and the complexity of the issues involved in deregulation. For example, this can be seen in the benefits of administrative activities. A draft letter to an industry body included the argument that 'the record keeping requirements imposed by Government can also bring a managerial benefit by improving the efficiency and, as a result, the profitability of a small business' (TNA: FV96/61, p. 2). The limits of deregulation were also expressed by the CBI:

> ... the exercise to reduce form filling had gone too far in some areas and was now affecting businesses ability to monitor its markets ... the quality of the aggregated statistics was being affected by these shortcomings in a number of particular areas and that it would be better to educate small firms about the benefits to be obtained by using Government statistics than continuing to seek cuts in coverage.
>
> (TNA: FV96/62, p. 1)

This range of challenges to the deregulation agenda limited the extent to which significant, widespread change was introduced, for example in terms of considering new regulations or managing how new or small businesses would engage with regulatory environments. The agenda remained an issue in the 1992 election and was subsequently 'relaunched.'

Relaunching the Deregulation Agenda

The Deregulation Initiative was relaunched within the DTI in 1992 (following the Conservatives' successful re-election, see Chapter 10) and led by Neil Hamilton. It had three objectives:

> ... better existing regulation, by cutting unnecessary burdens on business and reducing compliance and enforcement costs; effective new regulation, by ensuring that potential costs and the views of business are accounted for in framing and implementing new regulation; and greater official awareness of the views and needs of business.
>
> (Hansard, HC Deb. 19 October 1992 vol.212 col.230)

A Departmental Deregulation Minister was appointed in each government department, seeking to address the difficulties previous attempts had faced with resistance or lack of engagement. There were also attempts to support small firms' engagement with regulations, with the establishment of Local Business Partnerships. These were forums for local business communities and local authorities to discuss regulation-related issues, argued for as something of particular benefit for smaller, newer businesses. Hamilton (1994: 30) explained:

> The aim is to help business understand their responsibilities under regulations so making it easier for them to comply, while also helping

local authorities understand how regulations are operating on the ground so helping them to focus enforcement effort on those flouting the law.

Perhaps the most significant development was the replacement of the EDU with a new, high-profile Task Force formed by Michael Heseltine (Secretary of State for Trade and Industry). This consisted of representatives of large companies, a couple of academics and Lord Sainsbury as an adviser.

The work of this new group was focused on seven sectoral task forces, generally related to specific areas of regulation and those with appropriate expertise leading in each area. For example, Chair of the Construction Task Force was the Chairman of Bovis Construction Ltd with the task force composed of other construction company directors and partners. In 1994, the Task Force produced a report (DTI, 1994a, *Deregulation Task Forces Proposals for Reform*) that proposed 605 ways of reducing regulatory burdens.

The work of these predominantly large business-led task forces included consideration of the effects of regulation on small business. The first section of the report was titled 'Small Businesses' and included 13 proposals. These tended to make the case for universality and against the case for differential treatment of small businesses. For example:

> Do not create exemptions, barriers and thresholds for small business regulation. Regulate only where essential—and then universally.
>   Make regulators and enforcers into "enablers" not "threateners". Punish persistent and deliberate offenders. Help the ignorant, the uninformed and the hard-pressed to do better.
>
> (p. 1)

In this way, there was a shift in focus of the deregulation effort to general market liberalisation, less tied to small businesses. For example, it was proposed that, in relation to the British Standards Institution, a simple guide be produced for small firms with clear advice, including recommended consultants they should use. However, while recommending the avoidance of exemptions, the Task Force did nonetheless recommend that consideration of small businesses be given when formulating regulation:

> When drafting regulations, assume all businesses are small. Use the "small business litmus test".
>
> (ibid)

This litmus test was described in detail by Hamilton (1994: 29):

> In recognition of the particular difficulties faced by small firms with regard to complying with regulation, the Government has introduced

a small business litmus test as part of carrying out compliance cost assessments. This will normally take the form of departments identifying two or three typical small firms in the sector affected by the proposed regulation and discussing with them the practicality of the measure and the impact it will have on their business. Departments may carry out an alternative form of test where this would give a better and clearer picture of the impact on small firms.

The 1996 guidance for Compliance Cost Assessment under the Deregulation Initiative highlights the introduction of the 'small business litmus test.' Prime Minister John Major, in the foreword to the document, wrote that he was 'particularly pleased to see the inclusion in this new guidance of a small business litmus test, requiring consultation with some typical small businesses on the practicality of new regulatory proposals.'

An area where a distinctive approach to small firms was recommended was that the small company audit threshold 'should be raised substantially' (p. 45). The idea of employee status in small firms was also revisited, here in relation to the challenges in the construction industry and need for 'flexibility': 'An individual should be able to agree with an "employer" whether to be treated as an employed or self-employed person, accepting that he/she will be bound by that decision' (p. 65). Again, this is less in relation to small business exceptionalism and more about the industry as a whole, challenging the nature of employment rights and the nature of employment within the desired free market.

At the same time, the White Paper *Deregulation: Cutting Red Tape* (DTI, 1994c) set out the deregulation agenda and particular actions that were being taken across government departments. It argued that, without deregulation, there were dangers of fewer jobs, higher prices and less choice. This paper listed existing changes and those that were planned, including detailing where proposals from the Task Force were not accepted, for example, the recommendation for changes in the Treasury. The Treasury did not agree with the interpretation of the law presented by the Task Force and, on this basis, did not accept that the proposals would have the intended effects or would create significant risks for investors. Task Force recommendations that were adopted included raising the VAT threshold and statutory audit requirements so as to exclude many small firms (based on turnover): '500,000 of the smallest companies no longer need to have their accounts audited' (DTI, 1996: 86).

The Deregulation and Contacting Out Act (1994) made over 30 specific deregulatory changes to the law. It also informed the creation of a new Select Committee to consider new deregulation orders in terms of their potential burdens within 60 days. This introduced a power to amend or repeal primary legislation to reduce burdens meaning that, in order to remove a perceived burden, secondary legislation could be used to amend primary legislation. This raised significant concerns (including from the Labour Party) about the transfer of powers from Parliament to Whitehall, that is, away from the democratic process (Hansard, HC Deb. 24 November 1994 vol.250 cols.764–789). Although the broader issue of what are sometimes referred to as 'Henry VIII powers' would continue to be a topic of heated debate, especially with the passing of the EU (Withdrawal) Bill in 2018.

During the 1995–1996 session, 19 Deregulation Orders were submitted before parliament, but the following year this dropped to 12, then 5 and then 4. Examples included removing the need for three yearly re-authorisations of deductions of union subscriptions from salary; permitting bookings at registry offices up to 12 months in advance instead of 3; and relaxing the restrictions on opening hours of licensed premises over Millennium Eve. Nonetheless, despite the limited use of these mechanisms, concerns about the approach led to a consultation in cabinet in 1999 and to a paper called 'Proposed Amendments to the Deregulation and Contracting Out Act 1994.' The negotiations between the government and Parliament led to the approval of the Regulatory Reform Act 2001.

More generally, the DTI (1996: 87) set out the new approach to deregulation:

> The Government has introduced a requirement that no Department may bring forward new regulatory proposals that affect business without a Risk Assessment and a Compliance Cost Assessment. Ministers must personally certify that the cost to business of any proposal is justified by its benefits and that, if the proposal implements an EU requirement, no gold plating or double banking is included without full justification

This represented a further formalisation of the deregulation agenda and a further attempt to ensure different government departments attended to the government's objectives in this area.

DTI (1996) also provided examples of achievements of the Deregulation Initiative such as lifting restrictions on Sunday shopping and pub hours and revising food regulations 'that allow development of innovative products like fromage frais' (p. 85). It listed ongoing efforts to further reduce regulatory burdens ('without reducing necessary protection,' p. 85) including in relation to statistical returns, tax, health and safety, labour, planning, financial services, food, with over 1000 regulations identified for repeal and amendment.

The extent of deregulatory efforts, the White Papers produced and the task forces assembled led to a further criticism of this agenda expressed in the House of Commons in 1996:

> Deregulation has spawned an entire new layer of bureaucracy, created new buzz words and produced a new layer of Government. The Leader of the House, a Cabinet appointee and the Prime Minister are

all concerned with deregulation—without it, some might not even have jobs. There is a deregulatory Minister in every Department.

Pamphlets, circulars, booklets and departmental reviews are churned out. Experts and advisers are to be found in local government, and even the Institute of Directors has deregulation advisers. The cost is enormous.

The Select Committee is just one deregulatory initiative. Lord Sainsbury's task force, which has been taken over by Francis Maude, is another. The task force suggested that 605 pieces of legislation were ripe for repeal, and the Prime Minister added another 400. Of more than 1,000 measures identified, 643 have been repealed—but few have had the impact that Conservative Members would like. Comparing that figure with the 7,845 statutory instruments added to our legislation since January 1994 puts the matter in perspective. Admittedly, many of those instruments correct complicated or inadequate primary legislation such as the Jobseekers Act 1995 and the Children Act 1989, but that does not explain the need for 3,243 new statutory instruments already this year.

(Hansard, HC Deb. 22 May 1996 vol.278 cols.250–257)

The critique of increased bureaucracy and complexity around a deregulation agenda that was growing in scale but failing to achieve significant, demonstrable gains is one that would persist as the subsequent Labour government continued to pursue this agenda (and the coalition and Conservative governments that were to follow, see Chapter 11). In some ways, this area of policymaking represents an example of how small government advocates created larger government machinery in their efforts to achieve their aims. We will see another example of this when we discuss Business Link in the next chapter.

Conclusion

The development of enterprise policy under the Conservative administrations of the 1980s and 1990s saw a significant new role for the private sector in regional policy and therefore a key platform for the development and delivery of enterprise policies, for example with the creation of LEAs. Not only were these organisations private sector–led, they also had to compete for financial support from the private sector more widely, creating new forms of influence on the policies developed and delivered. This approach also provides an important example of where government finance increased rather than simply being replaced with money from the private sector. This included forms of conditionality attached to central government money exerting powerful mechanisms of control over regional bodies and limiting the extent to which these bodies represent forms of decentralisation, truly independent of central government.

Instead, it was the powers of local authorities that were reduced in this period.

The Conservatives also prioritised deregulation, not only in specific areas of regeneration classified as enterprise zones, but for the country as a whole. This agenda may have exacerbated rather than resolved some of the country's problems. For example, Piore and Sabel (1984: 182) argue that 'by pushing industries into unfamiliar situations and promoting radical restructurings, deregulation also lowered productivity, and it may have raised unemployment.' The deregulation agenda was also limited in the extent to which it could meaningfully impact the activities of small businesses.

A key element in this limited impact was the lack of commitment from other government departments, despite the role of the deregulation agenda in the broader aims of market liberalisation. The lack of commitment to an enterprise policy agenda can be seen as limiting the scope and impact of the policies. Enterprise policy agendas have often struggled to have sufficient profile to achieve significant cross-government support, even during the 'enterprise culture' period. In this case, it may also have reflected the limited degree to which government departments were willing to limit or compromise the regulations they introduced in the name of start-ups or small business growth.

10 Tackling Deadweight and Displacement Through Consultancy

This chapter discusses the concerns over how to tackle ineffectiveness in enterprise policies. It will explore this topic in terms of the increasing recognition of deadweight and displacement effects that had, as we have seen in previous chapters, limited the effectiveness of many enterprise policies. In this context, there was an increasing emphasis on improving management skills, in particular by encouraging engagement with consultants and forms of training. This would, in principle, then develop greater impact from enterprise policymaking and, more generally, maximise the potential for additionality in the benefits of economic growth through self-employment and small businesses.

We discuss the creation and development of Training and Enterprise Councils that saw training policy largely taken away from national government to be led by locally oriented, private sector bodies with a substantial responsibility for enterprise policy development and delivery. However, this discussion demonstrates that private sector–led enterprise policies often fail to involve small firms themselves and that the interests of small businesses can take less of a priority compared to the interests of larger businesses.

Business Link is then discussed as representative of the 'business improvement' agenda and a substantial development in the provision of business support services and the promotion of consultancy. This new enterprise policy initiative went far beyond previous schemes that provided support to businesses applying for financial assistance or signposted to existing services. The case draws out an important and ongoing tension between government and private sector support for small businesses and entrepreneurship. This discussion also links to quality management standards and the Investors in People accreditation.

The Enterprise Initiative

Following the 1987 election, Thatcher maintained a significant majority against a more centre-left Labour Party led by Neil Kinnock. The Conservative government therefore continued to pursue its agenda, including the development of enterprise policymaking. Where enterprise policy in the early 1980s was focused largely on creating more small firms and increasing levels of self-employment (e.g. through the Enterprise Allowance Scheme, see Chapter 8), the 1988 DTI White Paper *The Department for Enterprise* marked a move towards improving the quality of these businesses. This paper shifted attention 'to concentrate resources on improving the competitiveness of small and medium-sized firms' (Wren, 1996: 185; see also North et al., 1997; Greene et al., 2008).

DTI (1988) set out the 'Enterprise Initiative' as the collection of policies and forms of support available to small businesses and entrepreneurs as an alternative approach to industrial policy. Promotional material associated with this initiative highlighted the types of scheme discussed in the previous two chapters together with provision by the Small Firms Service (SFS) of a free telephone advice line ('telephone 100 and ask for "freephone enterprise"'). This, in part, reflected how the SFS had gradually begun to move beyond simply signposting to offer advice and counselling and beyond new ventures to also more actively supporting those small firms seeking to grow. More broadly, the government sought to encourage small firms to engage with private sector consultancy.

The Subsidising of Consultancy

The promotion of business consultancy services to SMEs was not a new initiative. Since its inception, enterprise policy had included forms of advice and support attached to particular schemes such as financial assistance or industrial estates (see Chapters 3 and 4). Kipping and Saint-Martin (2005) observe that, during the 1950s, Germany had established public funding schemes to promote the use of consultants to SMEs, while in late 1960s Britain, the Labour government had piloted a subsidy scheme to support these businesses in accessing consultancy services (see Chapter 5). Subsequently, the small firms information centres had offered a signposting service to existing support services (see Chapter 6).

In 1985, following a review, several smaller-scale DTI services were brought together as the Business and Technical Advisory Service (BTAS). These services included the Manufacturing Advisory Service, the Design Advisory Service and the Quality Assurance Support Scheme, all of which involved non-governmental, sectoral bodies and focused on areas such as productivity, efficiency and quality management (and later extended to include support for marketing), ultimately with the aim of improving international competitiveness (Hansard, HC Deb. 8 April 1987 vol.114 cols.271–272).

To encourage engagement with consultancy services, BTAS offered SMEs (defined as having fewer than 500 employees) grants towards 75% of the cost of 15 person-days of consultancy relating to its areas of focus. Wren (1996: 166) notes that such heavily subsidised consultancy services proved so popular that, in 1986, restrictions had to be introduced to limit support, now at 66%, to independent businesses and with the requirement that the consultancy was tied to a clear business plan. By July 1987, 15 000 firms had made use of BTAS, the majority of firms with fewer than 200 employees (Hansard, HC Deb. 17 July 1987 vol.119 cols.649–650).

From 1988, the Business Development Consultancy Initiative replaced existing advisory schemes, offering subsidised consultancy support to SMEs (remaining firms with fewer than 500 employees), now with a grant worth 50% (continuing at 66% for businesses in those areas of the UK designated as requiring additional support at this time). This subsidised consultancy continued to be popular and was actively promoted, including through Local Enterprise Agencies. From April 1988 to September 1989, it attracted 31 415 applications with 24 081 applications approved, costing the government an estimated total of £56.4m (Hansard, HC Deb. 1 November 1989 vol.159 col.260). A Segal Quince Wicksteed (1991) evaluation of the scheme questioned its relevance for most firms but identified that it did promote an awareness of consultancy services. Kipping and Saint-Martin (2005) comment that the DTI's expenditure for SME consultancy represented a significant boost for the management consultancy industry.

A Business Growth Training scheme was proposed in the 1988 White Paper *Employment in the 1990s* (DoE, 1988). In 1989, it was launched with the aim of improving the competitiveness of small firms with a budget of £55m per year and four major components:

> Help for smaller firms with fewer than 500 employees to obtain outside advice to improve their performance through better training. Up to £15,000 will be available to meet up to half the costs of professional assistance to plan for the training of their employees as part of a strategy for managing change; associated training of managers and supervisors; purchase of open learning materials, and other forms of training new to the firm;
>
> training of owners and managers of very small businesses in better management and business skills in order to help them run and develop their business;
>
> projects to demonstrate how new approaches to training and development can help employers meet their business needs more effectively. Selected firms will be given up to half of the agreed costs, up to a maximum of £60,000, to mount the projects and to disseminate the results to other employers;
>
> projects to help to start up partnerships between businesses on a national sectoral basis or locally, to define needs for training in key skills, and to develop a long-term strategy for improving the supply of those skills. Funding will be limited to a maximum of £60,000, up to half the costs. The Training Agency will draw up priorities for responding to applications for this pump-priming funding.
>
> (Hansard, HC Deb. 24 January 1989 vol.145 col.552)

This scheme therefore consolidated and refined the existing provision in seeking to develop the quality of small businesses. By December 1989, 30 000 firms were taking part (Hansard, HC Deb. 5 December 1989 vol.163 col.207).

Training and Enterprise Councils

The 1979 Conservatives 'initially had no clearly discernible policy on training' (Tuckman, 1996: 141) except that it should be driven by market forces. However, a policy approach began to develop from some of the principles of regional policymaking and consolidation of existing schemes. The Business Growth Training scheme was subsequently grouped together with the Enterprise Allowance Scheme and the advice provided by the Small Firms Service. A new form of organisation, Training and Enterprise Councils (TECs), was created to deliver this package of enterprise policies and, more broadly, to contract Local Enterprise Agencies and others to provide support to small firms. The way in which Local Enterprise Agencies (see Chapter 9) became contractors working to the TECs represented a significant shift in the government's desired approach from grants to contracting (Bennett, 1995).

TECs were modelled on American Private Industry Councils (Boocock et al., 1994) and the principle that 'above all it is about people as our key resource' (DoE, 1988: 3, from the preface by Secretary of State for Employment Norman Fowler). The Department of Employment (1988) White Paper set out how TECs would move away from the traditional centralisation of training policy to identify local requirements in terms of skill needs, secure appropriate training provision and manage training programmes. Continuing the policy of private sector involvement instead of local authority control of regional policy provision, TECs were to be led by local employers:

> At least two-thirds of (voluntary) TEC members should be employers at top management level drawn from the private sector. Others on the Councils will include senior figures from local education, training and economic development activities and from voluntary bodies and trade unions who support the aims of the Council.
>
> (ibid, p. 41)

TECs therefore replaced the Manpower Services Commission (MSC), which had been established by Labour in 1973 with responsibility for training, including aspects of employment such as the Jobcentres. Future Secretary of State for Trade and Industry Michael Heseltine (2000: 428) records:

> The MSC was seen as too static and bureaucratic. "We must bring in the private sector" was the cry. The Training and Enterprise Council

(TECs) were born out of the MSC, and brought in a quality of private sector support and management that had hitherto been absent.

Training policy and provision would now lie with businesses rather than politicians. A National Training Task Force was established to assist in setting up TECs and invited local groups to submit proposals. By October 1991, 82 TECs had been approved. These new bodies were described by Coffield (1990: 70) as 'a national network of independent companies, led by chief executives from private industry in order to deliver training and enterprise locally.' TECs had boards of 15 members, 10 of whom had to be from the private sector, and with a local focus as primary. This meant the significant diminution in the role of national training policy.

TECs and Enterprise Policy

By design, enterprise policy was a central part of TECs. Barnes (1992) analysed 18 initial TECs' three-year plans. In the strategic objectives reviewed, the most frequent focus was on improving support services for new and small firms. TECs also had the potential to act as local catalysts in the development of networks. For example, there were attempts to improve links between venture capital and entrepreneurs through Business Introduction Services, akin to a matchmaking service between investors and firms (Harrison and Mason, 1996).

However, as TECs developed they tended not to involve smaller businesses and there was perhaps less innovative development of locally oriented enterprise policy initiatives than was originally envisaged. Boocock et al. (1994) surveyed the provision of TECs and found:

> The main form of assistance for start-up firms nowadays remains the 'old' Enterprise Allowance Scheme; the majority of TECs have renamed and revamped the scheme to include enterprise training as a condition of receiving the weekly allowance. Over and above the EAS, the TECs almost invariably provide business information services; most have set up Training Access Points, which provide information about vocational education and training opportunities in their locality.
>
> Nevertheless, our survey suggests that more TECs now direct their attention at established firms wishing to expand. The usual form of support is the provision, at a subsidised cost, of business skills seminars exploring such topics as corporate strategy and the management of change. A common approach is for groups of firms to work together on problems and to suggest solutions from within the group. On a different tack, direct funding is often available to SMEs for the purpose of diagnostic counselling (business 'health checks') and/or to

assist in business planning and management development activities; the funding usually subsidises the employment of a consultant.

(p. 13)

A scheme launched by all TECs was the Skills for Small Businesses in 1995, supporting employee training linked to business objectives. It sought to build on the Small Firms Training Loans that had launched in June 1994 by enabling firms to develop and implement training plans which met business needs, including helping their workforces to gain NVQs and trying to develop trainers in small firms. It also included a scheme offering funds to groups of 10 or more companies to propose coordinated training initiatives.

TEC Delivery

As appropriate to the design of the policy, there was significant variation in the degree to which TECs concentrated on small businesses or self-employment (Boocock et al., 1994). However, there were concerns about the ability of these private sector organisations to determine effectively what was most appropriate for their region or how to best address the needs that were identified. As Barnes (1992: 12) explains, 'The most regular criticism has been that the new system puts employers who have hitherto shown little or no foresight in meeting their own training needs in charge of providing the nation's skills requirements.' Further, in seeking to meet targets and to use their judgment on where to focus support efforts, contract delivery risked distorting provision, for example decreasing the proportion of support available to ethnic minority and women business owners (Bennett, 1995). Further, Christopher (1992: 24) records that 'a higher proportion of training providers are now operating measures which effectively exclude special needs trainees, such as setting entrance tests or insisting that trainees must find their own employer placements before undertaking training.'

These types of issue compounded concerns about a lack of accountability. By 1997, TECs were responsible for public funds of £1.25bn but faced allegations of not exercising sufficient control after multiple cases of fraud, for example involving bogus qualifications affecting 28 TECs and costing £5m (Clement, 1997). There were also concerns raised about the practices used by contractors to meet TEC and government-set targets, for example by temporarily hiring their own ex-trainees to meet post-training employment targets (Tuckman, 1996).

However, it is important not to overplay the freedom the TECs had. According to Huggins (1997), over 95% of their funds came from government sources, with much of the remainder coming from the European Regional Development Fund. In addition to the original bid to lead a TEC, the state-funded money could always have strings attached. For example, this can be seen with the Business Introduction Services, with the government sponsoring five schemes in English regions. The TECs were invited to bid for an initial £20 000 for two years (19 did so). In bidding for funds in this way to access further government money or subsidy, the activities of such bodies can become shaped by central government. Balancing this, it is also the case that some of the unsuccessful TECs went ahead with their own versions of the scheme (Lonsdale, 1997).

For the TEC board members themselves, these challenges were compounded by a lack of clarity from the government. Robinson (1992: 15) records that 'many of the non-executive TEC board members with whom I have spoken have not been very clear as to what is expected of them nor that their valuable time is necessarily being used to best effect.' Tuckman (1996) cites reports in the newspapers that TEC representatives are said to have complained about the impossibility of delivering on their goals in the midst of budget cuts as well government inflexibility and an overall lack of ambition. The original TEC three-year plans were hampered in their strategic development by having to respond to long-term uncertainty and only annual announcements from the Treasury on funding. Barnes (1992: 37) presents a comment by the Chief Executive of the Devon and Cornwall TEC: 'We have been given the task to increase and improve the level of training. But we are measured by bums on seats.' As we saw in Chapter 9, these types of concern reflected a tension between locally oriented, private sector–led bodies developing and delivering initiatives and the dependence on central government funds that tended to utilise forms of conditionality to maintain central control.

Major Replaces Thatcher

In 1990, a Conservative Party worried about their position in the polls and the relative popularity of Labour removed Thatcher as Prime Minister and installed John Major as her replacement. By the 1992 General Election, all three parties were making manifesto commitments concerning advisory and support services, demonstrating the general acceptance of the increasing emphasis on improving the 'quality' of small businesses. Major won a small majority, keeping the Conservatives in power for another five years.

The Major government continued a significant emphasis on enterprise policy and small business as part of the broader agenda of market liberalisation. The DTI (1994b) audit of the UK's economic performance gave, as an example of success, the fact that 'the small firms sector grew faster in the 1980s than in the rest of Europe, Japan and the US; and . . . privatisation and liberalisation have had an enormous impact' (p. 2).

Following a 1995 Competitiveness White Paper (DTI, 1995, *Competitiveness: Forging Ahead*), the government sought to identify the key challenges facing small businesses. A series of 11 conferences was held with the key representatives of small businesses, the Institute of Directors, Chambers of Commerce, Confederation of British Industry, Federation of Small Business, Forum of Private Businesses and the TEC National Council, amounting to a total of 1500 delegates, half of which were small business owners. These events established 10 priorities for government: late payments; retained profits; uniform Business Rates; quality of business support services; government grants; inconsistent application of regulations (especially EU); inflexible, unhelpful government inspectors; administrative burden of taxes; quality standards; and the skills gap.

The 1996 Competitiveness White Paper (DTI, 1996, *Competitiveness: Creating the Enterprise Centre of Europe*) set out the government's ongoing commitment to 'enterprise':

> Enterprise, like the whole of the competitiveness agenda, is about firms' ability to win. Enterprise is a quality of people: it involves individual initiative and dynamism, self reliance, the ability to mobilise resources and a willingness to take risks. It is vital in firms of all sizes, and in public administration, but it is particularly important in small firms, which develop new markets, exploit new products and services, and which exemplify the essence of enterprise and lay the foundations for many of tomorrow's medium and large companies. . . . An enterprise society is one that encourages and fosters this quality by removing obstacles and sharpening incentives, giving itself more of the entrepreneurial spirit and skills needed to succeed in world markets. . . . An enterprising business will recognise and invest in the potential of its people.
>
> (p. 22)

The White Paper set out five strands to the enterprise policy agenda: economic stability (focused on inflation); education and training; reducing tax; deregulation (including greater flexibility in the labour market); and providing 'practical, pro-active assistance to business' (p. 22).

Small Business Finance in the 1990s

In addition to encouraging engagement with consultancy services, the government's 'pro-active assistance' continued to include a focus on finance for small businesses. For example, the Small Business Initiative launched in 1996, following a pilot in Norfolk and Suffolk. This scheme saw the major banks offer reduced interest rates or charges to those small businesses that undertook financial skills training.

Schemes also continued to try and incentivise investment in small firms. For example, Enterprise Investment Schemes (EIS) and Venture Capital Trusts (VCTs), both announced in 1993, were successors to the Business Start-Up Scheme and subsequent Business Expansion Scheme and focused on individual investors rather than tackling financial indus-try limitations. They were based on providing tax relief for equity inves-tors (allowing companies to raise up to £1m per year), with incentives for long terms investments (no capital gains tax liability for realisation of the investment after five years) and against failure (further tax relief if the company were to fail). VCTs allowed investors to further protect against risk by spreading the risk across a range of small companies. Investors were also encouraged to become engaged in the management of the firms, seeking to improve their 'quality,' as well as providing finance.

However, Lonsdale (1997) notes the limited success of EIS due to its excessive complexity (even for accountants, who did not consider unrav-elling the complexity worth their while) and the reputational shadow of BES (where investors lost money). In the case of VCTs, there were also high fees paid to structure investments.

One Stop Shops

Throughout the 1980s, there had been repeated discussion around the concept of 'one stop shops' for small business support services. For example, an inter-departmental communication from the Department of Employment in September 1984 discussed the idea (apparently raised as a possibility by the Prime Minister) to use Jobcentres to provide advice and information to small firms (TNA: FV96/64). It was suggested that such an approach would 'constitute a possible way of simplifying matters for businessmen by making advice and information more readily avail-able' (p. 1). Suggestions for developing the idea included the Small Firms Service and Jobcentres working more closely, with Jobcentres acting as gateways or having small firm contact points. The DTI (1985a) *Burdens on Business* White Paper suggested the need to experiment with helplines and a one stop shop that could be run with the help of the Chambers of Commerce. As the proliferation of sources of support and guidance for small firms continued with the growing prominence and funding for enterprise policy, there was thought to be value in somehow consolidat-ing this provision. The prominence of the idea is suggested by the fact that all three major parties featured proposals for consolidating small business advice services in their 1992 manifestoes.

Robinson (1992: 17) points out that, by the early 1990s, TECs were a logical focus for developing the one stop shop idea. However, as they were not the only one, they were 'likely to perceive themselves as being in competition with others who could fulfil such a role.' Heseltine (2000: 428–429) explains how, with the creation of TECs, there were now:

> . . . two local organisations competing for the attention of local com-panies, as there was no coordination with the chambers [of Com-merce, plus] the growing network of enterprise agencies. In many

cases, local authorities had also moved into providing advisory services and support for small companies, as had the DTI itself, and there were numerous services funded by various European Community programmes. To make matters worse, some of the TECs were about to move into the business of recruiting individual members, thus intensifying the rivalry with the chambers. . . . The question I faced was simple: how did we create a single, effective support service for British companies? . . . First, the TECs and chambers needed to come together to create a one-stop shop for small businesses and, secondly, the quality of the support available to businesses up and down the country had to be greatly improved. By good fortune, responsibility for small firms had been transferred from the Employment Department to the DTI and we inherited a budget of £30 million a year earmarked for this purpose. In addition, we had £60 million from the DTI's consultancy support schemes. . . . Business Link was born.

We now had to persuade as many of the local players . . . to co-locate and provide a centrally managed service. We offered to include certain of the Department's regional and export services through this same local network. From the start we received powerful support from the national umbrella organisations.

The creation of Business Link represented a new, large-scale development in the history of UK enterprise policy.

The Creation of Business Link: A One Stop Franchise

Business Link was set up in 1992. Bennett and Robson (2004: 862) cite the principal objectives for Business Link set out by the Department of Trade and Industry:

1. To bring integration and coherence between the main public sector suppliers of business services.
2. To achieve this by partnerships between these agents.
3. To improve the overall professionalism and quality standards.
4. To have a physical presence—an office or shop with maximum colocation of partners.
5. To develop a network to cover the whole country.
6. To combine DTI resources with local inputs from partners.
7. But to move to 'self-sufficiency' as rapidly as possible; in part based on charging fees for services.
8. To be bound by a contract to government, in partnership with other agents, thus aligning partners within a single framework set by DTI.
9. To give a primary emphasis to stimulating manager and employee commitments to training through a programme called Investors in People (IiP). [See a following section for discussion of IiP.]

Heseltine (2000), who was instrumental in pushing the scheme through against significant opposition from within his own party, saw it as a way of relieving small business owners of the bureaucracy and time wasted on paperwork. It was set up to integrate support and provide a single entry point, albeit through local franchisees, encouraging greater coop-eration amongst competing providers. This approach therefore moved away from the earlier Enterprise Initiative to a more decentralised model.

The government's preferred model for the franchises was mergers of TECs and Chambers of Commerce, but this was rarely taken up. None-theless, some involvement of these local organisations was a requirement and TECs were therefore effectively the anchor for Business Link ser-vices, in theory empowering the TECs further and leading to a lack of competition in bids since, for each locality, there were not multiple TECs to create proposals and Business Links were regionally focused. This cre-ated a spatial fragmentation of the availability of guidance and support for SMEs, with business owners being funnelled into local Business Link services with a local monopoly rather than accessing a national market for such services in the ways that a large firm might do (Bryson and Dan-iels, 1998).

The Function of Business Link

As we have seen with other forms of decentralised, locally focused ini-tiatives, central government nonetheless sought to shape the function of Business Links. Heseltine (2000: 430) notes, 'We were instantly criticised for too prescriptive and centralised an approach.' However, he suggests that, where control was loosened to support innovation, service provi-sion tended to revert back to the problematic levels of service that Busi-ness Link had been set up to overcome. The DTI (1995a) outlined how Business Links should be used to disseminate best practice (as identified to the DTI and CBI from leaders of the UK's 100 most successful firms), quality standards, training qualifications and to develop local busi-ness clubs. They could also bid for money to deliver 'locally-designed business development programmes' (p. 116) in addition to support for exports and technology. This involved Business Links and Chambers of Commerce promoting government work on understanding the potential impacts of technology and Business Links working with the patent office to support small firm innovation.

The Business Link brand itself was carefully controlled, with govern-ment keen to ensure a certain level of service (Heseltine, 2000). Further, all Business Link operators had to get ISO9001 (a quality standard) and Investors in People accreditation (see a following section). The gov-ernment's Advisory Group on Business Excellence (involving the Brit-ish Standards Institution, Investors in People, Institute of Directors, CBI, Management Charter Initiative, British Quality Foundation, TEC National Council, Quality Infrastructure Task Force and government) was set up after the 1995 *Competitiveness* White Paper 'to promote a more coherent approach to quality through Business Links' (DTI, 1995a: 154). This included providing written materials for use in the Business Links to guide this work.

Business Link Delivery

By 1996, government spending on Business Link had reached £130m per year, including £81m for business support services and £49m for Business Link pump-priming (Hansard, HC Deb. 6 November 1996 vol.284 col.1222). Personal Business Advisors were being driven by targets with a push towards commercialisation of the service to help reduce the need for government support. However, this target-driven approach, as with TECs, risked damaging the discrimination and focus of the support provision amidst an emphasis on 'selling' Business Link products and services (Lean et al., 1999). Also, similar to TECs (as discussed previously), there was some evidence of Business Link failing to address wider social inequalities. Bennett (2008), in an extensive review of Business Link usage and satisfaction data, found that it is 'government services themselves, particularly Business Link, that are some of the major sources of unequal access [to business support services]' (p. 395).

There were also challenges in meeting some of the central targets, for example in focusing support on high-growth firms. Initially, Business Link services targeted SMEs with a widely adopted definition of small firms as 9–49 employees and medium-sized as 50–249 employees (employment only, dropping any financial element such as turnover). Micro businesses were not turned away but not targeted at either. However, it is not as easy to determine what a 'high-growth' firm actually looks like, and SMEs that can be considered in these terms are very rare (Priest, 1999; Bennett, 2008). Forte (2011), who worked in Business Link and wrote a history of the service, recounts that there was a lack of clarity on how to define or identify these businesses and this contributed to a more general variability of provision (Bennett and Robson, 2004).

Nonetheless, Forte (2011) describes how Personal Business Advisors were given quite a lot of free reign in identifying appropriate firms and what services to provide. At times this led to the advisors providing consultancy for free or at reduced rates (that is, subsidised by the tax payer), which meant displacing services provided in the consultant marketplace. Lean et al. (1999) surveyed Personal Business Advisors and found relatively high levels of staff turnover (the survey suggesting due to low pay), potentially damaging relationships and continuity of service, potentially resulting in quite variable service.

While Business Link was developed in response to a survey of SME needs, there are arguments that some of the services provided were not in response to market demand. For example, it was not clear that there was a market failure in terms of available consultants, necessitating the provision of the Personal Business Advisors. Bennett (2012: 90) argues that the variable outcomes he identified for Business Link franchises 'confirm the expectation, going back to Bolton, that there is limited market gap for government-backed advice.' Bennett therefore concludes that 'Business Link was expanded beyond most client needs; resulting in massive inefficiencies' (ibid). These problems were potentially exacerbated by the change in focus from start-ups to supporting business growth, involving a broader range of challenges businesses might face but that were arguably already catered for in the marketplace (albeit not at a subsidised rate).

Mole et al. (2008) identified that, for firms seeking entry into new product markets, intensive support increased employment growth, on average by 11.7% (much greater than the 4.1% for firms not seeking this type of expansion). They also identified that some firms were more likely to benefit from Business Link support, for example, those with a formal business plan increased the average employment growth benefits from 3.9% to 6.7%. However, this suggests one of the potential problems in that those best equipped to benefit from the support, such as firms with formal business plans, highly developed forms of organisation or the ability to maximise learning, are those least likely to have experienced a market failure in support provision. Further, instead of strengthening those businesses that can and do access the support, there is a risk that targeted, localised support may produce forms of dependency and clientalism (Bennett, 2008).

If government becomes involved in service provision there will be effects on broader sources of provision. Instead of providing alternative support structures, government can also subsidise existing providers and, partly due to its particular franchise systems, Business Link was seen by some commentators as essentially a nationalisation of business support services, which led to increased service availability and, by some measures, quality, but also to a reduction in local diversity (Priest, 1999). However, Priest also identified an unwillingness to charge fees, suggesting difficulties in moving away from the subsidised model (although fee income did later increase, especially in relation to the Personal Business Advisors; Bennett and Robson, 2004).

Perhaps because of the government involvement, Business Link made a significant impact on the market for SME support. It had some positive impacts for firms, too. Bennett and Robson (2004), surveying participating SMEs, found that the impact of Business Link, as perceived by the SMEs themselves averaged in the *little-moderate* range. Nonetheless, overall satisfaction levels were found to increase, from 58% in 1997 to 81.5% in 2002. These types of aggregate figure suggest something of the overall character of the provision, but they may hide particular strengths in some areas and weaknesses in others.

For Heseltine (2000), the more successful Business Links operated where the varying interests and organisations worked effectively together. Bennett (2012) suggests that Chambers of Commerce and A4E were successful at delivering Business Link because of the synergies with their existing activities, for example for A4E and their training business (although there were also problems, for example A4E's £105m bill for running the Business Link website for three years, Cellan-Jones, 2010). Bennett and Robson (2004) analysed the different types of franchise holders operating Business Link and found a very variable service, even within types of franchise (e.g. Chambers of Commerce, local government, private sector), with striking variations in terms of market penetration, impact and satisfaction. This has important implications when one considers the effective monopoly that Business Link franchises exert (albeit in the context of government threats to remove failing service providers). Bennett and Robson suggest that this variability provides strong evidence against these types of government-financed support services.

Investors in People and Quality Standards

As we have seen, the Enterprise Initiative aimed at improving the quality of businesses in terms of performance and competitiveness, for example by addressing the perceived weakness in relation to quality of management in small firms. North et al. (1997) explain that 'small firms were told that implementing a formal quality management system would increase their efficiency, reduce waste and raise their marketing profile' (p. 112). A further important way in which this agenda was developed was through quality standards and forms of accreditation, especially through the development of Investors in People (IiP).

ISO9000 was first published in 1987 by ISO (International Organization for Standardization) and based on the BS5750 series of standards developed with the British Standards Institution (BSI) in 1979. Such approaches established formalised, standardised systems of quality improvement. However, North et al. (1997) argue that the formal quality standards promoted by government, drawing on large firm best practice, are simply not relevant to many small firms. Where they are adopted, this is often as a marketing strategy rather than a deeply embedded change in practices. North et al. also argue that, were small firms to fully comply and rigorously adopt this formalisation, it would limit certain of the key advantages relating to flexibility that small firms rely upon to compete.

The idea for IiP was introduced by the 1990 Conservative government. It was developed by the National Training Task Force (made up of senior industry figures), CBI and Trade Union Congress, with the aim of upskilling the workforce to improve productivity and competitiveness. This was, at least in part, a response to several reports in the 1980s that had identified higher skill levels in competitor countries like Germany and Japan.

CBI (1990: 31) explained the rationale:

> It is clear to the Task Force that the skills gap can be managed more effectively provided that best employer practice is adopted more widely. An Investor in Training has a clear view of the future based on appreciation of organisational and human strengths and values, built on a thorough-going commitment to securing the skills base needed for the 1990s and beyond.

It was therefore recommended that all employers, alongside supporting a wider engagement with NVQs, should support the training and development within their organisations through the adoption of a common definition of training activity and the measurable implementation and recording of such training. Further, the task force recommended that 'investment analysts and financial institutions should give particular attention to these reports' (p. 32). In this way, all employers were recommended to become Investors in Training and to be assessed in this work by their local TEC. There were challenges identified for SMEs, such as resource constraints and the lack of training owner-managers themselves may have had, but these challenges were seen as strengthening the case for smaller businesses to be sold on the benefits of training. To do so, it was suggested that training be promoted, by TECs but also, for example, by advisory services such as banks, and that a market be created in the provision of training services.

IiP was formally established in 1991 as a publicly funded, industry-led organisation that would offer guidance on skills and employment issues. It started out as a means of recognising businesses that invested in particular types of staff training and development (Ram, 2000; Hoque and Bacon, 2008) but, in some ways, it acted as an alternative to Business Link and similar forms of service provision for business development advice and support. One measure of success for IiP might be that it has since expanded its scope to a more general 'high performance' agenda and expanded its activities outside of the UK, to over 80 countries.

However, there were concerns that the owner-managers of SMEs perceived the assessment for IiP status to be overly bureaucratic (Hoque and Bacon, 2008) and inapplicable to the turbulent contexts and nature of smaller businesses (Alberga et al., 1997). These types of limitation may dissuade participation or limit the effectiveness of participation. The offer was therefore revised in 2000 to try and achieve a better fit for smaller businesses, and subsequent developments have also attempted to better target support, for example through the IiP Small Firms Initiative, which included government grants to facilitate small firm involvement (Hoque and Bacon, 2008). Where negative perceptions of relevance may represent less of an obstacle, for example where the accreditation is required by clients, an additional risk arises of IiP being obtained for external 'show' purposes rather than as a deep engagement with practices.

In Ram's (2000) study of IiP-accredited SMEs, he provides evidence that the award did little to influence day-to-day business practices. Instead, IiP was treated as a paper exercise that the businesses could use to promote themselves. In this, and other detailed qualitative studies, there is an important concern that the accreditation approach to SME support leads to a superficial adoption of advice and, as a result, it will not have the required impact on business efficiency or growth (beyond enabling some businesses to win particular contracts dependent on them having the accreditation).

Higgins and Cohen (2006) provide a different perspective on this idea of marketability in their analysis of IiP spending. They identified that, in 2004–2005, about £5m was received in grants and aid, with £1.8m spent on marketing, £1.6m on staff and £0.9m on administration. They conclude that IiP would therefore appear to be 'primarily a marketing agency, rather than a standard setter' (p. 6). They argue that this is important where, similar to Business Link and, to an extent, TECs, government-funded organisations distort markets and create near-monopolies.

Conclusion

Conservative government enterprise policy initiatives grew in terms of their scope and funding as their focus shifted from seeking to support a greater 'quantity' of small businesses and self-employment to focusing more attention on improving the 'quality' of these businesses. This agenda had the potential to overcome the deadweight and displacement effects that had proven to be persistent challenges for enterprise policies. This can be seen through the development of training (TECs), business support (Business Link) and quality standards (IiP) that were developed during this time, with these initiatives having high profiles and significant government funding.

However, the new approaches were not without problems of their own. Increasing use of private sector providers led to concerns about a lack of accountability, judgment and the exclusion of certain groups that might be more costly or difficult to reach but had previously received government support. Private sector–led bodies also caused concern about a lack of control over the substantial sums of government money being used and allegations of fraud or incompetence were made against some of those delivering services related to TECs and to Business Link.

A further problem developed with these relatively well-funded, high-profile initiatives. While they may have limited the types of deadweight or displacement effects that had accompanied geographically targeted, small-scale initiatives of the past, there were now concerns that organisations such as Business Link introduced new forms of market distortion. These state-subsidised organisations entered what were often already quite crowded marketplaces, creating monopolies in the provision of some services, channelling the customers for others. In the eyes of some observers, and somewhat surprisingly for the small state, free market Conservatives, the pursuit of an enterprise culture and international competitiveness had led the government to nationalise business support services.

11 Enterprise Policy as an Answer to Deprivation and Exclusion

The late 1990s and into the 2000s saw the New Labour government broaden the objectives for enterprise policy, encouraging a new push towards equality of opportunity for enterprise, attempting to boost access to self-employment in deprived areas and amongst excluded groups. The Labour government also attempted to simplify, join up and rationalise the wide range of enterprise policies that had developed. In this chapter, we discuss these objectives in relation to the Small Business Service, which sought to establish the voice of small business and respond to the key challenges facing these firms. We discuss what were, at this time, the three key elements of the enterprise policy agenda (regulation, advice and finance) and the degree to which the SBS achieved its aim of bringing coherence to this policy agenda (a more 'joined-up' approach).

The 2008 financial crisis renewed emphasis on enterprise policymaking as the government sought to support troubled firms and stimulate economic recovery. In the second half of the chapter, we will outline briefly how the familiar tools of enterprise policy that had been developed by this time were deployed in the aftermath of the financial crisis by governments including all three of the main, UK-wide political parties.

New Labour

By 1997, the traditional Conservative reputation for economic competence was tarnished by the failed Poll Tax and a troubled economy, experienced especially harshly among SMEs and with a substantial decline in SME numbers (Hughes, 2008). Labour, having implemented significant changes under Tony Blair and rebranded as 'New Labour,' claimed that 'support for small businesses will have a major role in our plans for economic growth' (Labour Party, 1997).

Labour won the 1997 election, securing a substantial majority in Parliament (albeit with fewer total votes than the Conservatives had won in 1992). Repositioning the party, Tony Blair's Labour Party (1997) had proposed ending 'the bitter political struggles of left and right that have torn our country apart for too many decades. Many of these conflicts have no relevance whatsoever to the modern world—public versus private, bosses versus workers, middle class versus working class.' Instead, Blair offered the vision of:

> ... a country in which people get on, do well, make a success of their lives. I have no time for the politics of envy. We need more successful entrepreneurs, not fewer of them. But these life-chances should be for all the people. And I want a society in which ambition and compassion are seen as partners not opposites—where we value public service as well as material wealth.

Forming their first government in 18 years, Labour had formally rejected their socialist aims and appeared to have accepted much of Thatcherism. For example, this could be seen in the approaches taken to privatisation, relatively low taxes and a limited role for trade unions. In terms of enterprise policy, it could also be seen in the development of an entrepreneurial society of 'responsible risk-takers' (Wilson, 2000).

More specifically, and, to an extent, more distinctively, New Labour developed an increasing interest in self-employment and SMEs that was shaped by their focus on regional development, including help for disadvantaged groups and communities. In this way, new policy areas were brought within the scope of enterprise policy with these businesses, and entrepreneurship more generally, seen as a potential solution to a range of economic and societal challenges.

Stephen Timms, the then Financial Secretary (HM Treasury, 1999), provided a foreword to the *Enterprise and Social Exclusion* report produced by the National Strategy for Neighbourhood Renewal, in which he identified 'a vital role that enterprise can play in helping to renew our poorest and most marginal communities.' Bringing jobs and services to areas affected by crime and unemployment, enterprise would stimulate the 'self-confidence and determination in local people and communities' to bring about regeneration. Timms goes on to emphasise particularly the broader significance of the enterprise-as-renewal message:

> This report was prepared to contribute to work on neighbourhood renewal. But it should also be seen as a contribution to the Government's goal of helping to build an enterprise society. The proposals here are one facet of that broader task—alongside encouraging high growth businesses, and removing barriers to the success of all business. I see no tension between promoting enterprise in our worst estates and in, say, our leading universities. Both are needed if we want to build a society in which enterprise thrives.

A new government with an espoused priority for enterprise and business growth and the development of an 'enterprise society' led to a range of new policy initiatives.

The Small Business Service

The development of the Small Business Service was announced in the March 1999 budget, with the details developed by Stephen Byers, Secretary of the State for the DTI, following a formal consultation process (Bennett and Robson, 2000). It was then established in 2000 as a 'Next Steps Agency.' These new bodies were described in the following way:

> Next Steps Agencies are designed to deliver Government services and other executive functions in a more efficient and effective way. . . . Agencies work within a framework of policy, targets, and resources set by Ministers, to whom the Chief Executive of the Agency is accountable. An Agency Steering Board, including the Chief Executive and senior officials from the DTI, as well as private sector representatives, will be put in place to advise on management and performance issues.
>
> (DTI, 1999: 13, cited in Curran and Blackburn, 2000: 182)

In keeping with similar approaches under the previous Conservative government, these bodies were to be kept at an arm's length from government. They were to provide centres of expertise including, in the case of the SBS, acting as a voice for small business. This included the somewhat superficial change from pursuing an 'enterprise culture' to an 'enterprise society' (although sometimes still referred to as an enterprise culture, e.g. SBS, 2004).

Byers (DTI, 1999: 3) set out the agenda for small businesses ('some of the most dynamic, enterprising and ambitious firms in the country'). He identified particular challenges facing these businesses in terms of: access to information and finance; costs of R&D; lack of experience and skills; lack of resources for regulatory compliance; and less opportunity to influence government thinking. In response to these challenges, the SBS would have three main tasks:

- to act as a voice for small business at the heart of Government;
- to simplify and improve the quality and coherence of Government support for small businesses; and
- to help small firms deal with regulation and ensure small firms' interests are properly considered in future regulation.

To achieve these aims, the SBS would be advised by the Small Business Council, a non-departmental public body comprising members drawn from small businesses, modelled on the US Small Business Administration (Bennett, 2014). This was in addition to the Small Business Investment Task Force (to advise on access to finance) and the Ethnic Minority Business Forum (Bourn, 2006).

Early successes were claimed in terms of issues perceived to be affecting the small business population, such as compulsory insolvencies resulting from short-term difficulties. The Inland Revenue changed how they dealt with companies facing compulsory redundancy to 'help viable companies through a difficult period by sympathetic consideration of company voluntary agreements [which would] potentially benefit thousands of small businesses, allowing them to overcome short-term difficulties' (Hansard, HC Deb. 2 November 2000 vol.355 col.828). We will consider the work of the SBS, and related bodies and initiatives, in relation to four key areas of enterprise policymaking at the time: better regulation; business support and advice; access to finance; and coherence in the enterprise policy agenda. We will then consider a broader set of initiatives supported by SBS that sought to develop a more inclusive approach to enterprise policies (addressing a perceived 'enterprise gap') through projects supported by the Phoenix Fund.

Better Regulation

The 1997 election saw political manifestoes introduce the idea of 'better' regulation alongside deregulation. After 18 years in government, the Conservatives' 1997 manifesto claimed they had 'abolished over a thousand regulations.' Campaigning for re-election, they explained that if they were to be re-elected, new regulations would 'only be introduced if it is clear that their benefits exceed their costs and they do not place an undue burden on a small firm.' However, the Conservatives were defeated by a rebranded Labour Party that promised to 'cut unnecessary red tape' and, after four years in government, later proposed that 'regulation should be introduced, where it is necessary, in a light-touch way [and they would also] examine opportunities to put time limits on regulations, deregulate by secondary legislation, and offer help to small firms' (Labour Party, 2001).

The introduction of the idea of 'better regulation' perhaps reflected a recognition that, despite a long-standing agenda of deregulation, it is the nature of governments to create new regulations. While perhaps gaining greater prominence, there was not much that was new here, for example the agenda essentially recycled ideas from the previous Conservative government, such as compliance cost assessments or a 'small business litmus test' (see Chapter 9). For Labour, new regulation was required to meet a 'think small first' test (DTI, 1999: 6) and this would be supported by the Small Business Service working closely with the Regulatory Impact Unit. The shift from deregulation to better regulation was captured as the Deregulation Unit became the Better Regulation Unit and, later, the Better Regulation Executive. These developments were also happening in a wider context of the European Union with its own initiatives, which included a Regulatory Scrutiny Board that reviewed regulatory impact assessments on draft initiatives and 'fitness checks' on existing legislation.

The Better Regulation Task Force (BRTF) also replaced the previous Conservative government's Deregulation Task Force. The BRTF identified five key principles to test whether any regulation was 'fit for purpose,' that it should be: proportionate; transparent; accountable; consistent; and targeted (Hansard, 1 April 1998 vol.309 cols.1246–1247). The taskforce produced reports and offered advice on the better regulation agenda for government and, from January 2006, became the Better Regulation Commission, 'with additional responsibilities to challenge departments and regulators on their performance against the better regulation targets' (Arculus, Head of BRTF at the time, 2005).

Recommendations accepted by government included, for example, that regulators should produce Regulatory Impact Assessments on all new major policies and initiatives. Explanations of the impact assessments should then be attached to new bills presented to Parliament, ensuring that the impacts of regulation were fully considered in its design and enactment. Further, the 2001 Regulatory Reform Act established a fast-track procedure to amend regulations where they were identified to be creating 'burdens' (defined as 'a restriction, requirement or condition,' Regulatory Reform Act, 2001).

In 2005, the Better Regulation Task Force produced a report titled *Regulation—Less is More: Reducing Burdens, Improving Outcomes.* This proposed the concept of 'regulatory budgets,' the report having been provoked by the development of this type of practice in the Netherlands. This was based on the principle of 'One-in, One-out,' that no new regulation should be introduced without other regulation, of equal impact, being removed. Importantly, there was a recognition of the benefits of regulation as well as the costs, although this was underdeveloped.

Alongside the *Less is More* report, the Treasury published the Hampton Report, *Reducing Administrative Burdens: Effective Inspection and Enforcement.* The recommendations from this report that were accepted by government included risk assessments being implemented more thoroughly and comprehensively ('entrenching the principle of risk assessment throughout the regulatory system, so that the burden of enforcement falls most on highest-risk businesses, and least on those with the best records of compliance,' Hampton, 2005: 8).

These developments and innovations led to the UK's better regulation agenda (specifically in terms of a balance between removing barriers to business from existing regulations while at the same time considering the potential impacts of new regulations) being commended by the OECD and becoming influential in the European Union (OECD, 2010). Nonetheless, other commentators, such as Boyfield (2006), writing in a publication from the Institute of Economic Affairs (a free market think tank), saw that 'regulation has certainly proved one of the boom industries of the twenty-first century' (p. 7), resulting in concerns about over-regulation harming economic growth.

New regulations that were particularly significant for small businesses included the introduction of a national minimum wage (NMW) and the working time directive, which sought to limit overwork by reducing the hours in the average working week. The NMW in particular was expected to cause significant compliance costs for smaller businesses. However, its impact was not as simple as compliance cost studies might suggest and resulted in a broad range of effects determined by a range of factors within and external to businesses (Heyes and Gray, 2001; Arrowsmith et al., 2003). There were also new regulations of potential benefit to small firms, such as regulating late payments (e.g. the work of the Better Payment Group set up in 1998) or the Enterprise Act (2002), which included an attempt to strengthen the UK's competition framework and approach to bankruptcy (including creating the Office of Fair Trading). These changes, and their myriad effects on small businesses, indicated something of the complexity of regulation and the difficulties in fully capturing its effects in compliance cost assessments or 'regulatory budgets.'

Kitching and Smallbone (2010: 14) argue that 'quantifying costs and benefits is . . . extremely difficult, particularly where these are intangible and/or likely to accrue over a long period of time.' There are significant difficulties in attempting to quantify all costs and benefits (Hahn, 1998; Chittenden et al., 2009). Robust assessment requires a more rounded, contextualised view of organisations to appreciate the varied significance of regulations to different businesses along with the indirect and dynamic effects of regulations (Mallett et al., 2019).

Business Support and Advice

The SBS was given responsibility for Business Link (DTI, 1999) after TECs were removed from any role in Business Link contracting. The existing 81 Business Link contracts were discontinued and bids invited for 45 new Business Link franchises. These bids included requirements that sought to overcome some of the challenges discussed in Chapter 10, for example needing to increase income and to avoid duplicating services already available in the market. In part, this reflected the return to the idea of this type of service operating as a gateway and signposting service.

In addition to a telephone helpline, Business Link had an online presence from 1996 that grew in terms of its significance, size and centrality to the Business Link service. It was part of a commitment to ensure the online availability of 25% of government services by 2002 and 100% by 2008. In 2004, the Business Link online advisory service was established as a one stop shop where businesses could access advice on starting up, regulatory requirements, exporting, accessing finance for growth and other information. The Business Link website included an online training directory promoted in partnership with the main high-street banks which offered a range of online courses and a directory of 750 000 other courses across the UK. The website was outsourced to Serco in 2005 (and transferred to HRMC in 2007). Over three years, the set-up and running of the website was reported to cost a substantial £105m (Cellan-Jones, 2010).

However, the one stop shop principle, while in theory preserved by the gateway and signposting function, was somewhat compromised by a proliferation of additional services (including those through the Phoenix Fund, discussed later in this chapter, that targeted particular groups). Other business support services included the New Enterprise Support Initiative, a helpline for employers and prospective employers, created in 1999. This included a range of support for new and small employers to help minimise the cost of complying with payroll obligations. There was also an increase in both the size and scope of the work carried out by the NESI helpline for new employers which, by 2002, was set to receive half a million calls from employers and prospective employers in the year (Hansard, HC Deb. 6 March 2002 vol.381 col.397). The size of the Inland Revenue Business Support Teams were also doubled. These Teams would offer new employers a detailed visit to take them through various payroll issues and were supported with £20 million for a new call centre and web-based advice and information service to answer the basic questions people have when starting or running a small firm. There was therefore a huge amount of advice and support available (without even considering that available outside government services).

Access to Finance

Access to finance for small business remained a key issue. The Enterprise Fund was established in 1999 having been announced in a previous *Competitiveness* White Paper. It had a budget of £180m and was to be managed by the SBS. DTI (1999) outlined the proposal for a scheme that would build on the existing Small Firms Loan Guarantee Scheme (SFLGS, see Chapter 8) by focusing on equity finance through venture capital funds that would be formed through partnerships funded by both the public and private sectors and would target high-growth businesses.

In 2003, a review was initiated into the SFLGS led by Teresa Graham, an accountant by background who had worked with various iterations of the government's deregulation/better regulation bodies. The resulting Graham Review of the Small Firms Loan Guarantee was published in 2004 and recommended that the scheme become less administratively complex, including for lenders to make guaranteed loans without government approval, and more targeted on the firms most in need of help. These recommendations were accepted by government.

According to a Freedom of Information request (FOI Release, 2013), for the period 1/12/2005–31/1/2009, there were 8680 SFLGS loans made totalling £675m. A total of 4305 claims had been made against the guarantees, costing the government £183m. This represents quite a substantial subsidy and, for some, may have suggested a scheme in need of change. In 2008, responsibility passed to a non-departmental public body, Capital for Enterprise Limited and, in January 2009, SFLGS was replaced by the Enterprise Finance Guarantee Scheme, which sought to reduce costs by capping departmental expenditure at 20% of each lender's annual lending through the scheme.

There was also a range of other finance initiatives, such as the Early Growth Funds set up between 2002 and 2004, which provided £8.5m to encourage risk funding for start-ups and growth firms, in particular focused on innovative and knowledge-intensive businesses. The funds were managed by professional fund managers and operated on a commercial basis, generally with match-funding from the private sector. Fund managers were also deployed in managing the Regional Venture Capital Funds (2004), here supported by the Regional Development Agencies (see the following discussion). This initiative provided £74m of risk capital finance for regions across England for SMEs demonstrating 'growth potential.' The intended focus of the Regional Venture Capital Funds on innovation and technology was also echoed in other schemes such as the Research and Development Tax Relief scheme begun in 2000 (SMEs engaged in R&D projects could deduct an extra 130% of their qualifying costs from their yearly profit or claim a tax credit if the company was loss making, worth up to 14.5% of the surrenderable loss).

The SBS also focused on the SMEs that were seeking to obtain finance, creating six 'investment readiness' demonstration projects to provide intensive education to SMEs, raise their awareness and understanding of the different financing options available and how best to access them. However, a potential problem with so many different schemes and qualifying criteria is that small businesses can become reliant on their accountants or networks to know about these schemes or initiatives, with associated costs, creating confusion or even some resentment from those who find out 'too late.'

Joined Up Enterprise Policymaking

As becomes apparent from the overview presented, there were now a huge number of schemes and initiatives stemming from the multifaceted enterprise policy agenda. This created a new problem: how to overcome the fragmentation and complexity of small firm services.

An SBS (2004) White Paper, *A Government Action Plan for Small Business: Making the UK the Best Place in the World to Start and Grow a Business*, sought to bring together the different areas of UK enterprise policy into one strategic document. There was also an accompanying document that reviewed the evidence base, seeking to ensure that enterprise policy was evidence-based and that the SBS could exert influence as a centre of expertise within government.

The report draws out seven key themes for analysis of the evidence base:

- Building an enterprise culture.
- Encouraging a more dynamic start-up market.
- Building the capability for small business growth.
- Improving access to finance for small businesses.
- Encouraging more enterprise in disadvantaged communities and under-represented groups.
- Improving small businesses' experience of government services.
- Developing better regulation and policy.

(p. 7)

The report's evidence base supplement drew upon a range of sources to describe the problems (e.g. a relatively low level of entrepreneurial activity in the UK), tied to clear measures of success. However, it provided less consideration of the more fundamental questions around whether there was a role for government or evaluating different policy approaches to address the problems identified. While these documents attempted to bring some order and coordination to the somewhat chaotic form that enterprise policy had taken, there remained significant concerns about the extent to which these interventions were really 'joined up' in design or delivery.

Huggins and Williams (2009) analysed the New Labour enterprise policy agenda and found that there had been some successful measures, for example in making longer-term cultural changes such as through the education system. However, there remained insufficient attention on how different areas of enterprise policymaking inter-relate. Huggins and Williams conclude that there had been 'an explosion in the number of new and often uncoordinated initiatives, each seeking its own segment of the policy playing field. This has meant that joined-up thinking across enterprise-policy areas has been significantly neglected' (pp. 34–35). Mole (2002) also highlights the potential for 'street-level technocracy' through the design of Business Links and the role of Personal Business Advisors. This could undermine efforts for coherence in enterprise policymaking such as that pursued by SBS, for example through the reliance on advisors' tacit knowledge and therefore their ability to modify or adapt enterprise policy support.

The Enterprise Gap

The SBS activities that we have described were generally in familiar enterprise policy areas and with limited degrees of innovation. An area where SBS sought to address some of the failings of the private sector–led model developed under the Conservatives was in terms of inclusivity. The DTI

(1999: 5) explained, for example, that SBS 'will encourage enterprise in deprived communities.' In this approach, Beresford (2015) identifies a distinctive, consistent Labour approach drawing on their values of inclusiveness, fairness, solidarity and community, which Beresford argues is particularly evidenced by the focus on regional development, including disadvantaged groups and communities.

While enterprise policy has a long history of involvement in relation to deprived areas (as discussed, for example, in Chapter 4), under New Labour it was extended in scope to targeting a perceived 'enterprise gap' among particular, underrepresented social groups. In effect, this broadened the range of questions to which 'entrepreneurship' was the answer and therefore shifted the emphasis of enterprise policymaking. This included a range of research projects commissioned by the DTI to look at entrepreneurship in deprived areas, amongst women and ethnic minorities, for example, a three-day conference at Durham University on female entrepreneurship ('Shifting the Gears' 10–12 September 2001, see Hansard, HC Deb. 10 December 2001 vol.376 col.660).

In response to this agenda, the Phoenix Fund was launched by the SBS in 2000 to tackle social exclusion by supporting innovative demonstrator projects providing business support in disadvantaged areas and with groups underrepresented among business owners. These projects would identify best practice and innovative new ideas that could then be developed with SBS. The scheme had an initial budget of £30m, with additional funds allocated such that the annual budget was generally maintained at this level. This supported initiatives across two phases in 2000 and 2001, receiving over 600 bids (including from Business Link franchises) for funding resulting in 96 projects (DTI, 2004).

According to DTI (2004: 5), bidders were asked to devise projects which would help people to:

- Explore the possibility of enterprise as a positive career choice
- Develop business ideas
- Consider the practicalities of setting up and running a business
- Start up new enterprises
- Grow existing businesses

Projects targeted support for a range of groups or areas including ethnic minorities; the long-term unemployed; refugees; particular sectors; women; people with disabilities; social enterprises; disadvantaged communities; over 50s; rural areas; ex-offenders; and young people. Twenty of the projects were focused specifically on women entrepreneurs and the development of a 'Strategic Framework for Women's Enterprise' focused on the areas of business-support provision, access to finance, childcare and caring responsibilities and transition from welfare benefits to self-employment. However, this framework was criticised for a lack of engagement with empirical evidence and potentially omitting key areas such as the structural barriers women face (Wilson et al., 2004).

A significant example of one of these projects was 'Prowess,' a women's enterprise advocacy organisation that sought to bring together representatives of business support organisations targeting help at women entrepreneurs. This project, as recognised by government, 'highlighted their role in raising awareness of the needs of women entrepreneurs and the need to work towards equal numbers of women and men starting in business' (Hansard, HC Deb. 7 November 2002 vol.392 col.748). In addition to activities such as an annual conference, the project offered training and advice for business support organisations as well as an award in recognition of the support offered to women entrepreneurs.

Other schemes supported by the Phoenix Fund introduced innovations that tended to focus on service delivery such as child minders at training sessions to support lone parents, home visits for those lacking the confidence to attend external sessions and the introduction of IT services and online support. There were also projects aimed at network building. For example, in addition to Business Incubators, there was a Social Enterprise Visit Programme that sought to facilitate shared learning and experience across the sector and the Business Volunteer Mentoring Scheme could also be used to access mentors for new and early stage businesses from a national network of volunteers (by 2013, 15 000 mentors could be accessed through a national mentoring portal). At heart, many of the projects were still focused on traditional business advice services but adapted or developed to support targeting specific groups and communities.

Community Development Finance Institutions (CDFIs) were developed to provide finance to businesses unable to obtain it from other sources and claimed to work towards a 'responsible' finance industry. Other initiatives (e.g. the 2002 establishment of Community Investment Tax Relief) also attempted to stimulate the flow of private finance to support enterprise in the UK's deprived communities. By the end of 2003, CDFIs had made over 1050 loans totalling over £6.5m million, which the government claimed had created 1860 jobs in over 1000 new and existing businesses (Hansard, HC Deb. 12 February 2004 vol.417 cols.1627–1628). By 2010, CDFI lending had reached £200m.

Evaluating SBS

In 2004–2006, the National Audit Office (Bourn, 2006) conducted extensive fieldwork to look in detail at SBS's work in terms of its four key areas: regulation, advisory services, access to finance and joining-up government. In terms of regulation, the review found that the SBS had often been limited in its ability to make meaningful impact due to a lack of timely engagement from relevant government departments (a longstanding problem, see, for example, Chapter 9). The report highlighted the Government Action Plan as a meaningful attempt to bring together the various areas of enterprise policy. While it was noted that the plan was widely welcomed, there were, again, significant concerns about the influence held by SBS across government in terms of being able to deliver.

For finance, SBS estimated that, annually, 150 000 small firms struggled to access finance and that the Small Firms Loan Guarantee helped around 6000 businesses access finance each year, supporting turnover and net increases in employment. However, there were default rates of almost nine times higher than for commercial lending and high-level displacement of existing business. Again, this represented persistent problems in terms of a lack of scope (if seeking to fill the perceived 'gap' in finance) and significant displacement effects, with concerns about a lack of additionality. The report did identify an improvement in the quality and volume of services provided by Business Link while it was managed by SBS and noted the value of a single online portal.

Other evaluations and commentators also identified limitations in the work of SBS. In relation to ethnic minority businesses, while there were successes there were also concerns that 'a complex and uneven picture emerges in which examples of good practice . . . exist within a system that is often characterised by a lack of coherence, instability, and fragmentation' (Ram and Jones, 2008: 359). A report by the Small Business Network went further, arguing that 'the SBS is a bureaucratic waste of time and money' (a condemnation that was used to criticise the SBS in the House of Lords, Hansard, HL Deb. 10 February 2005 vol.669 cols.895–897).

In 2003, SBS staff were moved from government offices and co-located with the Regional Development Agencies (see the following section). By 2005, the government was starting to pull back from the SBS, halving its staffing from 400 to 200 and with reduced direct involvement in the delivery of programmes and greater emphasis on its role as a voice for small business. In 2006, despite being claimed as a success (for example, 'saving business at least £85 million annually,' Hansard, HC Deb. 22 October 2006 vol.450 cols.95–97), SBS was downgraded from an Executive Agency to being a policy unit within the DTI's Enterprise and Business Group as part of an argument that support services needed to be streamlined and delivered at a regional level. As part of this, Business Link was devolved to a regional level of control through the Regional Development Agencies.

New Labour and Regional Development

Regional Development Agencies (RDAs) were created in April 1999 and existed until 2010 as a central part of the Labour government's economic development aims. RDAs took a similar form to the Conservatives' private sector–led regional bodies, chaired by business people with boards consisting of private sector, local government, trade union and voluntary organisations. Again, similar to previous bodies, this often tended not to include small businesses. In some ways, this represented a (limited) return to local government influence, but RDAs still responded to top-down, centralised targets.

The RDAs were designed to lead on regional investment and identify skills training needs appropriate to the local economy. They took responsibility for administering European Regional Development Funds and, from April 2005, they were also responsible for the Business Link operator contracts. Selected RDAs would also create Women's Enterprise Units. The 2006 budget announced a structured programme of intensive coaching and assistance for high-growth SMEs to be rolled out by Regional Development Agencies. In these ways the RDAs were often expected to respond to central government priorities or to implement initiatives designed centrally. Regional Selective Assistance (2000–2004), for example, provided discretionary grants to encourage firms to locate or expand in those areas designated as 'Assisted Areas,' with the aim of either creating new employment or safeguarding jobs. As with previous locally oriented bodies, there remained, therefore, significant constraints and central government direction in relation to the enterprise policy agenda.

In particular, this related to a national government concern for more inclusive economic growth and to tackling areas of deprivation. The Local Enterprise Growth Initiative (LEGI), for example, was announced in the 2005 budget and implemented the following year. Consistent with the broad policy agenda concerning the role that enterprise could play in regional development, LEGI aimed to 'release the economic and productivity potential of the most deprived local areas across the country through enterprise and investment—thereby boosting local incomes and employment opportunities and building sustainable communities' (DCLG, 2010: 5; DCLG, 2006).

The Department for Communities and Local Government supported 20 LEGI area partnerships (10 in February 2006, followed by a further 10 in December 2006). Although mostly located in the North of England, LEGI areas were spread across most English regions, apart from the South West, and covered a wide range of activities. In the government's *National Evaluation of the Local Enterprise Growth Initiative*, the nature of these activities included support for existing businesses to grow, supporting new ventures and helping residents gain skills and jobs, as well as investments in local areas to help attract business activity (DCLG, 2010).

The programme ceased in March 2011, following a change in government. Assessments of its impact have been somewhat mixed. The government's own evaluation, conducted by an external consultancy, highlighted that 'performance in terms of the "core" LEGI activity areas of creating new business and supporting existing businesses, met or exceeded expectations in the vast majority of areas' (DCLG, 2010: 9). Moreover, in concluding, the report noted that, on-balance, the scheme generated greater value than it cost and that it had overcome some of the failures of existing programmes. Nevertheless, the report also noted that the management costs associated with the scheme were higher than expected and observed that 'levels of additionality, especially with regard to support for existing businesses and its impacts, seem to be low' (2010: 13). This was also highlighted by a more critical review by Einiö and Overman (2016: 23) who concluded that 'if the ultimate objective was to improve economic outcomes for residents then this represents a costly policy failure.'

Perhaps one of the most damning criticisms of the SBS is that all the issues it was set up to tackle persisted after its demise, including the need for more coherent, joined-up enterprise policymaking.

Simplifying Small Business Support

Gordon Brown succeeded Tony Blair as Labour leader and Prime Minister in 2007, having previously been influential in shaping New Labour's agenda as Chancellor of the Exchequer since 1997. The new administration did not present a clear set of political principles or an explicit agenda for government (Beech, 2009) and much of the legacy of Brown's time in office was shaped by the financial crisis of 2008 (see the following section).

In terms of enterprise policy, this was the moment for addressing what had become its bloated, overly complex, labyrinthine nature. As in many areas of enterprise policy, this did not involve significant disagreement between the main political parties but more a general trend as the idea was explored by both Labour and the Conservatives. In opposition, the Conservative Party commissioned a report by high-profile entrepreneur Douglas Richard (the Richard Report, 2008), which estimated that expenditure on the enterprise policy agenda in the UK had reached £12bn, with over 3000 schemes, little rigorous evaluation and alleging significant waste (e.g. on administration costs). The report recommended that 'government should only intervene when reasonable access to appropriate business advice or support is not practically possible and any intervention must then satisfy key objective criteria' (p. 5).

This report was, in part, a response to Labour's 'Simplifying Business Support' initiative and the Business Support Simplification Programme that was first discussed in 2007. This aimed to make it easier for start-ups and small businesses to access government support, in part by reducing the number of support schemes from 3000 to 100 by 2010. The plan to achieve this centred on Business Link and thematically grouped forms of assistance. The BERR (2008) paper *Simple Support, Better Business: Business Support in 2010* provided the rationale:

> . . . many businesses say they are confused. Little coordination, numerous schemes and multiple providers mean that some companies, particularly time and cash strapped SMEs, are put off seeking

help. The Annual Small Business Service Survey 2005 found that over 50% of small businesses want government help, but struggle to find their way through the maze of provision. This means the businesses that will benefit most from support are often those least likely to access it. In addition, such confusion means the system is neither cost-effective nor efficient to deliver.

This is not good for business customers, for tax-payers who foot the bill, or for public funding providers, who do not get full return on their investment.

(pp. 2–3)

There was also a similar initiative in Europe with the Small Business Act (EU) in 2008. However, a lot of these intentions were thrown into disarray by wider events that would reshape the government's approach to enterprise policymaking in the midst of crisis.

The 2008 Financial Crisis

In the immediate aftermath of the 2008 financial crisis, Mathiason (2008) described the magnitude of the event:

> It was the year the neo-liberal economic orthodoxy that ran the world for 30 years suffered a heart attack of epic proportions. Not since 1929 has the financial community witnessed 12 months like it. Lehman Brothers went bankrupt. Merrill Lynch, AIG, Freddie Mac, Fannie Mae, HBOS, Royal Bank of Scotland, Bradford & Bingley, Fortis, Hypo and Alliance & Leicester all came within a whisker of doing so and had to be rescued.

Trillions of dollars were provided by countries including the UK to try to stabilise the economy and to save the financial institutions in peril. It was a return to a scale of international financial crash and crisis of 1929–1931, in which UK enterprise policy had first been developed in response to the Macmillan gap (Chapter 3).

The crisis not only played out at the international or national levels but, as with the financial crisis aftermath through the 1930s, it also had severe regional implications. To take one example, the collapse of the Northern Rock bank had significant impacts on local communities in the North East of England. The regional policy infrastructure that was already in place would therefore need to be deployed in response. For example, a statement by the Chancellor of the Exchequer (Alistair Darling) set out how he had:

> . . . asked the chief executive of the Regional Development Agency, ONE NorthEast, to lead the Government's response. ONE North-East have already begun constructive discussions with Northern

Rock and will work with local authorities, Jobcentre Plus, Business Link NorthEast, the Learning and Skills Council and Northern Rock's management to co-ordinate the Government's support for those involved.

(Hansard, HC Deb. 18 March 2008 vol.473 cols.53–54)

Enterprise policy also came to the fore, for example in response to the characterisation of SMEs as credit-constrained when the availability of bank lending and other forms of finance was reduced, particularly for firms with high demands or perceived as otherwise risky (Fraser et al., 2013). Cowling et al. (2012: 794) have found that, in a recession where available funding reduced generally, 'lending institutions appear to use firm size as their primary lending criterion, with micro-business in particular being restricted in its access to capital.' However, it is also important to note that small firms are likely to reduce demand for finance owing to perceived high risk in volatile economic conditions.

The concerns about access to finance and the importance of new and small businesses to the recovering economy led to several new schemes as part of the 'Real Help Now' initiative. For example, the Capital for Enterprise Fund was set up to provide 'equity or mezzanine investment aimed at releasing or sustaining growth potential for SMEs that are over-geared and have exhausted traditional forms of bank finance' (BIS, 2010). The Small Firms Loan Guarantee Scheme was also extended in the 2008 budget, which announced a temporary 20% increase in the funds available. It also extended eligibility for SFLGS to businesses over five years old with growth aspirations.

Later in the year, the SFLGS was replaced by the Enterprise Finance Guarantee. This was a £1.3bn scheme that sought to support bank lending of 3 months to 10 years to UK businesses unable to access finance, with the decision to lend left to the lending institution. The scheme was initially only available until 31 March 2010, but the 2010 budget extended it for a further year and substantially increased its budget. The 2012 budget then extended eligibility for lenders to further incentivise them to loan to SMEs. Such schemes or initiatives do not seem to be as easy to close as is sometimes assumed by those who initiate them. For example, Entrepreneurs' Relief (2008) was a capital gains tax relief of 10% available to those selling or giving away their business. This scheme also became extended in later budgets with a large number of changes that made it difficult to evaluate or to investigate (for example, when a sudden increase in costs might be due to misuse of the scheme, Morse, 2014).

There were also renewed attempts to improve the regulatory environment, including the 2008 Regulatory Enforcement and Sanctions Act. This established the Local Better Regulation Office which sought to support more effective local authority coordination around regulatory enforcement and the development of 'primary authorities.' This was a statutory scheme, supporting businesses to connect with a local authority to support their effective engagement with regulations, with the ultimate aim of reducing the burdens and complexities of regulatory compliance. In 2009, the government also introduced the Small Firms Impact Test, the latest iteration of guidance for policymakers in considering the impact of regulations on firms with fewer than 20 employees. This provided a flow chart and checklist encouraging consideration of the different ways in which small firms might be disproportionately affected by regulation and encouraging differential treatment for these firms (including exemptions or simplified reporting procedures).

Austerity Britain

Ahead of the election in 2010, the Conservatives promised 'more diverse forms of affordable credit for small businesses [through] a national loan guarantee scheme' on the basis that 'lack of access to credit remains a problem, especially for SMEs' (Conservative Party, 2010). The Labour Party promised to 'create a new Small Business Credit Adjudicator with statutory powers ensuring that SMEs are not turned down unfairly when applying to banks for finance' (Labour Party, 2010). In this way, post financial crisis, access to finance remained the dominant fixation for enterprise policymaking, just as it had for many of the previous 80 years.

The election resulted in an abrupt end for Gordon Brown's premiership, and a new government was formed by a coalition of the Conservatives and Liberal Democrats. Elected in the ongoing aftermath of the 2008 financial crisis, the 2010 UK coalition government set about 'combining a far-reaching public sector restructuring with exceptionally large and rapid cutbacks' to lower debt and spending and pursue market-led growth (Taylor-Gooby, 2012: 77). In terms of the enterprise policy responses, there was little change, with new Prime Minister David Cameron (2011) providing a familiar call to arms:

> We are the party of enterprise. And let me tell you—right now, right here today in Britain 2011, we have got the most almighty job to do. Because for over a decade in this country the enemies of enterprise have had their way. Taxing. Regulating. Smothering. Crushing. Getting in the way.

David Young, an influential member of the Thatcher governments and their push for an 'enterprise culture' (see Chapter 8) was appointed as advisor to the Prime Minister on enterprise. He authored a series of influential reports proposing ideas such as supporting access to funding (praising the Start Up Loans scheme, see the following section) and facilitating business growth. Young highlighted a need to better market government initiatives, placing a particular emphasis on technology and the ease of establishing a modern business. He returned to many of the themes he had pursued in the 1980s, for example arguing that universities were failing to provide graduates with the skills for business or enterprise (leading to the establishment of the Small Business Charter as an accreditation for UK Business Schools in their support for small firms and entrepreneurship). Young also provided his take on the Bolton Report, which he praised for acknowledging the problems caused for new and small businesses by bureaucracy but argued that 'the issue I believe to have impaired business and entrepreneurship most was the confiscatory levels of personal taxation that mitigated against people wishing to work for themselves' (Young, 2012: 2).

The government's *The Plan for Growth* set out four ambitions centred on the aim of making 'the UK one of the best places in Europe to start, finance and grow a business' (HM Treasury and BIS, 2011: 6). This plan included, for example, a focus on deregulation (cutting 'red tape,' including 'an unprecedented moratorium exempting micro and start-up business from new domestic regulation for three years,' p. 7) and on finance for new and growing businesses (through extending forms of tax relief and a proposed business angel co-investment fund).

Coalition Enterprise Policy

Enterprise policy, in addition to more internal government issues such as supporting smaller businesses in accessing government procurement contracts, continued to focus on areas of deregulation, access to finance, business support and regional development. We will provide a brief overview of these areas as they developed in this period.

The Beecroft Report (2011) recommended excluding small or micro firms from some areas of employment law, arguing that 'much of employment law and regulation impedes the search for efficiency and competitiveness' (p. 2). It was therefore suggested that, by lessening employee rights (e.g. making it easier to lay off workers), more jobs would be created by the more successful businesses that would result ('by making our businesses more competitive and hence more likely to grow,' p. 2). While Beecroft's recommendations were not fully enacted, deregulation continued to be a core issue of relevance to enterprise policy.

The coalition government launched its 'Red Tape Challenge' (RTC), setting out to remove or revise around 3000 regulations across 29 themes that were argued to hamper growth. This strategy involved aiming to 'remove or simplify existing regulations that unnecessarily impede growth' and assessing regulations in terms of their costs to support a 'one in, one out' approach (later 'one in, two out') such that any new regulation was accompanied by a 'deregulatory measure (an "OUT"), which relieves business of the same net cost as any "IN"' (HM Government, 2011: 3). This agenda continued under the subsequent Conservative government elected in 2015 through the Red Tape Challenge programme which '. . . allows Business to tell Government how it can cut red tape and reduce bureaucratic barriers to growth and productivity within their sector' (HM Government, 2016).

Reporting on progress in January 2014, Cameron remarked that removing and revising regulations would:

> ... make it easier for you to grow, to create jobs and to help give this country the long-term security we are working towards. More than 1.3 million new jobs have been created since I came to office—many of them by small businesses. And I know many of you want to grow further—or may be thinking of employing your first person—but have been put off or held back by red tape.
>
> (Cameron, 2014)

Through the RTC, changes have been made in various aspects of employment-related law, such as to increase the qualifying period in employment for unfair dismissal claims from one year to two and dissuade access to employment tribunals by workers through mandatory conciliation with the Advisory, Conciliation and Arbitration Service and the introduction of application fees.

Access to finance also retained a prominence in the austerity era of UK politics, with the emphasis of this agenda continuing to focus on supporting the financial industry. The Seed Enterprise Investment Scheme provided tax benefits for investors in small businesses and start-ups in combination with the Enterprise Investment Schemes and Venture Capital Trusts. The flagship Funding for Lending Scheme was launched in 2012. This was a scheme that provided cheap money to banks so that they, in turn, could lend to small businesses at more attractive rates. Although the scheme was designed initially for mortgage and small business lending, it was revised in November 2013 to focus only on the latter, promoting the idea of bank debt to SMEs. More recently, the Chancellor's Autumn Statement in 2014 extended the scheme for a further year, as well as allocating £500m to the Enterprise Finance Guarantee Scheme.

Other initiatives focused on SME funding included more direct interventions such as Start Up Loans (2012), an independently managed, government-funded scheme for those wanting to start or grow a business but unable to access finance. Advice on the scheme was provided by the British Business Bank, which was set up in 2014 as a government-owned, privately managed business development bank to make finance markets work better for small businesses. Start Up Loans were initially targeted at young people but later extended. The scheme operated under a fixed interest rate and provided pre-application support as well as 12 months of free mentoring. By the end of January 2016, this scheme had provided over £185m in funds to over 30 000 applicants. An SQW Ltd and PRG Durham University (2016) evaluation found that opportunity-based motivations (such as having a business idea) were more common than necessity-based ones (such as a lack of other employment opportunities).

However, nearly a third of those in receipt of loans had missed payments of three consecutive months or more. These types of challenge fed into concerns about a lack of transparency and whether the scheme was achieving its aims of wider economic growth

Business advice and support also continued as a policy focus. A recommendation from Young's (2013) *Growing Your Business: A Report on Growing Micro Businesses* was to develop a voucher scheme that would help small businesses to access support that would help them to grow. The resultant scheme, which was developed by the Department for Business, Innovation and Skills with the Cabinet Office 'Nudge Unit' (the Behavioural Insights Team, which drew on behavioural science to attempt to develop innovative policy solutions), subsidised 50% of the costs of the consultancy, up to a maximum of £2000. The scheme focused on supporting access to expert advice in areas such as accessing finance, management, staff development and marketing. An initial assessment was made (either face to face or online) by advisers from partner organisations to identify business needs, and then vouchers were given to pay for the business advice from a list of accredited suppliers (listed on an external organisation's business support marketplace).

A government evaluation six months after the intervention compared those using the vouchers with a control group. The evaluation identified impacts on skill levels, business growth and (sales) turnover, as well as increasing the self-reported likelihood of seeking and paying for further business advice (BIS, 2016). However, by August 2015 there were only 7000 successful recipients who made use of their voucher (against a government target of 20 000) and only £3.6m out of £30m available funding was utilised (Guardian, 2015).

The regional development agenda under the coalition government focused on the creation of Local Enterprise Partnerships (LEPs). Bentley et al. (2010) suggest that the policy for LEPs was firstly about abolishing the RDAs, which the government suggested had been organised to administrative boundaries rather than reflecting local needs. One of the key changes from RDAs to LEPs was a greater focus on LEPs bidding for funding. Bentley et al. (p. 549) emphasise the ways in which this introduced forms of centralised control (familiar from earlier chapters of this book): 'government can decide what it wants to see . . . if LEP proposals are not constituted in the way government wants, and if LEPs propose to do what government does not want, the government will reject them.' Harrison's (2011) detailed, early examination of LEPs indicates that with only 69 days to prepare submissions, 'many areas had to go with what they already knew' (2011: 8) rather than propose radical plans.

The LEPs were intended to take on a range of different roles such as working with government and local employers to deliver economic and social outcomes. This involved infrastructure, support of high-growth businesses, tackling unemployment, housing and accessing European Regional Growth Fund money. LEPs also supported initiatives such as

Skills Support for the Workforce, which was designed to meet the local skills needs LEPs identified in relation to those employed in SMEs. Some of the responsibilities held by the RDAs that LEPs were to replace, such as inward investment, innovation and access to finance, were now held by central government (Ward, 2019).

There was also a range of other initiatives developed as part of the government's pursuit of an 'enterprise led' recovery, for example the Business Growth Service or the Scale Up Challenge, which sought local-level initiatives to support additionality in the pursuit of high-growth firms led by a private sector consultancy. However, overall, the initiatives and schemes developed were within these familiar areas of enterprise policy, some of which returned to formats developed by the previous Conservative government, others extensions or refinements of what had happened under Labour.

The Post-Coalition Conservative Governments

The 2015 election returned the Conservatives with a slim majority, after a collapse in the Liberal Democrat vote, and huge gains for the Scottish National Party proved a significant setback for Labour. The Conservative government was elected promising a referendum on Britain's membership of the European Union.

Newly appointed ministers Sajid Javid and Anna Soubry announced their plans for an Enterprise Bill that would form the basis of the latest iteration of UK enterprise policy. Javid explained that 'small businesses are Britain's engine room and the success of our whole economy is built on the hard work and determination of the people who run and work for them.' They proposed an agenda that would 'sweep away burdensome red tape, get heavy-handed regulators off firms' backs and create a Small Business Conciliation Service to help resolve disputes,' with later plans producing a target of reducing £10bn of regulatory costs for business. There were also proposals for support for small firms in accessing finance and ensuring receipt of debts owed to them in the form of late payments (Javid and Soubry, 2015).

At the time of writing this book, the most recent election was called by Teresa May (who had replaced Cameron following the loss of his 'remain' position in the EU referendum) in 2017, ostensibly looking to extend her majority and strengthen her position in government. To conclude our journey through the historical development of enterprise policy in the UK it is interesting to briefly look at the position of enterprise policy in each of the three main UK-wide political parties (albeit with UKIP obtaining a significant public prominence but without winning any MPs and parties from Scotland, Wales and Northern Ireland maintaining a significant presence, especially the Scottish National Party, which significantly exceeded the Liberal Democrats in terms of number of seats, and the Democratic Unionist Party, which was now in position to provide a voting majority for May's Conservatives).

In the run up to the election, the Labour Party (2017) stated that it planned to 'put small businesses at the centre of our economic strategy,' stating that, unlike the Conservatives, it understood the challenges facing small businesses. This included proposing changes to the financial system (e.g. a National Investment Bank) to address a gap in lending to small businesses, changes to the tax system and that they would 'declare war on late payments.' The Conservative Party (2017) also highlighted tax and business rates as well as addressing the 'barriers' facing small businesses, including 'reducing the bureaucracy and regulation that prevent small businesses from flourishing.' The Liberal Democrats (2017) talked about 'tackling the shortage of equity capital for growing firms and providing long-term capital for medium-sized businesses,' creating a start-up allowance, changing business rates, developing the provision of mentoring support and pledging to 'Reform the Regulatory Policy Committee to remove unnecessary regulation, reduce regulatory uncertainty, and support new markets and investment.' This therefore represented another election with little to differentiate the political parties in terms of enterprise policymaking.

Conclusion

The New Labour government that came to power in 1997 continued to expand and develop the enterprise policy agenda, now centred on a Small Business Service. The SBS focused on familiar areas of deregulation (albeit now reframed as a 'better regulation' agenda), access to finance and business advice and support. It is difficult to conclude that the SBS made a significant impact in any of these areas, but the most meaningful change in this period was the expansion of enterprise policy to seek to address not only deprivation and unemployment but wider forms of social disadvantage and exclusion as well. Through the range of policies supported by the Phoenix Fund, existing enterprise policies were adapted and developed to better meet the needs of, for example, self-employed women with childcare responsibilities and ethnic minorities.

In overcoming some of the limitations of previous target-driven enterprise policy initiatives that had excluded certain groups, this more inclusive approach was a welcome development, if potentially lacking in broad scale or significant impact. However, the enterprise policy agenda had now become so large and with so many schemes and initiatives that a dominant issue became how to ensure that this agenda was coherent and 'joined up.' By 2007, there was a cross-party consensus that the enterprise policy agenda needed to be slimmed down and simplified in search of accessibility, coherence and value for money. However, this approach was overtaken by events, and the financial crisis of 2008 prompted new and expanded enterprise policies to try and support economic recovery.

Our brief overview of the governments that came after the financial crisis indicates the degree of repetition in enterprise policymaking. There were also variations in emphasis, for example, in the degree of support for regional development or the ways in which central government worked with local authorities and the private sector. However, overall, much of the enterprise policymaking that had been utilised in the decade after the financial crisis by Labour, Conservative and Liberal Democrat members of government have been broadly similar and lacked much that was innovative or sought to address the problems embedded in the policies that had been delivered by successive prior governments.

A key observation that can be made of not only the decade following the financial crisis, the 20-year period covered in this chapter or, to an extent, the period covered in this book as a whole, is the political consensus around enterprise policymaking. Of course, there are changes in focus, increasing use of the internet to deliver services or focusing on specific sectors (such as high technology or green technology) but, ultimately, the core themes remain. One is left to wonder, after so many years of government initiatives to address a finance gap or to reduce the burdens of regulation, why more initiatives are still required. This persistence more than anything suggests that the enterprise policy agenda that has developed over the past 100 years may have had significant limitations in its effectiveness.

12 Conclusion

In this final chapter of the book, we offer an extended conclusion, drawing out the themes and insights from the preceding analysis. Utilising an historical institutionalist approach focused on interests, ideas and institutions, we discuss the development and interplay of enterprise policy interventions and consider the development, or otherwise, of enterprise policy over time. Finally, we present a set of suggestions for how enterprise policy might be advanced.

The Development of Small Firms as an Interest Group

Historically, the relative prominence accorded to small business and entrepreneurship has fluctuated, as has the emphasis placed on enterprise policies intended to facilitate or support these ventures. Across the period of our study, ideas about small businesses and entrepreneurs, along with the nature of those ventures, have changed. In the nineteenth century, they were simply businesses, operating at a local level and not considered as anything like a distinct grouping of business type, exerting some influence locally, regulated by national government in other areas. This situation changed as large businesses came to dominate, reshaping the economy and government attitudes towards industrial policy, with small businesses viewed as the remnants of a bygone era. Furthermore, as the economy began to transform, large businesses began to fragment and sub-contract and small businesses and entrepreneurs became seen as the keys to economic and social progress. It was only once this later phase began, in the second half of the twentieth century, that small firms were again able to exert influence through government in shaping their institutional environment.

The emergence of enterprise policy in the UK can be tied to small business interests being represented to the Macmillan Committee. While the ideas of small businesses as a distinct grouping and of their difficulties in accessing long-term finance did not radically alter the work of the Committee (which did little to evidence or substantiate the problem), they did take hold; the latter complaint being known as the Macmillan gap and persisting in some form in enterprise policies to the present day. However, the development of enterprise policies concerning access to finance and regional development that followed were less in response to small firms' demands and more an attempt to support economic recovery following severe economic and social crises by governments that were out of ideas and desperate to counter extreme unemployment and poverty. Some forms of intervention were enacted repeatedly, but there was little attempt to get to the fundamental causes of the perceived market failure (which for some at the time related not to the nature of small firms per se but rather to the changing nature of the finance industry and the loss of small, local banks). It was the influence of other interest groups (the financial industry) that limited the scope and impact of enterprise policies intended to aid small businesses in gaining access to long-term investment funds. In this way, the early enterprise policy agenda reinforced and maintained the 'rules of the game' and privileged the interests of the existing financial institutions.

For a long time (and to a degree throughout the period analysed in this book), government approaches to industrial policy have been dominated by the interests of large businesses, especially in key industries. This arrangement played a central role in limiting the scope and potential effectiveness of enterprise policies. The centralised approach of government, focused after the Second World War on tripartite negotiations with industry and labour, also began to demonstrate the degree to which the owners of smaller businesses and the self-employed, and their potentially very different agendas, were excluded from such arrangements. There was a degree of ideational capture in which the answers to problems were to be identified and developed through a political process that excluded the majority of the firms in the economy (while the CBI, in theory, was to represent all businesses, many of its small firm members repeatedly claimed that this was not the case and the policies of this period would appear to bear this out). This continued as representatives of large business tended to dominate the organisations established as part of the decentralisation of important areas of enterprise policies in regional initiatives (albeit with significant central government influence often retained).

It is important to note that this emergence of the small firm in government thinking, and the substantial expansion of enterprise policymaking, coincided not with an ideological breakthrough on the part of government but primarily the changing approach of large businesses. Unpredictability, a fluctuating economy and significant labour unrest marked a turbulent decade in the 1970s. This created a very different operating environment for the large businesses that had come to rely on economies of scale that left them potentially vulnerable. In response, these businesses began to look for new ways to organise in order to manage the risks and uncertainties they were facing. This tended to result in forms of fragmentation and the development of sub-contracting arrangements and complex supply chains, leading to a substantial increase in the number of small firms and self-employed as large business sought to externalise uncertainty and risk.

Responding to the interests represented in this mass of new and small businesses, operating in difficult, highly competitive and often exploitative environments, was the task of the Small Firms Division, which cemented a place for small firms as a distinct interest group within government. However, enterprise policy agendas have often struggled to have sufficient profile to achieve significant cross-government support, even in the period of the 'enterprise culture.' For example, in the case of deregulation, many efforts were limited by government departments with their own agendas and their own aims in creating regulation.

Outside government, there was a brief period of relative militancy (threats of action, such as withholding taxation) marshalled by new representative groups and a period of organisation around small business and self-employment interests. However, the rhetoric of the enterprise culture and, perhaps, the fundamentally heterogeneous nature of these businesses, led to many of these movements running out of steam. The representative groups that remained moved from outsider to insider status, working with the machinery of government. In some ways, government's preference for engaging with such groups, or with business leaders from large corporates, instead of the messy plurality of the businesses within the 'SME' or 'small business' labels, can lead to a misunderstanding of these businesses.

Framing the diversity of enterprises under a homogeneous 'SME' label simultaneously creates a constituency with a set of concerns, interests and needs that can be targeted through government interventions while somewhat perversely ensuring that such interventions do little to benefit the vast majority of enterprises grouped under the SME label. The outcome is a political discourse and a policy approach that is internally consistent but fails to reflect the experiences of the typical enterprises it purports to support.

Enterprise Policy Ideas

For analytical clarity, we have tended to focus on the key aspects of particular enterprise policies that targeted access to finance, regional development, deregulation or guidance and support. Of course, creating a distinction between different types of intervention is somewhat false. If small businesses and entrepreneurs are able to bring about economic and social regeneration, then there is a rationale for government to do all within its power to help, or at least not hinder, the action of these ventures. The same might be said of their role in maintaining competitive markets or bringing forward innovations to disrupt incumbents. This can be clearly seen in the development of a regional policy agenda that frequently draws on a range of enterprise policy ideas, often delivered together (e.g. advice and guidance accompanying financial assistance or access to affordable premises). A lot of the core ideas in enterprise policy-making were developed in the 1930s, including various schemes to support access to finance, regional development or early attempts to provide guidance and support in areas such as management practices.

While the Bolton Committee and its report were clearly influential, it is debatable the extent to which their work innovated new ideas in enterprise policymaking. Instead, what the report largely functioned as was a common reference point that codified the key policy ideas that had been developed to-date and characterised the small business 'sector' for future policymakers to respond to. The Committee also framed small businesses as being entrepreneurial and providing the seedbed for future growth ventures. Cast in this new, dynamic light, the case for government intervention becomes stronger, if not compelling when weighed against other priorities.

This did not have an immediate impact on policymaking but things changed significantly with the arrival of the Thatcher government and a new place for small businesses within a wider set of political ideas that can be summarised as neoliberalism. For policymakers, this shift presented a change in policy paradigm, structuring how they viewed the world and responded to challenges. These changes framed the new 'enterprise culture' as promoting individualism and personal responsibility, with these values represented in small businesses and the 'entrepreneur.' This saw a new prominence for enterprise policy in the UK and the expansion of the enterprise policy agenda and a large number of initiatives. It also saw a greater willingness to remove the 'barriers' and 'burdens' that held small businesses back, such as through making high-profile commitments to deregulation.

Taking the longer view of the development of enterprise policy in the UK reveals the apparent repetition of concerns and enterprise policy responses. As such, this perspective allows us to raise questions about the nature of enterprise policy and its development. Why is it that, after decades of intervention, the same or similar problems seem to persist? There are various possible answers, or partial answers, on which we might speculate.

The Failure of Ideas

One explanation for the apparent failure of enterprise policy agendas is that successive governments have failed to really understand the small business sector (Boswell, 1973). Certainly, questions have been raised about how far politicians and civil servants can appreciate what small businesses need (Bennett, 2008) and how effectively small businesses have represented their interests to government (Bolton, 1971). It is fair to say that, in recent decades, the mainstream political parties have settled on a broadly consistent framing of small businesses and their problems, albeit not always one that is aligned with available evidence (Leyshon,

1982; Wapshott and Mallett, 2018) or learning from previous errors (Blackburn and Schaper, 2012; Arshed et al., 2014). In other words, the ideas around small businesses and entrepreneurs appear to have become structured into persistent norms, or tropes, that exert isomorphic pressure on appropriate ways to think about and address small businesses and entrepreneurs.

Gibb (2000) describes how policy has tended to create support structures that involve subsidised programmes of training, finance and counselling; reinforcing an image of SMEs as being in need of assistance from an industry of advisers, consultants and accountants. As a result, smaller businesses become customers and government intervention is focused upon the market that is subsequently created, rather than any underlying problems. Ram et al. (2013) suggest that such a subsidised industry creates vested interests where many intermediaries are constantly having to ensure that they win government funding to secure their own futures, further perpetuating the original underlying assumptions that developed the policy agenda in the first place.

The types of underlying, or at least unquestioned or undebated, assumptions that have shaped enterprise policymaking can be seen with the focus on supply-side issues. As we have seen throughout the book, attempts to address the challenges of accessing finance for new and small businesses have tended to focus on supply-side problems. For example, initiatives have sought to stimulate private sector investors to address the perceived gap in finance for investment by demonstrating the commercial returns that could be achieved. However, the demand-side is rarely considered, for example the potential lack of businesses that represent valuable investments, an aversion on the part of many small business owners to sell equity and applicants who are not investment-ready, for example because of their present stage of development or levels of expectations (Mason and Harrison, 2003). With high-profile schemes such as Business Link, the amount of take-up relative to the numbers of SMEs in the economy is very small. This is despite very high awareness levels amongst the public and researchers have generally concluded that enterprise policy schemes and initiatives have not suffered due to a lack of marketing (Curran and Blackburn, 2000). Instead, it may simply be the case that business owners or entrepreneurs feel that what is on offer is not what they want or need. Again, there may be demand-side issues, perhaps relating to wider considerations around the outlook of many business people such as a reluctance to engage with external advice from people who do not understand their business, which would be understandable.

A further, significant challenge across many of the enterprise policy schemes discussed in this book are the concerns about the degree to which they really made a difference. For example, questions have been raised about whether job creation initiatives simply displaced jobs or economic activity from one area to another, or whether the provision of additional guarantees or tax relief for investors simply created better outcomes for those who were going to invest anyway. Concerns about displacement, deadweight and a lack of additionality have persisted and raise important questions about enterprise policymaking. This has also fed into criticisms of the evaluation of these policies, which should be the basis of their expansion or development but are often not. Curran (2000) suggests that the evaluation of enterprise policies has tended to lag behind their proliferation, suggesting, perhaps, that the benefits of such initiatives are taken as an act of faith rather than rigorous judgement.

A further explanation for the inability of enterprise policies to overcome the problems they seek to address is that terms such as 'enterprise policy,' 'SME' or 'small business' are deceptively broad. They offer a sense of cohesion to disparate realities, to an extent that limits effective intervention. Under this explanation, enterprise policy could be both effective and ineffective at the same time, depending on which small businesses are being considered. Currently in the UK, there are approximately 5.7m 'SMEs' representing some 4.3m businesses without employees, 1.1m micro businesses (if we discount those with no employees), 0.2m small and 35 000 medium-sized businesses. Even without considering the diversity that might be increased were business sector, business goals and so on to be included, it would be surprising if all these businesses shared problems and could also share the benefits of a common solution. This represents a fundamental problem for any 'enterprise policy' that seeks to address these businesses, which represent virtually all businesses in the UK (99.95%). However, it would be a brave politician who announced that nothing was being done for small firms!

If the businesses homogenised under labels such as SME are significantly mischaracterised and the differences between them in terms of their concerns, interests and needs are obscured, then it is not, for example, the scope or delivery mechanism of specific policies that needs greatest attention but the assumptions underlying these policies. Importantly, these assumptions are shared across the mainstream, national political parties in the UK, creating a lack of critical debate or the development of new ideas. Ultimately, the failure of ideas in enterprise policymaking has to therefore be, at least in part, attributable to the lack of political debate.

The Future of Enterprise Policy

This conclusion has sought to reiterate and question the underlying assumptions and path-dependent nature of much of the policies and policymaking in the area of enterprise. The implications of this analysis are important in terms of the future of enterprise policy in the UK and support the development of a number of proposals for future general directions in enterprise policy further afield.

Work by political scientists in the historical institutionalism tradition has been framed as '*historical* because it recognizes that political development must be understood as a process that unfolds over time [and] *institutionalist* because it stresses that many of the contemporary implications of these temporal processes are embedded in institutions— whether these be formal rules, policy structures or norms' (Pierson, 1996: 126). In our analysis, we have sought to demonstrate how enterprise policymaking has been limited in its development by particular rules (e.g. those of particular government departments, especially the Treasury), policy structures (e.g. the ways in which government engages with small firms or evaluates and develops enterprise policies) and norms (the unquestioned, underlying assumptions that drive a great deal of enterprise policymaking). Dominant, if unhelpful, ideas such as the mischaracterisation of SMEs, create forms of path dependency, limiting the scope for institutional change, and these limitations have been repeatedly reinforced by particular interest groups.

> *We suggest that it is vital that the underlying assumptions about enterprise policy are rigorously questioned, including the core rationale for the policies themselves.*

> *We suggest that, where governments do seek to act, the problems should be rigorously investigated and understood and policies should be piloted and evaluated to ensure they can meet clearly specified goals. Where policies are evaluated as ineffective in achieving their goals, steps should be taken to terminate those policies.*

Blyth (2002: 257) argues that 'specific types of state structures may be more prone to ideational capture and intellectual path-dependence than others.' Our analysis suggests that something in the nature of enterprise policy has led to a similar outcome. While significant funds have been deployed for enterprise policies in the more recent era, the underdeveloped political machinery and a lack of influence across wider government often leads to a lack of scope in ambition or implementation. Often, an existing set of ideas are drawn upon that are 'safe' and have appropriate levels of support both within and outside government.

> *We suggest that governments review how they engage with SMEs and ensure they attend to the heterogeneity of this grouping and the wide range of experiences and viewpoints that may be expressed. Given the sheer number and variety of businesses grouped under this label, representative organisations might not be able to capture fully the diversity of SMEs.*
> *We suggest that governments engage in further detail with SMEs. Better understanding of SME characteristics that are relevant to policymaking and implementation can inform these processes. For example, appreciating how independent business owners might be reluctant to seek and take external advice or guidance.*

We suggest that large businesses might not be best placed to shape, develop and deliver enterprise initiatives and policies. The experiences of operating and managing in large ventures might not provide a useful knowledge base on small businesses. The policies and practices that are often necessary for a large business to operate might be unsuitable for much smaller ventures.

Perhaps most radically, given the focus of our book, in order to address the points we have set out above:

We suggest that governments reject the homogenising label of SMEs and find new ways of engaging with businesses that are not large corporations or multinationals.

Ultimately, we want this book to act as a call to question the underlying assumptions about enterprise policy. There is a great need for research-informed debate across the political spectrum.

We suggest that innovations in enterprise policy should stem from extensive debate, be tied to clear, evidence-based policy and clearly articulated goals about the political decisions that drive the relationships among government, small business and entrepreneurship.

Methodological Appendix

In this Methodological Appendix, we describe the approach taken to identifying and analysing the different types of sources used in the book. We feel it is appropriate to set out our approach for two reasons: firstly, in the interests of transparency, so that others can examine and critique our work; secondly, to note the historical institutionalist perspective we have adopted in tackling the subject, as set out in Chapter 1.

Sources

The research project underpinning this book draws on various kinds of source. Academic books and journal articles across a range of disciplines were typically used as a starting point through which to gain others' insights and discover paths to further relevant literature and important primary sources.

We referred to written documents generated through the business of government such as White Papers, Parliamentary research reports and policy evaluations. We have also examined records of Parliamentary proceedings collected in Hansard, 'an edited verbatim record of what was said in Parliament' that also includes details of votes and written statements (Hansard, 2019).

Where available, under public records and data protection rules, we studied the proceedings of prominent commissions and committees via records held at The National Archives in Kew, London. Reading how the uncertainties of the day were framed, evaluated and addressed by different ideas and interests helped build understanding of how enterprise policies have developed.

Various political manifestoes, pamphlets and books from political parties and think tanks, often held at the British Library in London and Boston Spa, were consulted to access contemporary perspectives on political debates and pledges regarding enterprise policy. Speeches, biographies and autobiographies of prominent actors in the enterprise policy story were also consulted for gaining insight into the personal motivations for action or subsequent reflections on how events unfolded.

Naturally, inherent in our task are challenges concerning the constructed nature of archives (Brooks, 1969; Grigg, 1991; Hill, 1993), and other sources. As appropriate, sources were subjected to critical consideration through questions of authenticity, validity, credibility and representativeness (Lipartito, 2014). Furthermore, we faced hurdles such as those with language where the precise meaning of terms as they were used at the time is hard to fully grasp (see Bloch, 1954). We sought to address these matters through our wider reading, although we recognise this as an ongoing challenge.

Our Approach

Historical Institutionalism

With enterprise policy relating to action by governments to support entre-preneurship and smaller business ventures, taking a long-view of how different challenges have been viewed and responded to helps to reveal the persistence, or otherwise, of ideas and interests. Examining enter-prise policy over time highlights how, regardless of sustained attention, complaints around finance and those concerning regulation are virtually ever-present. Similarly, policy responses, whether through measures to stimulate enterprise in particular locations or to support business growth more generally, emerge and re-emerge with some frequency. The extent to which such efforts and responses seem to arise might suggest degrees of path dependency, limiting the extent to which problems can be reframed radically or tackled through innovative responses.

Studying enterprise policy over time reveals the apparent repetition of problems and solutions in operation. Adopting a broadly historical institutionalist approach to examining this topic suggests that recent attention on enterprise policy, and the problems it is directed towards addressing, carries echoes of previous debates and interventions. To this extent, questions might be raised about the prospects for enterprise pol-icy fulfilling the hopes apparently pinned on it for addressing the wide range of problems it targets.

Book Structure

In constructing a book from these analyses we were influenced by Bloch's (1954: 153) remark that '. . . the periodicity of the generations is by no means regular. As the rhythm of social change is more or less rapid, the limits contract or expand. There are, in history, some generations which are long and some which are short,' and it is only by looking that we come to understand the turn of events. To this extent, balancing cohesion in terms of policy interventions and chronological order has represented an ongoing tension. It has also meant that some periods and areas of activity have required more attention than others, but the intention has been to capture both a sense of the times in a given period and the detail of how enterprise policy was deployed in such circumstances.

References

Alberga, T., Tyson, S. and Parsons, D. (1997). An evaluation of the Investors in People standard. *Human Resource Management Journal*, 7(2): 47–60.

Aldcroft, D.H. (1964). The entrepreneur and the British economy, 1870–1914. *The Economic History Review, New Series*, 17(1): 113–134.

Aldrich, H.E. (2010). 'Beam me up, Scott(ie)!' Institutional theorists' struggles with the emergent nature of entrepreneurship. *Institutions and Entrepreneurship*, published online, 12 March 2015, pp. 329–364. Available at: https://doi.org/10.1108/S0277-2833(2010)0000021015 Accessed: 30.9.19.

Alford, B.W.E. (1972). *Depression and recovery? British economic growth 1918–1939*. London: The Macmillan Press.

Anderson, A.R., Drakopoulou-Dodd, S.L. and Scott, M.G. (2000). Religion as an environmental influence on enterprise culture: The case of Britain in the 1980s. *International Journal of Entrepreneurial Behavior & Research*, 6(1): 5–20.

Appleyard, K.C. (1939). Government sponsored trading estates. *Journal of the Royal Society of Arts*, 87(4519): 843–863.

Arculus, D. (2005). Foreword, better regulation task force Annual Report for 2004/5. *Better Regulation Task Force*. Available at: www.eesc.europa.eu/resources/docs/designdelivery.pdf Accessed: 30.9.19.

Arrowsmith, J., Gilman, M.W., Edwards, P. and Ram, M. (2003). The impact of the national minimum wage in small firms. *British Journal of Industrial Relations*, 41: 435–456.

Arshed, N., Carter, S. and Mason, C. (2014). The ineffectiveness of entrepreneurship policy: Is policy formulation to blame? *Small Business Economics*, 43(3): 639–659.

Atkinson, R. (2000). Narratives of policy: The construction of urban problems and urban policy in the official discourse of British government 1968–1998. *Critical Social Policy*, 20(2): 211–232.

Bache, I. (1999). The extended gatekeeper: Central government and the implementation of EC regional policy in the UK. *Journal of European Public Policy*, 6(1): 28–45.

Bache, I. and Jordan, A. (2006). Europeanization and domestic change. In: I. Bache and A. Jordan (eds.) *The Europeanization of British politics*. London: Palgrave Macmillan, pp. 17–33.

Baines, S. and Wheelock, J. (1998). Reinventing traditional solutions: Job creation, gender and the micro-business household. *Work, Employment & Society*, 12(4): 579–601.

Baker, M. and Collins, M. (2010). English commercial banks and organizational inertia: The financing of SMEs, 1944–1960. *Enterprise & Society*, 11(1): 65–97.

Balchin, P.N. (1990). *Regional policy in Britain: The North-South divide.* London: Paul Chapman Publishing Ltd.

Bannock, G. (1989). Changing viewpoints. In: G. Bannock and A. Peacock (eds.) *Governments and small business.* London: Paul Chapman Publishing Ltd, pp. 12–23.

Barlow, M. (1940). The dispersal of industry. *The Spectator*, 1 March 1940, p. 10. Available at: http://archive.spectator.co.uk/article/1st-march-1940/11/the-dispersal-of-industry Accessed: 29.9.19.

Barnes, G. (1992). *An examination of the formulation of policies by Training and Enterprise Councils.* Coventry, UK: Warwick Business School.

Bartrip, P.W.J. (1983). State intervention in mid-nineteenth century Britain: Fact or fiction? *Journal of British Studies*, 23(1): 63–83.

Bechhofer, F. and Elliott, B. (1981). Petty property: The survival of a moral economy. In: F. Bechhofer and B. Elliott (eds.) *The petite bourgeoisie.* London: Palgrave Macmillan, pp. 182–200.

Beech, M. (2009). A puzzle of ideas and policy: Gordon Brown as Prime Minister. *Policy Studies*, 30(1): 5–16.

Beecroft, A. (2011). *Report on employment law.* London: Department for Business, Innovation & Skills. Available at: www.gov.uk/government/publications/employment-law-review-report-beecroft Accessed: 30.9.19.

Beesley, M.E. and Wilson, P.E.B. (1981). Government aid to small firms in Britain. In: P. Gorb, P. Dowell and P. Wilson (eds.) *Small business perspectives.* London: Armstrong Publishing/London Business School, pp. 254–308.

BEIS. (2018). Business population estimates for the UK and regions 2018. *Department for Business, Energy & Industrial Strategy*, published online 11 October 2018. Available at: https://assets.publishing.service.gov.uk/government/uploads/system/uploads/attachment_data/file/746599/OFFICIAL_SENSITIVE_-_BPE_2018_-_statistical_release_FINAL_FINAL.pdf Accessed: 29.9.19.

Bendix, R. (1956). *Work and authority: Ideologies of management in the course of industrialization.* London: Chapman & Hall.

Bennett, D.C. (1983). State aids to small firms in the European Community. *International Small Business Journal*, 2(1): 27–37.

Bennett, R.J. (1995). The re-focusing of small business services in enterprise agencies: The influence of TECs and LECs. *International Small Business Journal*, 13(4): 35–55.

Bennett, R.J. (2008). SME policy support in Britain since the 1990s: What have we learnt? *Environment and Planning C: Government and Policy*, 26(2): 375–397.

Bennett, R.J. (2011). *Local business voice: The history of Chambers of Commerce in Britain, Ireland, and revolutionary America 1760–2011.* Oxford: Oxford University Press.

Bennett, R.J. (2012). Government advice services for SMEs: Some lessons from British experience. In: R. Blackburn and M. Schaper (eds.) *Government SMEs and entrepreneurship development: Policy, practice and challenges.* Farnham: Gower Publishing, pp. 185–198.

Bennett, R.J. (2014). *Entrepreneurship, small business and public policy: Evolution and revolution*. Abingdon, OX: Routledge.

Bennett, R.J. and Robson, P. (2000). The Small Business Service: Business support, use, fees and satisfaction. *Policy Studies*, 21(3): 173–190.

Bennett, R.J. and Robson, P. (2004). Support services for SMEs: Does the 'franchisee' make a difference to the Business Link offer? *Environment and Planning C: Government and Policy*, 22(6): 859–880.

Bennett, R.J., Smith, H., van Lieshout, C., Montebruno, P. and Newton, G. (2020). *The age of entrepreneurship: Business proprietors, self-employment and corporations since 1851*. Abingdon, OX: Routledge.

Bentley, G., Bailey, D. and Shutt, J. (2010). From RDAs to LEPs: A new localism? Case examples of West Midlands and Yorkshire. *Local Economy*, 25(7): 535–557.

Beresford, R. (2015). New labour and enterprise policy: Continuity or change? Evidence from general election manifestos. *British Politics*, 10(3): 335–355.

BERR. (2008). Simple support, better business: Business support in 2010. Available at: https://webarchive.nationalarchives.gov.uk/20090609065902/www.berr.gov.uk/files/file44988.pdf. Accessed: 26.8.19.

Billings, M., Mollan, S. and Garnett, P. (2019). Debating banking in Britain: The Colwyn committee, 1918. *Business History*. Online before publication.

Birch, D.L. (1981). Who creates jobs? *The Public Interest*, Fall: 3–14.

BIS. (2010). Early assessment of the impact of BIS Equity Fund Initiatives. Available at: https://assets.publishing.service.gov.uk/government/uploads/system/uploads/attachment_data/file/32234/10-1037-early-assessment-bis-equity-fund-initiatives.pdf Accessed: 30.9.19.

BIS. (2016). Growth vouchers programme evaluation. Cohort 1: Impact at six months. Available at: https://assets.publishing.service.gov.uk/government/uploads/system/uploads/attachment_data/file/498329/BIS-16-30-growth-vouchers-programme-evaluation-cohort-1-impact-at-6-months.pdf Accessed: 28.8.19.

Blackaby, F.T. (1978). Narrative. In: F.T. Blackaby (ed.) *British economic policy, 1960–74*. Cambridge: Cambridge University Press, pp. 11–76.

Blackburn, R.A. and Schaper, M.T. (2012). Introduction. In: R.A. Blackburn and M.T. Schaper (eds.) *Government, SMEs and entrepreneurship development: Policy, practice and challenges*. Farnham: Gower Publishing, pp. 1–15.

Blank, S. (1973). *Industry and government in Britain: The Federation of British Industries in Politics, 1945–65*. Farnborough: Saxon House/Lexington Books.

Bloch, M. (1954). *The historian's craft* (trans. Peter Putnam). Manchester: Manchester University Press.

Blyth, M. (2002). *Great transformations: Economic ideas and institutional change in the twentieth century*. Cambridge: Cambridge University Press.

Bolter, H. (1971). Bolton Committee Report: New DTI Division and Minister should sponsor small firms. *Financial Times*, 4 November 1971.

Bolton, J.E. (1971). *Committee of inquiry on small firms*. London: HM Stationery Office.

Bolton, J.E. (1982). The future of small businesses: A review of developments since the committee of inquiry (1969–71). *Journal of the Royal Society for the Encouragement of Arts, Manufactures and Commerce*, 130(5310): 305–320.

Boocock, G., Lauder, D. and Presley, J. (1994). The role of the TECs in supporting SMEs in England. *Journal of Small Business and Enterprise Development*, 1(1): 12–18.

Booth, A. (1978). An administrative experiment in unemployment policy in the thirties. *Public Administration*, 56(2): 139–157.

Booth, A. (1982). The Second World War and the origins of modern regional policy. *Economy and Society*, 11(1): 1–21.

Boswell, J. (1973). *The rise and decline of small firms*. London: George Allen & Unwin.

Bourn, J. and National Audit Office. (2006). Supporting small business: Full report. Available at: www.nao.org.uk/wp-content/uploads/2006/05/0506962. pdf Accessed: 23.8.19.

Boyfield, K. (2006). Editorial: Better regulation without the state. Available at: http://iea.org.uk/sites/default/files/publications/files/upldeconomicAffairs 325pdf.pdf Accessed: 25.8.19.

Brebner, J.B. (1948). Laissez faire and state intervention in nineteenth-century Britain. *The Journal of Economic History*, 8(S): 59–73.

Bridge, S. (2010). *Rethinking enterprise policy*. Houndmills, Basingstoke: Palgrave.

Brockway, A.F. (1932). *Hungry England*. London: Victor Gollancz.

Brooks, P.C. (1969). *Research in archives: The use of unpublished primary sources*. Chicago, IL: University of Chicago Press.

Brown, R., Hayton, J., Sandy, C. and Brown, P. (1976). *Small businesses: Strategy for survival*. London: Conservative Political Centre, CPC 592.

Bruton, G.D., Ahlstrom, D. and Li, H.L. (2010). Institutional theory and entrepreneurship: Where are we now and where do we need to move in the future? *Entrepreneurship Theory & Practice*, 34(3): 421–440.

Bryson, J.R. and Daniels, P.W. (1998). Business link, strong ties, and the walls of silence: Small and medium-sized enterprises and external business-service expertise. *Environment and Planning C: Government and Policy*, 16(3): 265–280.

Burrows, R. (1991). The discourse of the enterprise culture and the restructuring of Britain. In: J. Curran and R.A. Blackburn (eds.) *Paths of enterprise: The future of the small business*. London: Routledge, pp. 17–33.

Cain, P.J. and Hopkins, A.G. (1980). The political economy of British expansion overseas, 1750–1914. *The Economic History Review, Second Series*, XXXIII (4): 463–490.

Cameron, D. (2011). Speech to Conservative Spring Conference, Cardiff, 6 March 2011. Full transcript published in *The Spectator*, 6 March 2011. Available at: www.newstatesman.com/2011/03/enterprise-government-party Accessed: 29.9.19.

Cameron, D. (2014). Federation of Small Businesses speech. Available at: www. gov.uk/government/news/supporting-business-david-cameron-announces-new-plans Accessed: 1.8.16.

Carnevali, F. (2005). *Europe's advantage: Banks and small firms in Britain, France, Germany, and Italy since 1918*. Oxford: Oxford University Press.

Carnevali, F. and Scott, P. (1999). The Treasury as a venture capitalist: DATAC industrial finance and the Macmillan gap, 1945–60. *Financial History Review*, 6(1): 47–65.

CBI. (1968a). Speech by John Davies, 6 June 1968 available, TNA: BT360/4/1/ ANNEX A.

CBI. (1968b). *Britain's small firms: Their vital role in the economy*. London: Confederation of British Industry.

CBI. (1990). *Towards a skills revolution*. London: Confederation of British Industry.

Cellan-Jones, R. (2010). The £105m website. Available at: www.bbc.co.uk/ blogs/thereporters/rorycellanjones/2010/07/the_105m_website.html. Accessed: 28.9.19.

Chataway, C. (1972). *New deal for industry: Government and industry on the threshold of Europe*. London: Conservative Political Centre, CPC No. 515.

Chittenden, F., Iancich, S. and Sloan, B. (2009). Techniques available for estimating the impact of regulations. In: A. Nijsen, J. Hudson, C. Müller, K. van Paridon and R. Thurik (eds.) *Business regulation and public policy*. New York, NY: Springer, pp. 43–59.

Christopher, T. (1992). Countering disadvantage now. *Policy Studies*, 13(1): 22–29.

Ciliberto, F. (2010). Were British cotton entrepreneurs technologically backward? Firm-level evidence on the adoption of ring spinning. *Explorations in Economic History*, 47: 487–504.

Civil Service. (1970a). The reorganisation of Central Government. Presented to Parliament by the Prime Minister and Minister for the Civil Service, Cmnd. 4506.

Civil Service. (1970b). New policies for public spending. Presented to Parliament by the Chancellor of the Exchequer, Cmnd. 4515.

Clemens, E.S. and Cook, J.M. (1999). Politics and institutionalism: Explaining durability and change. *Annual Review of Sociology*, 25: 441–466.

Clement, B. (1997). Training fraud cost taxpayer £5m. Available at: www. independent.co.uk/news/politics-training-fraud-cost-taxpayer-pounds-5m-1293377.html Accessed: 28.9.19.

Coffield, F. (1990). From the decade of the enterprise culture to the decade of the TECs. *British Journal of Education & Work*, 4(1): 59–78.

Coleman, D.C. and Macleod, C. (1986). Attitudes to new techniques: British businessmen, 1800–1950. *The Economic History Review*, 39(4): 588–611.

Commission of the European Communities. (1981). *Eleventh report on competition*. Luxembourg: Office for Official Publications of the European Communities.

Conservative Party. (1966). Conservative party general election manifesto: Action not words: The new Conservative programme. Available at: www. conservativemanifesto.com/1966/1966-conservative-manifesto.shtml Accessed: 16.9.19.

Conservative Party. (1970). Conservative party general election manifesto: A better tomorrow. Available at: www.conservativemanifesto.com/1970/1970-conservative-manifesto.shtml Accessed: 16.9.19.

Conservative Party. (1979). General election manifesto. Available at: www. margaretthatcher.org/document/110858 Accessed: 22.9.19.

Conservative Party. (1983). General election manifesto: The challenge of our times.

Conservative Party. (2010). Conservative party general election manifesto: Invitation to join the government of Britain. Available at: www.conservatives.com/~/media/Files/Manifesto2010 Accessed: 29.9.19.

Conservative Party. (2017). Forward together: The conservative manifesto. Available at: www.conservatives.com/manifesto Accessed: 31.8.19.

Conzelmann, T. (2006). Regional policy. In: I. Bache and A. Jordan (eds.) *The Europeanization of British politics*. London: Palgrave Macmillan, pp. 265–279.

Coopey, R. (1994). The first venture capitalist: Financing development in Britain after 1945, the case of ICFC/3i. *Business and Economic History*, 23(1): 262–271.

Coopey, R. and Clarke, D. (1995). *3i: Fifty years investing in industry*. Oxford: Oxford University Press.

Coutts, K., Tarling, R., Ward, T. and Wilkinson, F. (1981). The economic consequences of Mrs Thatcher. *Cambridge Journal of Economics*, 5(1): 81–93.

Cowling, M., Liu, W. and Ledger, A. (2012). Small business financing in the UK before and during the current financial crisis. *International Small Business Journal*, 30(7): 778–800.

Cowling, M. and Mitchell, P. (2003). Is the small firms loan guarantee scheme hazardous for banks or helpful to small business? *Small Business Economics*, 21(1): 63–71.

Cox, A. (1986). State, finance and industry in comparative perspective. In: A. Cox (ed.) *State, finance and industry: A comparative analysis of post-war trends in six advanced industrial economies*. Brighton: Wheatsheaf Books, pp. 1–59.

Crafts, N. (2012). British relative economic decline revisited: The role of competition. *Explorations in Economic History*, 49: 17–29.

Croxford, G.G., Wise, M.M. and Chalkley, B.B. (1987). The reform of the European Regional Development Fund: Preliminary assessment. *Journal of Common Market Studies*, 26(1): 25–38.

Curran, J. (2000). What is small business policy in the UK for? Evaluation and assessing small business policies. *International Small Business Journal*, 18(3): 36–50.

Curran, J. and Blackburn, R.A. (2000). Panacea or white elephant? A critical examination of the proposed new small business service and response to the DTI consultancy paper. *Regional Studies*, 34(2): 181–189.

Curran, J. and Stanworth, J. (1981). The social dynamics of the small manufacturing enterprise. *Journal of Management Studies*, 18(2): 141–158.

Curran, J. and Stanworth, J. (1982). Bolton ten years on – a research inventory and critical review. In: J. Stanworth, A. Westrip, D. Watkins and J. Lewis (eds.) *Perspectives on a decade of small business research: Bolton ten years on*. Aldershot: Gower Publishing Company Ltd, pp. 3–27.

Curran, J. and Storey, D.J. (2002). Small business policy in the United Kingdom: The inheritance of the Small Business Service and implications for its future effectiveness. *Environment and Planning C: Government and Policy*, 20(2): 163–177.

Daily Telegraph. (1969). Minding their business. Available from BT360/5/47 (Committee of Inquiry on Small Firms: proposals for an inquiry), The National Archives of the UK.

Dannreuther, C. and Perren, L. (2013). *The political economy of the small firm*. Abingdon, OX: Routledge.

Dardot, P. and Laval, C. (2014). *The new way of the world: On neoliberal society*. London: Verso.

Davis, R. (2017). Euroscepticism and opposition to British entry into the EEC, 1955–75. *Revue Française de Civilisation Britannique/French Journal of British Studies*, XXII(2): 1–16.

DCLG/Department for Communities and Local Government. (2006). Strong and prosperous communities. The Local Government White Paper, Cm 6939-I. Available at: https://assets.publishing.service.gov.uk/government/uploads/system/uploads/attachment_data/file/272357/6939.pdf Accessed: 29.8.19.

DCLG/Department for Communities and Local Government. (2010). National Evaluation of the Local Enterprise Growth Initiative Programme-Final report. Available at: https://assets.publishing.service.gov.uk/government/uploads/system/uploads/attachment_data/file/6289/1794470.pdf Accessed: 29.8.19.

Deakin, N. and Edwards, J. (2005). *The enterprise culture and the inner city*. London: Routledge.

Dell, E. (1997). *The Chancellors: A history of the Chancellors of the Exchequer, 1945–90*. London: Harper-Collins.

Dennison, S.R. (1939). *The location of industry and the depressed areas*. Oxford: Oxford University Press.

Denver, D. and Garnett, M. (2014). *British General Elections since 1964: Diversity, dealignment, and disillusion*. Oxford: Oxford University Press.

Department of Employment. (1988). *Employment for the 1990s*. London: HMSO.

Desai, R. (1994). Second-hand dealers in ideas: Think-tanks and Thatcherite hegemony. *New Left Review*, 203: 27–64.

Devlin, P. (1972). *Report of the Commission of Inquiry into industrial and commercial representation*. London: ABCC/CBI.

DTI. (1985). *Burdens on business: Report of a scrutiny of administrative and legislative requirements*. London: HMSO.

DTI. (1986). *Building businesses-Not barriers*. London: HMSO.

DTI. (1994a). *Deregulation task forces proposals for reform: The detailed proposals of the seven business deregulation task forces*. London: HMSO.

DTI. (1994b). *Competitiveness: Helping business to win*. London: HMSO.

DTI. (1994c). *Deregulation: Cutting red tape*. London: HMSO.

DTI. (1995). *Competitiveness: Forging ahead*. London: HMSO.

DTI. (1996). *Competitiveness: Creating the enterprise centre of Europe*. London: HMSO.

DTI. (1988). *The department for enterprise*. London: HMSO.

DTI. (1999). *The small business service: A public consultation*. Great Britain: Department of Trade and Industry. URN 99/815.

DTI. (2004). *Leading lights: Experiences from the Phoenix Development Fund*. Sheffield: Small Business Service.

Dundon, T., Grugulis, I. and Wilkinson, A. (1999). Looking out of the black-hole. *Employee Relations*, 21(3): 251–266.

Economist. (1971). No case for aid. Available from T342/116 Treasury Press Cutting Section (selected extracts from Press comment), The National Archives of the UK.

Einiö, E. and Overman, H.G. (2016). The (displacement) effects of spatially targeted enterprise initiatives: Evidence from UK LEGI. SERC Discussion

Paper 191, Spatial Economics Research Centre, London School of Economics. Available at: http://eprints.lse.ac.uk/66493/1/sercdp0191.pdf Accessed: 29.8.19.

Elbaum, B. and Lazonick, W. (1986). An institutional perspective on British decline. In: B. Elbaum and W. Lazonick (eds.) *The decline of the British economy*. Oxford: Oxford University Press, pp. 1–17.

Fairclough, N. (1992). *Discourse and social change*. Cambridge: Polity Press.

Fazey, I.H. (1987). *The pathfinder: The origins of the Enterprise Agency in Britain*. London: Financial Training Publications Ltd.

FOI Release. (2013). Small Firms Loan Guarantees (SFLG) scheme. Available at: https://assets.publishing.service.gov.uk/government/uploads/system/uploads/attachment_data/file/200224/foi-130470-small-firms-loan-guarantees-scheme.pdf Accessed: 29.9.19.

Foreman-Peck, J.S. (1985). Seedcorn or chaff? New firm formation and the performance of the interwar economy. *Economic History Review*, 38(3): 402–422.

Forte, E. (2011). *Intervention: The battle for better business*. Available at: https://www.battleforbetterbusiness.co.uk/ Accessed 18.11.19.

Fotopoulos, G. and Storey, D. (2019). Public policies to enhance regional entrepreneurship: Another programme failing to deliver? *Small Business Economics*, 53(1): 189–209.

Fraser, S., Bhaumik, S. and Wright, M. (2013). What do we know about the relationship between entrepreneurial finance and growth? ERC White Paper No.4. Enterprise Research Centre.

Frost, R. (1954). The Macmillan Gap 1931–53. *Oxford Economic Papers*, 6(2): 181–201.

Galbraith, J.K. (1972). *The new industrial state* (2nd edition). Harmondsworth: Penguin Books.

Galbraith, J.K. (1992). *The great crash 1929*. London: Penguin Books.

Gamble, A. (1974). *The conservative nation*. London and New York, NY: Routledge & Kegan Paul.

Ganguly, P. (1985). *United Kingdom small business statistics and international comparisons*. London: Sage Publications.

Gibb, A.A. (2000). SME policy, academic research and the growth of ignorance, mythical concepts, myths, assumptions, rituals and confusions. *International Small Business Journal*, 18(3): 13–35.

Gilbert, B.A., Audretsch, D.B. and McDougall, P.P. (2004). The emergence of entrepreneurship policy. *Small Business Economics*, 22(3–4): 313–323.

Glynn, S. and Booth, A. (1996). *Modern Britain: An economic and social history*. London: Routledge.

Gordon, S. (1972). Two monetary inquiries in Great Britain: The MacMillan Committee of 1931 and the Radcliffe Committee of 1959. *Journal of Money, Credit and Banking*, 4(4): 957–977.

Gorman, T. (1985). *Business still burdened: More regulations for the scrapheap*. CPS Policy Study No. 76. London: Centre for Policy Studies.

Gray, C. (1998). *Enterprise and culture*. London: Routledge.

Greene, F.J., Mole, K. and Storey, D.J. (2008). *Three decades of enterprise culture: Entrepreneurship, economic regeneration and public policy*. Houndmills, Basingstoke: Palgrave.

Griffiths, B. (1974). Two monetary inquiries in Great Britain: Comment. *Journal of Money, Credit and Banking*, 6(1): 101–114.

Grigg, S. (1991). Archival practice and the foundations of historical method. *The Journal of American History*, 78(1): 228–239.

Grylls, M. and Redwood, J. (1980). *The National Enterprise Board: A case for euthanasia*. London: Centre for Policy Studies.

The Guardian. (2015). Government growth voucher scheme branded a failure. Available at: www.theguardian.com/business/2015/aug/16/government-small-business-scheme-branded-a-failure Accessed: 30.9.19.

Hahn, R.W. (1998). Policy watch: Government analysis of the benefits and costs of regulation. *The Journal of Economic Perspectives*, 12: 201–210.

Halcrow, M. (1989). *Keith Joseph: A single mind*. London: Macmillan Press.

Hall, P.A. (1986). The state and economic decline. In: B. Elbaum and W. Lazonick (eds.) *The decline of the British economy*. Oxford: Oxford University Press, pp. 266–302.

Hall, P.A. (1991). The British enterprise zones. In: R.E. Green (ed.) *Enterprise zones: New directions in economic development*. London: Sage Publications, pp. 179–191.

Hall, P.A. (1992). The movement from Keynesianism to monetarism: Institutional analysis and British economic policy in the 1970s. In: S. Steinmo, K. Thelen and F. Longstreth (eds.) *Structuring politics: Historical institutionalism in comparative analysis*. Cambridge: Cambridge University Press, pp. 90–113.

Hall, P.A. (2009). Historical institutionalism in rationalist and sociological perspective. In: J. Mahoney and K. Thelen (eds.) *Explaining institutional change: Ambiguity, agency. power*. New York, NY: Cambridge University Press, pp. 204–224.

Hamilton, N. (1994). The government's deregulation initiative. *Economic Affairs*, 14(4): 28–30.

Hampton, P. (2005). *Reducing administrative burdens: Effective inspection and enforcement*. Norwich: HMSO.

Hannah, L. (1983). *The rise of the corporate economy* (2nd revised edition). London: Methuen.

Hannah, L. (2004). A failed experiment: The state ownership of industry. In: R. Floud and P. Johnson (eds.) *The Cambridge economic history of modern Britain*. Cambridge: Cambridge University Press, pp. 84–111.

Hansard. (2019). About Hansard. Available at: https://hansard.parliament.uk/ Accessed: 28.9.19.

Hansard

HC Deb. vol.255 col.1199, 20 July 1931. [Online]. Available at: https://hansard.parliament.uk Accessed: 7.9.19.

HC Deb. vol.359 col.1033, 7 April 1940. [Online]. Available at: https://hansard.parliament.uk Accessed: 13.9.19.

HC Deb. vol.376 cols.156–157, 18 November 1941. [Online]. Available at: https://hansard.parliament.uk Accessed: 6.9.19.

HC Deb. vol.435, cols.1837–1838, 1 April 1947. [Online]. Available at: https://hansard.parliament.uk Accessed: 10.9.19.

HC Deb. vol.436, col.27, 15 April 1947. [Online]. Available at: https://hansard. parliament.uk Accessed: 10.9.19.

HC Deb. vol.477 WS, 4 July 1950. [Online]. Available at: https://hansard. parliament.uk Accessed: 6.9.19.

HC Deb. vol.825 col.188, 3 November 1971. [Online]. Available at: https:// hansard.parliament.uk Accessed: 13.9.19.

HC Deb. vol.837 col.17, 15 May 1972. [Online]. Available at: https://hansard. parliament.uk Accessed: 20.9.19.

HC Deb. vol.852 cols.204–205, 8 March 1973. [Online]. Available at: https:// hansard.parliament.uk Accessed: 20.9.19.

HC Deb. vol.916 col.277, 28 July 1976. [Online]. Available at: https://hansard. parliament.uk Accessed: 20.9.19.

HC Deb. vol.928 col.496, 22 March 1977. [Online]. Available at: https://hansard. parliament.uk Accessed: 20.9.19.

HC Deb. vol.929 col.270, 29 March 1977. [Online]. Available at: https://hansard. parliament.uk Accessed: 22.9.19.

HC Deb. vol.935 col.117, 12 July 1977. [Online]. Available at: https://hansard. parliament.uk Accessed: 20.9.19.

HC Deb. vol.953 col.59W, 4 July 1978. [Online]. Available at: https://hansard. parliament.uk Accessed: 22.9.19.

HC Deb. vol.955 col.645, 3 August 1978. [Online]. Available at: https://hansard. parliament.uk Accessed: 20.9.19.

HC Deb. vol.957 col.1197, 9 November 1978. [Online]. Available at: https:// hansard.parliament.uk Accessed: 22.9.19.

HC Deb. vol.987 col.372, 30 June 1980. [Online]. Available at: https://hansard. parliament.uk Accessed: 20.9.19.

HC Deb. vol.1000 cols.781–782, 10 March 1981. [Online]. Available at: https:// hansard.parliament.uk Accessed: 23.9.19.

HC Deb. vol.24 cols.167–168, 17 May 1982. [Online]. Available at: https:// hansard.parliament.uk Accessed: 23.9.19.

HC Deb. vol.25 col.234, 15 June 1982. [Online]. Available at: https://hansard. parliament.uk Accessed: 23.9.19.

HC Deb. vol.34 col.214, 16 December 1982. [Online]. Available at: https:// hansard.parliament.uk Accessed: 23.9.19.

HC Deb. vol.36 col.69, 1 February 1983. [Online]. Available at: https://hansard. parliament.uk Accessed: 23.9.19.

HC Deb. vol.48 col.468, 16 November 1983. [Online]. Available at: https:// hansard.parliament.uk Accessed: 22.9.19.

HC Deb. vol.53 col.240, 1 February 1984. [Online]. Available at: https://hansard. parliament.uk Accessed: 23.9.19.

HC Deb. vol.59 cols.1196–1202, 10 May 1984. [Online]. Available at: https:// hansard.parliament.uk Accessed: 23.9.19.

HC Deb. vol.60 col.526, 25 May 1984. [Online]. Available at: https://hansard. parliament.uk Accessed: 23.9.19.

HC Deb. vol.88 col.192, 3 December 1985. [Online]. Available at: https:// hansard.parliament.uk Accessed: 23.9.19.

HC Deb. vol.96 cols.107–108, 22 April 1986. [Online]. Available at: https:// hansard.parliament.uk Accessed: 23.9.19.

HC Deb. vol.100 cols.262–263, 26 June 1986 [Online]. Available at: https:// hansard.parliament.uk Accessed: 27.9.19.

HC Deb. vol.107 col.524, 16 December 1986 [Online]. Available at: https:// hansard.parliament.uk Accessed: 27.9.19.

HC Deb. vol.114 cols.271–272, 8 April 1987 [Online]. Available at: https:// hansard.parliament.uk Accessed: 27.9.19.

HC Deb. vol.119 cols.649–650, 7 July 1987 [Online]. Available at: https:// hansard.parliament.uk Accessed: 27.9.19.

HC Deb. vol.123 col.602, 2 December 1987 [Online]. Available at: https:// hansard.parliament.uk Accessed: 27.9.19.

HC Deb. vol.1131 cols.833–835, 20 April 1988. [Online]. Available at: https:// hansard.parliament.uk Accessed: 25.9.19.

HC Deb. vol.138 cols.273–274, 27 July 1988 [Online]. Available at: https:// hansard.parliament.uk Accessed: 27.9.19.

HC Deb. vol.145 col.552, 24 January 1989 [Online]. Available at: https:// hansard.parliament.uk Accessed: 27.9.19.

HC Deb. vol.153 col.175, 16 May 1989 [Online]. Available at: https://hansard. parliament.uk Accessed: 27.9.19.

HC Deb. vol.155 col.174–175, 21 June 1989 [Online]. Available at: https:// hansard.parliament.uk Accessed: 27.9.19.

HC Deb. vol.157 col.329, 20 July 1989. [Online]. Available at: https://hansard. parliament.uk Accessed: 23.9.19.

HC Deb. vol.159 col.260, 1 November 1989 [Online]. Available at: https:// hansard.parliament.uk Accessed: 27.9.19.

HC Deb. vol.163 col.207, 5 December 1989 [Online]. Available at: https:// hansard.parliament.uk Accessed: 27.9.19.

HC Deb. vol.167 col.497, 19 February 1990. [Online]. Available at: https:// hansard.parliament.uk Accessed: 23.9.19.

HC Deb. vol.194 col.156, 3 July 1991. [Online]. Available at: https://hansard. parliament.uk Accessed: 25.9.19.

HC Deb. vol.212 col.230, 19 October 1992 [Online]. Available at: https:// hansard.parliament.uk Accessed: 27.9.19.

HC Deb. vol.250 col.764–789, 24 November 1994 [Online]. Available at: https:// hansard.parliament.uk Accessed: 27.9.19.

HC Deb. vol.278 cols.250–257, 22 May 1996 [Online]. Available at: https:// hansard.parliament.uk Accessed: 27.9.19.

HC Deb. vol.284 col.1222, 6 November 1996 [Online]. Available at: https:// hansard.parliament.uk Accessed: 27.9.19.

HC Deb. vol.309 cols.1246–1247, 1 April 1998 [Online]. Available at: https:// hansard.parliament.uk Accessed: 29.9.19.

HC Deb. vol.355 col.828, 2 November 2000 [Online]. Available at: https:// hansard.parliament.uk Accessed: 29.9.19.

HC Deb. vol.376 col.660, 10 December 2001 [Online]. Available at: https:// hansard.parliament.uk Accessed: 29.9.19.

HC Deb. vol.381 col.397, 6 March 2002 [Online]. Available at: https://hansard. parliament.uk Accessed: 29.9.19.

HC Deb. vol.392 col.748, 7 November 2002 [Online]. Available at: https:// hansard.parliament.uk Accessed: 29.9.19.

HC Deb. vol.417 cols.1627–1628, 12 February 2004 [Online]. Available at: https://hansard.parliament.uk Accessed: 29.9.19.

HC Deb. vol.450 cols.95–97, 22 October 2006 [Online]. Available at: https://hansard.parliament.uk Accessed: 29.9.19.

HC Deb. vol.473 cols.53–54, 18 March 2008 [Online]. Available at: https://hansard.parliament.uk Accessed: 29.9.19.

HL Deb. vol.669 cols.895–897, 10 February 2005 [Online]. Available at: https://hansard.parliament.uk Accessed: 29.09.19.

Harling, P. and Mandler, P. (1993). From 'fiscal-military' state to laissez-faire state, 1760–1850. *Journal of British Studies*, 32(1): 44–70.

Harris, R. (2004). Government and the economy, 1688–1850. In: R. Floud and P. Johnson (eds.) *The Cambridge economic history of modern Britain, Vol. 1: Industrialisation, 1700–1860.* Cambridge: Cambridge University Press, pp. 204–237.

Harrison, J. (2011). Local enterprise partnerships. Centre for Research in Identity, Governance, Society (CRIGS)/Globalization and World Cities (GaWC) research network. Available at: https://repository.lboro.ac.uk/articles/Local_enterprise_partnerships/9487037 Accessed: 28.8.19.

Harrison, R.T. and Mason, C.M. (1986). The regional impact of the small firms loan guarantee scheme in the United Kingdom. *Regional Studies*, 20(6): 535–549.

Harrison, R.T. and Mason, C.M. (1996). *Informal venture capital: Evaluating the impact of business introduction services.* Hemel Hempstead: Prentice Hall.

Hart, D.M. (2003). Entrepreneurship policy: What it is and where it came from. In: D.M. Hart (ed.) *The emergence of entrepreneurship policy: Governance, start-ups, and growth in the US knowledge economy.* Cambridge: Cambridge University Press, pp. 3–19.

Hawkins, A. (1998). *British party politics, 1852–1886.* Houndmills, Basingstoke: Macmillan Press.

Heath, E. (1965). *Putting Britain right ahead: A statement of Conservative aims.* London: Conservative and Unionist Central Office.

Heath, E. (1970). Leader's Speech, Blackpool 1970. Available at: www.britishpoliticalspeech.org/speech-archive.htm?speech=117 Accessed: 19.9.19.

Heim, C.E. (1986). Interwar responses to regional decline. In: B. Elbaum and W. Lazonick (eds.) *The decline of the British economy.* Oxford: Oxford University Press, pp. 240–265.

Heseltine, M. (2000). *Life in the jungle: My autobiography.* London: Hodder & Stoughton.

Heyes, J. and Gray, A. (2001). The impact of the national minimum wage on the textiles and clothing industry. *Policy Studies*, 22: 83–98.

Higgins, N.J. and Cohen, G. (2006). Investors in people: A critical review and evaluation of the Standard with regard to its commercial application in organisations. Available at: www.valuentis.com/Publications/Books/ISHCM_IiP_EvalStudy_030406.pdf Accessed: 22.9.16.

Hill, M.R. (1993). *Archival strategies and techniques.* London: Sage Publications.

Hirschberg, D. (1999). *The job-generation controversy: The economic myth of small business.* Armonk, NY: ME Sharpe.

HM Government. (2011). One-in, one-out: Statement of new regulation. Available at: www.gov.uk/government/collections/one-in-two-out-statement-of-new-regulation Accessed: 23.6.16.

HM Government. (2016). Cutting red tape. Available at: https://cutting-red-tape.cabinetoffice.gov.uk/ Accessed: 22.6.16.

HM Treasury. (1999). *Enterprise and social exclusion.* London: National Strategy for Neighbourhood Renewal, Policy Action Team 3.

HM Treasury. (2006). *A strong and strengthening economy: Investing in Britain's future.* Economic and Fiscal Strategy Report and Financial Statement and Budget Report March 2006; HM Treasury HC 968, London: The Stationery Office. Available at: https://webarchive.nationalarchives.gov.uk/20070701181706/ www.hm-treasury.gov.uk/media/B/3/bud06_completereport_2320.pdf Accessed: 29.9.19.

HM Treasury and BIS. (2011). The plan for growth. HM Treasury and Department for Business Innovation and Skills, (Crown Copyright ISBN 978-1-84532-842-9). Available at: www.gov.uk/government/uploads/system/uploads/attachment_data/file/31584/2011budget_growth.pdf Accessed: 26.8.19.

Hoare, A.G. (1985). Dividing the pork barrel: Britain's enterprise zone experience. *Political Geography Quarterly,* 4(1): 29–46.

Hobsbawm, E.J. (1968). *Industry and empire.* London: Penguin Books.

Holliday, R. (1995). *Investigating small firms: Nice work?* London: Routledge.

Hoque, K. and Bacon, N. (2008). Investors in people and training in the British SME sector. *Human Relations,* 61(4): 451–482.

Howlett, P. (1995). The thin end of the wedge? Nationalisation and industrial structure during the Second World War. In: R. Millward and J. Singleton (eds.) *The political economy of nationalisation in Britain, 1920–1950.* Cambridge: Cambridge University Press, pp. 237–256.

Hudson, P. (2004). Industrial organisation and structure. In: R. Floud and P. Johnson (eds.) *The Cambridge economic history of modern Britain, Vol. 1: Industrialisation, 1700–1860.* Cambridge: Cambridge University Press, pp. 28–56.

Hudson, R. (2000). *Production, places and environment: Changing perspectives in economic geography.* Harlow: Pearson Education.

Huggins, R. (1997). Training and Enterprise Councils as facilitators of a networked approach to local economic development: Forms, mechanisms, and existing interpretations. *Environment and Planning C: Government and Policy,* 15(3): 273–284.

Huggins, R. and Williams, N. (2009). Enterprise and public policy: A review of Labour government intervention in the United Kingdom. *Environment and Planning C: Government and Policy,* 27(1): 19–41.

Hughes, A. (2008). Entrepreneurship and innovation policy: Retrospect and prospect. *The Political Quarterly,* 79(S1): 133–152.

Hunt Committee. (1969). The Intermediate Areas: Report of a Committee under the Chairmanship of Sir Joseph Hunt. Presented to Parliament by the Secretary of State for Economic Affairs by Command of Her Majesty April, 1969. London: HMSO. Cmnd. 3998.

Ingham, G.K. (1970). *Size of organization and worker behavior.* London: Cambridge University Press.

Irwin, D. (2006). Local enterprise agency loan fund: A review of performance. National Federation of Enterprise Agencies Annual Conference (September 2006).

James, S. (1986). The central policy review staff, 1970–1983. *Political Studies*, XXXIV: 423–440.

Javid, S. and Soubry, A. (2015). New measures to support entrepreneurs and job creation have been set out in Sajid Javid's first speech as Business Secretary, 19 May 2015. Available at: www.gov.uk/government/news/sajid-javid-outlines-ambitious-enterprise-bill Accessed: 26.8.19.

Jones, C. (2006). Verdict on the British enterprise zone experiment. *International Planning Studies*, 11(2): 109–123.

Jones, L.J. (1983). Public pursuit of private profit? Liberal businessmen and municipal politics in Birmingham, 1865–1900. *Business History*, 25(3): 240–259.

Jones, M.T. (1979). An analysis of the accounts of small companies. In: *Studies of Small Firms' Financing: Research Report No 3*. London: HMSO. Part of Wilson Committee (no stated editor), pp. 3–29.

Jordan, G. and Halpin, D. (2003). Cultivating small business influence in the UK: The Federation of Small Businesses' journey from outsider to insider. *Journal of Public Affairs: An International Journal*, 3(4): 313–325.

Joseph, K. (1976). *Monetarism is not enough*. Chichester: Centre for Policy Studies.

Joseph, K. (1978). General election: Sir Keith Joseph to Angus Maude (contribution to manifesto). Available at: www.margaretthatcher.org/document/111829 Accessed: 29.9.19.

Kavanagh, D. (1990). *Thatcherism and British politics: The end of consensus?* Oxford: Oxford University Press.

Khavul, S., Chavez, H. and Bruton, G.D. (2013). When institutional change outruns the change agent: The contested terrain of entrepreneurial microfinance for those in poverty. *Journal of Business Venturing*, 28: 30–50.

Kindleberger, C.P. (1987). *The world in depression, 1929–1939*. Harmondsworth: Penguin Books.

King, R. (1979). The middle class revolt and the established parties. In: R. King and N. Nugent (eds.) *Respectable rebels*. London: Hodder & Stoughton.

Kinross, J.B. and Plant, A. (1967). Rt. Hon. The Lord Piercy, C.B.E. *Journal of the Royal Statistical Society: Series A (General)*, 130(2): 274–276.

Kipping, M. and Saint-Martin, D. (2005). Between regulation, promotion and consumption: Government and management consultancy in Britain. *Business History*, 47(3): 449–465.

Kitching, J. and Smallbone, D. (2010). *Literature review for the SME capability to manage regulation project, report for Inland Revenue*. Auckland: Government of New Zealand.

Labour Party. (1979). General election manifesto, the Labour way is the better way. Available at: http://labourmanifesto.com/1979/1979-labour-manifesto.shtml Accessed: 22.9.19.

Labour Party. (1997). New Labour because Britain deserves better.

Labour Party. (2001). General election manifesto: Ambitions for Britain.

Labour Party. (2010). The Labour Party Manifesto 2010: A future fair for all. Available at: www.cpa.org.uk/cpa_documents/TheLabourPartyManifesto-2010.pdf Accessed: 29.9.19.

Labour Party. (2017). For the many, not the few. Available at: https://labour.org.uk/manifesto/ Accessed: 31.8.19.

Lean, J., Down, S. and Sadler-Smith, E. (1999). An examination of the developing role of personal business advisors within Business Link. *Environment and Planning C: Government and Policy*, 17(5): 609–619.

Leslie Hays Consultants. (1990). *Evaluation of Regional Enterprise Grants*. London: HMSO.

Leyshon, A. (1982). The UK Government small business model: A review. *European Small Business Journal*, 1(1): 58–66.

Liberal Democrat Party. (2017). Our plan. Available at: www.libdems.org.uk/manifesto Accessed: 31.8.19.

Liberal Party. (1979). Liberal manifesto: The real fight is for Britain.

Liberal Party. (1987). SDP/Liberal Alliance manifesto, Britain united: The time has come.

Lipartito, K. (2014). Historical sources and data. In: M. Bucheli and R.D. Wadhwani (eds.) *Organizations in time: History, theory, methods*. Published to Oxford Scholarship Online: January 2014. DOI:10.1093/acprof: oso/9780199646890.001.0001

Lloyd George, D., Kerr, P.H. and Seebohm Rowntree, B. (1930). *How to tackle unemployment: The Liberal plans as laid before the government and the nation*. London: Liberal Party.

Lonsdale, C. (1997). *The UK Equity Gap: The failure of government policy since 1945*. Aldershot: Ashgate Publishing.

Lord, C. (1996). Industrial policy and the European Union. In: D. Coates (ed.) *Industrial policy in Britain*. Houndmills, Basingstoke: Macmillan Press, pp. 212–237.

Lundström, A., Vikström, P., Fink, M., Meuleman, M., Głodek, P., Storey, D. and Kroksgård, A. (2014). Measuring the costs and coverage of SME and entrepreneurship policy: A pioneering study. *Entrepreneurship Theory & Practice*, 38(4): 941–957.

MacMahon, J. (1996). Employee relations in small firms in Ireland: An exploratory study of small manufacturing firms. *Employee Relations*, 18(5): 66–80.

MacMillan, H. (1931). *Committee on Finance & Industry*. Report/Presented to Parliament by the Financial Secretary to the Treasury June 1931. Cmd 3897. London: HMSO.

Mallett, O. and Wapshott, R. (2017). Small business revivalism: Employment relations in small and medium-sized enterprises. *Work, Employment & Society*, 31(4): 721–728.

Mallett, O., Wapshott, R. and Vorley, T. (2019). How do regulations affect SMEs? A review of the qualitative evidence and a research agenda. *International Journal of Management Reviews*, 21(3): 294–316.

Marsh, D. and Grant, W.P. (1977). *The confederation of British industry*. London: Hodder & Stoughton.

Mason, C. and Harrison, R. (2003). Closing the regional equity gap? A critique of the Department of Trade and Industry's Regional Venture Capital Funds Initiative. *Regional Studies*, 37(8): 855–868.

Mathias, P. (1969). *The first industrial nation: An economic history of Britain 1700–1914*. London: Methuen & Co.

Mathiason, N. (2008). Three weeks that changed the world. Available at: www.theguardian.com/business/2008/dec/28/markets-credit-crunch-banking-2008 Accessed: 29.9.19.

Matthews, D. (2007). The performance of British manufacturing in the Post-War long boom. *Business History*, 49(6): 763–779.

Maville, A. (2012). Enterprise agencies: An English model of small business advice and support. In: R.A. Blackburn and M.T. Schaper (eds.) *Government, SMEs and entrepreneurship development: Policy, practice and challenges*. Abingdon, OX: Routledge, pp. 211–225.

Mayhew, H. (2017). London labour and the London poor. Available at: www.gutenberg.org/files/55998/55998-h/55998-h.htm Accessed: 4.9.19.

McAleavey, P. (1995). European regional development fund expenditure in the UK: From additionality to 'subtractionality'. *European Urban and Regional Studies*, 2(3): 249–253.

McCrone, G. (1969). *Regional policy in Britain*. London: George Allen and Unwin Ltd.

McHugh, J. (1979). The self-employed and the small independent entrepreneur. In: R. King and N. Nugent (eds.) *Respectable rebels*. London: Hodder & Stoughton, pp. 46–75.

Meadows, P. (1978). Planning. In: F.T. Blackaby (ed.) *British economic policy 1960–1974*. Cambridge: Cambridge University Press, pp. 402–417.

Merlin-Jones, D. (2010). *The industrial and commercial finance corporation: Lessons from the past for the future*. London: Civitas.

Michael, G. (1968). Mind the acorns. *The Spectator*, 25 October 1968, p. 35. Available at: http://archive.spectator.co.uk/article/25th-october-1968/35/mind-the-acorns Accessed: 16.9.19.

Middlemas, K. (1983). *Industry, unions and government: Twenty-one years of NEDC*. London: NEDC/The Macmillan Press.

Middlemas, K. (1986). *Power, competition and the state: Vol. 1: Britain in search of balance, 1940–1961*. London: Macmillan Press.

Middlemas, K. (1990). *Power, competition and the state: Vol. 2: Threats to the postwar settlement: Britain, 1961–74*. Houndmills, Basingstoke: Macmillan Press.

Miller, F. (1979). The British unemployment assistance crisis of 1935. *Journal of Contemporary History*, 14(2): 329–352.

Mills, C.W. (1951). *White collar: The American middle-classes*. Oxford: Oxford University Press.

Millward, R. (1995). Industrial organisation and economic factors in nationalisation. In: R. Millward and J. Singleton (eds.) *The political economy of nationalisation in Britain, 1920–1950*. Cambridge: Cambridge University Press, pp. 3–12.

Millward, R. and Singleton, J. (1995). The ownership of British industry in the post-war era: An explanation. In: R. Millward and J. Singleton (eds.) *The political economy of nationalisation in Britain, 1920–1950*. Cambridge: Cambridge University Press, pp. 309–320.

Mitchell, J.E. and Cattermole, C.N. (1979). CoSIRA and its customers. In: *Studies of small firms' financing: Research report No 3*. London: HMSO. Part of Wilson Committee (no stated editor), pp. 54–58.

Mitchell, J.E. and Clay, T. (1979). ICFC and its customers. In: *Studies of small firms' financing: Research report No 3*. London: HMSO. Part of Wilson Committee (no stated editor), pp. 59–68.

Mole, K. (2002). Street-level technocracy in UK small business support: Business Links, personal business advisers, and the Small Business Service. *Environment and Planning C: Government and Policy*, 20(2): 179–194.

Mole, K., Hart, M., Roper, S. and Saal, D. (2008). Differential gains from Business Link support and advice: A treatment effects approach. *Environment and Planning C: Government and Policy*, 26(2): 315–334.

Montebruno, P., Bennett, R., Van Lieshout, C., Smith, H. and Satchell, M. (2019). Shifts in agrarian entrepreneurship in mid-Victorian England and Wales. *Agricultural History Review*, 67(1): 71–108.

Moran, M. (2009). *Business, politics, and society: an Anglo-American comparison.* Oxford: Oxford University Press.

More, C. (2000). *Understanding the industrial revolution.* Abingdon, OX: Routledge.

Morris, P. (1991). Freeing the spirit of enterprise: The genesis and development of the concept of enterprise culture. In: R. Keat and N. Abercrombie (eds.) *Enterprise culture.* London: Routledge, pp. 21–37.

Morse, A. (2014). The effective management of tax reliefs. Available at: www.nao.org.uk/wp-content/uploads/2014/11/Effective-management-of-tax-reliefs.pdf Accessed: 26.8.19.

Mottershead, P. (1978). Industrial policy. In: F.T. Blackaby (ed.) *British economic policy 1960–1974.* Cambridge: Cambridge University Press, pp. 418–483.

Nightingale, P. and Coad, A. (2016). Challenging assumptions and bias in entrepreneurship research. In: H. Landstrom, A. Parhankangas, A. Fayolle and P. Riot (eds.) *Challenging entrepreneurship research.* London: Routledge, pp. 101–128.

North, D.C. (1990). *Institutions, institutional change and economic performance.* Cambridge: Cambridge University Press.

North, J., Curran, J. and Blackburn, R.A. (1997). Quality standards and small firms: A policy mismatch and its impact on small enterprise. In: D. Deakins, P. Jennings and C.M. Mason (eds.) *Small firms: Entrepreneurship in the nineties.* London: Paul Chapman, pp. 112–126.

OECD. (1962). OECD economic surveys: United Kingdom 1962. Available at: https://dx.doi.org/10.1787/eco_surveys-gbr-1962-en Accessed: 19.9.19.

OECD. (2010). *Better Regulation in Europe: United Kingdom.* OECD Publishing. Available at: https://www.oecd.org/gov/regulatory-policy/44912232.pdf Accessed: 18.11.19.

Orwell, G. (2000). Unemployment. In: P. Davidson (ed.) *A kind of compulsion 1903–1936.* London: Secker and Warburg.

Page, A.C. (1976). State Intervention in the Inter-War Period: The Special Areas Acts 1934–37. *British Journal of Law and Society*, 3(2): 175–203.

Pass, C. (1971). The Industrial Reorganisation Corporation: A positive approach to the structure of industry. *Long Range Planning*: 63–70.

Payne, P.L. (1972). *British entrepreneurship in the Nineteenth Century.* London: Macmillan Press.

Pemberton, H. (2004). Relative decline and British economic policy in the 1960s. *The Historical Journal*, 47(4): 989–1013.

Perkin, H. (1992). The enterprise culture in historical perspective: birth, life, death-and resurrection? In: P. Heelas and P. Morris (eds.) *The values of the enterprise culture: The moral debate.* London: Routledge, pp. 36–60.

Piercy, W. (1955). The Macmillan gap and the shortage of risk capital. *Journal of the Royal Statistical Society: Series A (General)*, 118(1): 1–7.

Pierson, P. (1996). The path to European integration a historical institutionalist analysis. *Comparative Political Studies*, 29(2): 123–163.

Pigou, A.C. (2016). *Aspects of British economic history: 1918–1925*. London: Routledge.

Piore, M.J. and Sabel, C.F. (1984). *The second industrial divide*. New York, NY: Basic Books.

Pitfield, D.E. (1978). The quest for an effective regional policy, 1934–37. *Regional Studies*, 12(4): 429–443.

Polanyi, K. (2001). *The great transformation: The political and economic origins of our time*. Boston, MA: Beacon Press.

Priest, S.J. (1999). Business Link services to small and medium-sized enterprises: Targeting, innovation, and charging. *Environment and Planning C: Government and Policy*, 17(2): 177–194.

Pugh, M. (2002). *The making of modern British politics 1867–1945* (3rd edition). Oxford: Blackwell.

Quince, R. (1994). Strategic programme for innovation and technology transfer (SPRINT): Mid-term review. *European Planning Studies*, 2(2): 225–232.

Radcliffe, C. (1959). *Committee on the working of the monetary system, report*. London: HMSO.

Rainnie, A. (1989). *Industrial relations in small firms: Small isn't beautiful*. London: Routledge.

Ram, M. (2000). Investors in people in small firms: Case study evidence from the business services sector. *Personnel Review*, 29(1): 69–91.

Ram, M. and Jones, T. (2008). Ethnic-minority businesses in the UK: A review of research and policy developments. *Environment & Planning C: Politics and Space*, 26(2): 352-374.

Ram, M., Jones, T., Edwards, P., Kiselinchev, A., Muchenje, L. and Woldesenbet, K. (2013). Engaging with super-diversity: New migrant businesses and the research-policy nexus. *International Small Business Journal*, 31(4): 337–356.

Raven, J. (1989). British history and the enterprise culture. *Past & Present*, 123: 178–204.

Rees, G. (1970). *The Great Slump: Capitalism in crisis, 1929–1933*. London: Weidenfeld and Nicolson.

Regulatory Reform Act. (2001). Available at: www.legislation.gov.uk/ukpga/1994/40/contents Accessed: 28.9.19.

Richard, D. (2008). Small business and government: The Richard Report. Available at: www.conservatives.com/pdf/document-richardreport-2008.pdf Accessed: 20.8.18.

Ritchie, J. (1991). Enterprise cultures: A frame analysis. In: R. Burrows (ed.) *Deciphering the enterprise culture: Entrepreneurship, petty capitalism and the restructuring of Britain*. London: Routledge, pp. 17–34.

Roberts, R.H. (1992). Religion and the 'enterprise culture': The British experience in the Thatcher era (1979–1990). *Social Compass*, 39(1): 15–33.

Robinson, G. (1992). Training and Enterprise Councils: The story so far. *Industrial and Commercial Training*, 24(9): 14–17.

Rogers, C. (2009). The politics of economic policy making in Britain: A re-assessment of the 1976 IMF crisis. *Politics & Policy*, 37(5): 971–994.

Rubinstein, W.D. (2003). *Twentieth-century Britain: A political history*. Houndmills, Basingstoke: Palgrave Macmillan.

Saul, S.B. (1985). *The myth of the Great Depression 1873–1896* (2nd edition). London: Macmillan Press.

SBS. (2004). *A government action plan for small business: Making the UK the best place in the world to start and grow a business.* London: HMSO.

Schmidt, V.A. (2002). Europeanization and the mechanics of economic policy adjustment. *Journal of European Public Policy,* 9(6): 894–912.

Schneiberg, M. (2007). What's on the path? Path dependence, organizational diversity and the problem of institutional change in the US economy, 1900–1950. *Socio-Economic Review* 5: 47–80.

Schumacher, E.F. (1973). *Small is beautiful: A study of economics as if people mattered.* London: Blond & Briggs/Abacus.

Scott, P. (1997). British regional policy 1945–51: A lost opportunity. *Twentieth Century British History,* 8(3): 358–382.

Scott, P. (2000). The Audit of Regional Policy: 1934-1939. *Regional Studies,* 34(1): 55–65.

Scott, P. and Newton, N. (2007). Jealous monopolists? British banks and responses to the Macmillan Gap during the 1930s. *Enterprise & Society,* 8(4): 881–919.

Segal Quince Wicksteed. (1991). *Evaluation of Regional Enterprise Grants: Second stage.* London: HMSO.

Selden, R. (1991). The rhetoric of enterprise. In: R. Keat and N. Abercrombie (eds.) *Enterprise culture.* London: Routledge, pp. 58–71.

Shutt, J. (1984). Tory enterprise zones and the labour movement. *Capital & Class,* 8(2): 19–44.

Shutt, J. and Whittington, R. (1987). Fragmentation strategies and the rise of small units: Cases from the North West. *Regional Studies,* 21(1): 13–23.

Skidelsky, R.J.A. (1967). *Politicians and the slump: The Labour government of 1929–1931.* Houndmills, Basingstoke: Macmillan Press.

Skidelsky, R.J.A. (2003). *John Maynard Keynes, 1883–1946: Economist, philosopher, statesman.* Houndmills, Basingstoke: Macmillan Press.

Smallbone, D. (1991). Partnership in economic development: The case of UK local enterprise agencies. *Review of Policy Research,* 10(2-3): 87–98.

Smiles, S. (2014). Self help: With illustrations of conduct and perseverance. Available at: www.gutenberg.org/files/935/935-h/935-h.htm Accessed: 4.9.19.

Smith, I.T. (1985). Employment laws and the small firm. *Industrial Law Journal,* 14(1): 18–32.

SQW Ltd and PRG Durham University. (2016). Evaluation of start-up loans: Year 1 report. *British Business Bank.* Available at: http://british-business-bank.co.uk/wp-content/uploads/2016/03/SUL-Evaluation-Year-1-Report-Final-March-2016.pdf Accessed: 28.8.19.

Stamp, J.C. (1931). The report of the Macmillan Committee. *The Economic Journal,* 41(163): 424–435.

Stedman Jones, D. (2012). *Masters of the universe.* Princeton, NJ: Princeton University Press.

Stevenson, J. and Cook, C. (1994). *Britain in the depression: Society and politics, 1929–1939.* London: Longman.

Storey, D.J. (1994). *Understanding the small business sector.* London: Routledge.

Storey, D.J. and Johnson, S. (1987). *Are small firms the answer to unemployment?* London: Employment Institute.

Taylor, A.J. (1972). *Laissez-faire and state intervention in nineteenth-century Britain.* London: Macmillan Press.

Taylor-Gooby, P. (2012). Root and branch restructuring to achieve major cuts: The social policy programme of the 2010 UK coalition government. *Social Policy & Administration*, 46(1): 61–82.

Thatcher, M. (1984). Speech to Small Business Bureau Conference. Available at: www.margaretthatcher.org/document/105617 Accessed: 29.9.19.

The National Archives (TNA)

BT262/20/CSF60, Committee Meeting Minutes, 28 October 1969.

BT262/21/CSF/357, Committee Meeting Minutes, 16 April 1971.

BT262/21/CSF273, Committee Meeting Minutes, 11 November 1970.

BT360/4/1, Brief for the President for a discussion with Mr John Davies of the CBI on 9 July.

BT360/4/2, Meeting with Mr John Davies about the problems of small companies, 11 July 1968.

BT360/4/15, NEDC Memorandum: The problem of the small firm, 19 September 1968.

BT360/5/1, Draft Paper for INO(B) The Problem of the Small Firm, Note by The Board of Trade, December 1968.

BT360/9/79, Advisory Services and Consultancy Grants.

BT360/10/CSF124, Committee of Inquiry into Small Firms: Sources of finance.

BT361/15, Draft speech for the Minister for Industry, Sir John Eden, for the dinner with the Southern Region Branch of the Engineering Industries' Association on 13 January 1971.

FV62/45, Letter from 10 Downing Street, 27 September 1971.

FV80/20, Entry into the EEC and small firms: The immediate impact (part 1 of SFD study).

FV96/61, p. 2, Correspondence with trade association, 29 December 1983.

FV96/62, Proposal from NFSE for change to tax, 7 March 1984.

FV96/62, p. 1, Discussion of reductions in form-filling for small firms, 6 May 1984.

FV96/62, p. 2, Death by Red Tape, 5 October 1984.

FV96/63, p. 1, Correspondence on VAT exemption, 28 September 1984.

FV96/64, Correspondence received by an MP from a constituent.

FV96/64, Letter discussing Job Centre proposals, 21 September 1984.

MH61/1/3, Press Cutting: New Area 'Distressed,' *Daily Express*, 24 November 1936.

PJ6/10/97, 'One in five failure' for small firms loan scheme, *The Times*, 12 August 1982.

T200/6/1, Committee on Finance and Industry, Notes on discussions, 20, 21, 27, 28 November and 4, 5 December 1930.

T200/6/5, Committee on Finance and Industry, Notes on discussions, 28 November 1930.

T200/8/6, Committee on Finance and Industry, Twenty-Ninth Day-Thirty-Fourth Day, 16 May-4 June 1930.

T328/235, Internal memo, 9 December 1968.

T342/115b, Committee of Inquiry on Small Firms correspondence, 5 November 1970.

T342/116, Qg/0226 Cabinet Office memorandum to the Department of Trade and Industry.

T390/742, Loan guarantee scheme for small and medium sized firms, 1981.

T430/470, Evaluation of the Loan Guarantee Scheme, a report by Pieda PLC for Employment Department, February 1992.

Thelen, K. (2004). *How institutions evolve: The political economy of skills in Germany, Britain, the United States, and Japan.* Cambridge: Cambridge University Press.

Thomson, A. (2016). *Small business, education and management: The life and times of John Bolton.* Abingdon, OX: Routledge.

Tolbert, P.S., David, R.J. and Sine, W.D. (2011). Studying choice and change: The intersection of institutional theory and entrepreneurship research. *Organization Science,* 22(5): 1332–1344.

Tomlinson, J. (1994). *Government and the enterprise since 1900.* Oxford: Oxford University Press.

Tomlinson, J. (2016). De-industrialization not decline: A new meta-narrative for post-war British history. *Twentieth Century British History,* 27(1): 76–99.

Tuckman, A. (1996). Labour, skills and training. In: D. Coates (ed.) *Industrial policy in Britain.* Houndmills, Basingstoke: Macmillan Press, pp. 135–155.

Wapshott, R. and Mallett, O. (2015). *Managing human resources in small and medium-sized enterprises: Entrepreneurship and the employment relationship.* Abingdon, OX: Routledge.

Wapshott, R. and Mallett, O. (2018). Small and medium-sized enterprise policy: Designed to fail? *Environment and Planning C: Politics and Space,* 36(4): 750–772.

Ward, M. (2019). Local Enterprise Partnerships. House of Commons Library Briefing Paper No. 5651, 28 March 2019.

Weatherill, B. and Cope, J. (1969). *Acorns to Oaks: A policy for small business.* London: Conservative Political Centre.

Wilks, S. (1999). *In the public interest: Competition policy and the Monopolies and Mergers Commission.* Manchester: Manchester University Press.

Williams, N. and Vorley, T. (2015). Institutional asymmetry: How formal and informal institutions affect entrepreneurship in Bulgaria. *International Small Business Journal,* 33(8): 840–861.

Williamson, P. (2003). *National crisis and national government: British politics, the economy and empire, 1926–1932.* Cambridge: Cambridge University Press.

Wilson, G. (2000). Business, state, and community: 'Responsible risk takers', New Labour, and the governance of corporate business. *Journal of Law and Society,* 27(1): 151–177.

Wilson, H. (1979). *The financing of small firms: An interim report of the committee to review the functioning of financial institutions.* Cmnd. 7503. London: HMSO.

Wilson, L., Whittam, G. and Deakins, D. (2004). Women's enterprise: A critical examination of national policies. *Environment and Planning C: Government and Policy,* 22(6): 799–815.

Winstanley, M.J. (1983). *The shopkeeper's world, 1830–1914.* Manchester: Manchester University Press.

Wise, M. and Croxford, G. (1988). The European regional development fund: Community ideals and national realities. *Political Geography Quarterly,* 7(2): 161–182.

Wood, E.G. (1974). Management advisory services for the small firm. *Aslib Proceedings*, 26(2): 74–82.

World Bank. (2014). *The big business of small enterprises: Evaluation of the World Bank Group experience with targeted support to small and medium-size enterprises, 2006–12.* Washington, DC: International Bank for Reconstruction and Development/The World Bank. DOI:10.1596/978-1-4648-0376-5

World Bank. (2019). Doing business 2019: Training for reform. Available at: www.worldbank.org/content/dam/doingBusiness/media/Annual-Reports/English/DB2019-report_web-version.pdf Accessed: 30.8.19.

Wren, C. (1996). *Industrial subsidies: The UK experience.* Houndmills, Basingstoke: Macmillan Press.

Young, D. (1992). Enterprise regained. In: P. Heelas and P. Morris (eds.) *The values of the enterprise culture: The moral debate.* London: Routledge, pp. 29–35.

Young, D. (2012). Making business your business: Supporting the start up and development of small business. Available at: https://assets.publishing.service.gov.uk/government/uploads/system/uploads/attachment_data/file/32245/12-827-make-business-your-business-report-on-start-ups.pdf Accessed: 20.9.19.

Young, D. (2013). Growing your business: A report on growing micro businesses. Available at: https://assets.publishing.service.gov.uk/government/uploads/system/uploads/attachment_data/file/198165/growing-your-business-lord-young.pdf Accessed: 30.9.19.

Index

Printed in the United States
by Baker & Taylor Publisher Services